Impasses of Divorce

Impasses of Divorce

The Dynamics and Resolution of Family Conflict

Janet R. Johnston
and Linda E. G. Campbell
with Foreword by *Judith S. Wallerstein*

THE FREE PRESS
A Division of Macmillan, Inc.
NEW YORK

Collier Macmillan Publishers
LONDON

SIMON & SCHUSTER
Rockerfeller Center
1230 Avenue of the Americas
New York, New York 10020

First Simon & Schuster paperback edition 1999

SIMON & SCHUSTER and colophon are trademarks
of Simon & Schuster Inc.

Manufactured in the United States of America

10 9 8 7 6 5 4 3 2 1

The Library of Congress has cataloged this edition as follows:

Johnston, Janet R.
Impasses of divorce : the dynamics and resolution
of family conflict / Janet R. Johnston and Linda E. G.
Campbell ; with foreword by Judith S. Wallerstein.
p.   cm.
Bibliography: p.
Includes index.
ISBN: 0-684-87101-7
1. Divorce—United States.   2. Divorce mediation—United States.
3. Divorced parents—United States—Attitudes.   4. Children of divorced
parents—United States—Attitudes.   5. Custody of children
—United States.   I. Campbell, Linda E. G.   II. Title.
HQ834.J45   1988
306.8'9—dc19   88-11224
CIP

Dedicated to
Kathryn, Benjamin, Alana, Kathryn, and Eric

Contents

Foreword

Divorcing parents who are locked in passionate, unremitting conflict over their children baffle and dismay judges, attorneys, and members of the mental health professions. Despite two decades of research on divorce and a decade of experience with mediation programs in the public and private sectors, these families continue to challenge our psychological understanding and our therapeutic expertise. Unable to move forward into a settled divorce and equally unable to move back into a working marriage, they remain, to use the central image of this work, at an impasse from which efforts to dislodge them often fail. The consequences are frequently tragic. The persistent quality of the conflict, combined with its enduring nature, seriously endangers the mental health of the parents and the psychological development of their children. Ironically, under the guise of fighting for the child, these parents may succeed in inflicting severe emotional suffering on the very person whose protection and well-being is the presumed rationale for the battle. Moreover, as we have seen all too often, the conflict may erupt into child-stealing and violence that destroys lives.

Efforts to modify or interrupt the driven, destructive, and self-destructive behaviors in which these families engage have been hampered by a dearth of relevant psychological theory and clinical experience. Because psychoanalytic theory and family systems theory have both been formulated almost entirely within the matrix of the intact family, we have lacked the theoretical concepts which could shed light on the family system when it comes apart. Moreover, families locked in the bitterest or most intractable divorce disputes represent a relatively unfamiliar group to the practitioner. Typically, people whose anger serves to ward off depression do not seek help. People whose symptoms are ego-syntonic or who regard themselves as saints and martyrs rarely apply for counseling or mediation. Few among this high-conflict population would bring themselves to the attention of the mental health professional at all were they not required by law to make decisions over their children that they are unable to resolve. As a result, these high-conflict families have remained a poorly understood population tragically in need of help, yet demonstrably resistive to the methods that clinician and mediator commonly employ.

This book represents a major contribution to understanding these families and to the development of new and effective ways of helping them. It has been my privilege to observe at close range the evolution, over several years, of the ideas and intervention methods described herein. During this time I have experienced a mounting regard for the original, sometimes audacious, conceptual thinking that the authors have essayed. I have been repeatedly impressed with their compassionate commitment to their very troubled clients, be they adults or children, and their persistent search for methods that would relieve the suffering of these families. The authors have moved the field significantly forward in expanding theoretical knowledge and in enhancing our capacity to intervene successfully.

The work described in this book has been built carefully over time. The intervention models that are presented are based on extensive clinical experience, since 1976, with hundreds of high-conflict families. The target population for the intensive intervention programs that are reported in detail here consists of 80 high-conflict families with 100 children. This population was small enough to enable the authors to know each of the families intimately, and to work personally with most of them. The sample was at the same time large enough to permit generalization and statistical analysis of the results, and to include a diversity of ethnic and racial backgrounds and socioeconomic levels.

The central theoretical formulation is that of the divorce transition impasse. Using vivid case material the authors develop the compelling idea that the impasses in which these families appear to be caught have been shaped by a confluence of powerful psychological and social forces. The protagonists within each of these intense family dramas are trapped by internal conflicts and external pressures into repetitive behaviors that they feel helpless to control.

The impasse itself is presented as a tri-level model drawing first on forces in the surrounding social world, which include extended kin and new partners as well as the legal and mental health systems and their representatives. A second set of forces has its roots in the complex interaction of the marital couple, their tangled history of love and hate, and its traumatic vicissitudes before and during the separation. Finally, a third set of forces is associated with the intrapsychic functioning of each individual, the impact of severe narcissistic injury, and the threats that powerful feelings pose to vulnerable people who fear not only depression but even psychic annihilation.

The value of the concept of *the impasse* as a working model for the mediator or clinician is in providing a way of understanding the sequence of events within each family, which can guide the intervention. In effect it provides a diagnostic tool which, in the hands of the mediator, will indicate whether the point of entry into the impasse and subsequent strategy should be centered upon the extended family and social setting, as for example when the conflict has taken on the characteristics of tribal warfare; whether the mediator should centrally address the traumatic events of the separation; or focus upon undoing the personal narcissistic injuries involved.

Surely these are not old ideas in new bottles. On the contrary, the authors argue for the complex integration of ideas—of factors drawn out of family systems theory, out of object relations theory in psychoanalysis, out of respect for the power of psychopathology, and out of the recognition (at long last) of the powerful impact of the legal and mental health systems—all combined to argue against simplistic one-sidedness and in favor of seeing integrations and linkages in their full, nondoctrinaire, real life complexity. Only then, they argue convincingly, will we be able to see how all of these internal and external psychological and social factors interact to shape, produce, and maintain the impotent rage that is the hallmark of these unfortunate clients. Without this complex vision, the authors aver, these clients cannot make use of the intrinsically rational processes of the mediation method. Using fresh and lively case material, the authors enable the practioner to see the immediate applicability of the ideas presented to the range of issues confronted daily. With this expanded view of mediation (which they spell out in detail) in family-centered, individual, and group interventions, we may proceed.

Finally, a major contribution of this work, and one of particular importance from my own perspective, are the poignant, sensitively drawn portraits of the children in these families. The suffering and disorganization of the children (many of them very young), who are caught in the parental crossfire, their anxiety-driven efforts to cope with their own fantasies and real terrors, their worry about their parents, their emotional isolation, their gallant efforts to maintain their integrity and survival within the storm—all of these aspects are reported with accuracy, compassion, and high respect. Not surprisingly, the work confirms that the family conflict sets off a range of severe psychopathological responses, which are likely to become consolidated within the developing conscience and character of the growing child. Fortunately, the children are not merely observed and then set aside, but are fully included within the purview of these interventions. Direct work with the children, using play and interview techniques, is presented in detail.

The plight of children of divorce who are caught up in the parental conflict has been of increasing concern. There is mounting evidence throughout this book, and in my own work as well, that many of these parents battle over children on whom one or both parents are intensely dependent. Children who are caught within these strange parent-child relationships appear to have taken on a key role in staving off the serious psychological deterioration of the adult. Often the adult cannot separate his or her own ego boundaries from those of the child. These relationships seriously jeopardize the present and future emotional and intellectual development of their children. Many of these youngsters are severely symptomatic at school and on the playground, where they display both aggressive and withdrawn/depressed behaviors. Others among them have difficulty in distinguishing fantasy from reality and suffer with intrusive, bizarre misperceptions that impede their daily functioning. Moreover, there is reason to assume that early identification with the parental role of aggressor, or victim, has long staying power and may surface again as the young person reaches adolescence and young adulthood. Unfortunately, it is improbable that settlement of the dispute between the parents and establishment of mutually agreed-upon arrangements over issues of custody or access will, by themselves, facilitate the child's recovery. Nor is it at all likely, as the authors note and I fully agree, that the brief intervention with the children that is envisioned here will be sufficient to free the child entirely to move ahead developmentally. The best we can hope for at the time is to relieve the child's immediate anxiety and to interrupt the continued infliction of suffering on the child by one or both parents. Beyond this, many, perhaps all, of these children will need the most skillful sustained psychotherapy that we can provide.

The needs of the very troubled families that this work addresses have for many years pushed us to the limits of our theoretical knowledge and our skills as clinicians and mediators. This book represents a major breakthrough for the individual practitioner as well as for the field as a whole. For its illuminating insights, for the complexity of its thinking that matches the complexity of the phenomena we confront, for its pioneering models and creative efforts to develop and refine a new range of intervention methods, I regard this work as one of the most important contributions of two decades of divorce research. We have finally broken through our own professional impasse and are, at last, on our way.

JUDITH S. WALLERSTEIN, PH.D.
Center for the Family in Transition
Corte Madera, California
March 1988

Preface

There is an emerging consensus that mediation is distinct from therapy and counseling and from the practice of law. The general trend is to view mediation as an issue-oriented, goal-directed, problem-solving endeavor whose primary aim is to resolve or manage interpersonal conflict so as to reach agreement. The resolution of conflicts of interest between parties is assumed to come about through the efforts of a neutral third party. The process involved the balancing of power between the disputants, while clearly defining issues, generating options, ordering priorities, and then negotiating and bargaining differences and alternatives. This economic model of the decision-making process—based on principles of conflict resolution drawn from the theory and practice of mediating industrial disputes but modified for the particular problems of the family—assumes a psychological model of rational man. The assumption is that by providing the right structure and techniques, divorcing parents who are contesting the custody and care of their children can become rational, focused, and goal oriented. It is believed that this rational decisionmaking process can produce a legally enforceable parenting agreement that is mutually more acceptable and likely to be sustained than one determined by an adversarial court procedure. Moreover, it allows parents to take responsibility for ordering their own lives, despite divorce, in ways that are more likely to have beneficial consequences for their children.

While there is growing evidence among a large proportion of the divorcing population to support these claims (Kock and Lowery, 1984; Pearson and Thoennes, 1982; 1984; Sprenkle and Storm, 1983), formal outcome studies of mediation and court experiences indicate that the present rational decision-making models of mediation have been ineffective with "enmeshed", "highly conflicted" couples who are ambivalent about their separation or who have "severe psychopathology" or "personality disorders" (Kressel et al., 1980; Pearson and Thoennes, 1980; Waldron et al., 1984). The present models are also considered inappropriate for dysfunctional families as evidenced by violence and abuse (Cauble et al., 1985; Little et al., 1985; Lyon et al., 1985). Further, the children of such families are particularly at risk because their parents are often severely limited in their capacity to cooperate and respond appropriately to their needs and to provide a consistent, secure environment.

It is clearly evident that misplaced and escalating personal and spousal conflicts, emanating from long-term difficulties or from separation-engendered conflict, result in resistances to mediation, questionable negotiation strategies, and unrealistic custody demands. Spouses who aim to spite and punish one another, whose desire to win the divorce at all costs, whose need for revenge and retribution is stronger than the wish for an equitable settlement who harbor intense ill will, unremitting anger, and chronic distrust or who nurture ambivalent reconciliation fantasies are not able to use a rational decision-making process. Because they cannot put aside their feelings, they will subvert the process in the service of their emotional and interpersonal conflicts.

Rather than characterize these high-conflict families as failures of mediation, we propose new methods and models of mediation to work with them. Rather than enjoin them not to fight or encourage them to avoid and contain their overwhelming emotional conflicts, we contend that the point of departure for a more appropriate mediation model is some understanding of why these parents are locked into chronic disputes. Based on this understanding, what is needed are strategic, focused interventions aimed at their impasse, which will prepare them to negotiate and make decisions more rationally. Rather than assume they know what is best for their children, we argue that their children need to be clinically assessed and that the mediator should be prepared to counsel and educate parents as to their needs and even to advocate on their behalf.

This book is intended to provide a conceptual framework for understanding the dynamics and resolution of high-conflict divorces. While the methods for working with divorcing families were forged in the crucible of the most entrenched disputes which constitutes the most rigorous test possible of their effectiveness, the conflict themes shown in stark relief are, in some form or degree, common to all divorces. Hence the book is relevant to understanding and working with less severely disputing families. In chapter 1 we present an overview of the components of disputes and describe the manner in which these reciprocally reinforce one another and become layered to form the divorce-transition impasse. In chapters 2–5 we develop each of the levels of the impasse in more detail, giving case illustrations and specific intervention strategies. The forces which hold the disputes in place come from the wider social system, from the couple or family system dynamics, and from individual intrapsychic processes. Consequently, each component force will be examined in order. We begin with the external (the least acknowledged but most easily understood contributant) and proceed to the internal personality factors (the most readily acknowledged but least understood aspect).

Specifically, in chapter 2 we describe the external components of the impasse: the typical ways in which a new lover or spouse, grandparents and other family members; and therapists, attorneys, and court personnel initiate or maintain custody disputes. Transforming allies who fuel disputes into supportive helpers who settle them is the theme of a series of practical strategies for intervening, illustrated by case vignettes. In chapter 3 we identify the interactional profiles of couples who appear to have complementary or symmetrical pathologies, as well as techniques for helping couples extricate themselves from these patterns. The focus is on two types of interactional conflicts: those in which couples hold onto idealized images of each other and those in which they have constructed negative polarized views of one another. Chapters 4 and 5 describe typical intrapsychic conflicts that revolve around separation-engendered feelings of rejection, humiliation, loss, and helplessness. We examine how parents with varying degrees of vulnerability to these feelings use fights with the ex-spouse in- and outside the court to ward off or manage these intolerable emotions. We also show how they use their children in the service of restoring self-esteem, replenishing loss, and reconstituting self-efficacy. Various counseling strategies are presented.

What sense do children make of the parents' conflict, and how do they react to witnessing arguments, verbal abuse, and physical aggression? How does the child's age make a difference? In chapters 6 and 7 we describe and illustrate children's age-specific responses to parental discord, their problems in making transitions from one parent's home to the other, and the quality of their attachment to each parent. As the children become older, they typically become more involved in the disputes—even enmeshed—and contribute actively and significantly to the drama, creating a family rather than a parental impasse. Of particular concern are the common coping or defensive styles these children appear to be developing, which place them at future risk in terms of their moral development and their capacity for satisfying interpersonal and intimate relations. Chapter 8 presents the elements of a method for doing brief work with these children, illustrated by three cases.

In chapters 9 and 10 we present our three-phase model of mediation with high-conflict families. During the first phase, the couple is prepared for conflict resolution by strategic counseling interventions into the impasse and by heightening their concern for their child. During the second phase, they negotiate their coparenting relationship and the actual agreement, and during the third, they are helped to implement their new plans. This basic mediation method has been adapted to groups of high-conflict families. We present special techniques for using group dynamics to resolve the parental impasse and for developing cooperative plans for children. The passages of two families through the individual family model and one through the group model illustrate the method.

Within each chapter we discuss the treatment prognosis for each kind of impasse, and in the Appendix we present the salient findings on outcome, both at the end of the counseling-mediation intervention and at the follow-up that was undertaken two to three years later. Specifically, we compare the individual and group models of intervention, address to what extent impasses have been resolved for these families, and consider what appears to be the legacy of conflict for the children, within families who have and have not settled their differences.

Acknowledgments

The work reported in this book was undertaken at the Child and Family Divorce Counseling Service, Psychiatric Services, Children's Hospital of San Francisco. We would like to express our appreciation to Jerome Oremland, MD, Chief of Psychiatry, and to Carolyn Hallowell, LCSW, Chief Psychiatric Social Worker, for institutional support.

Funds for this project were provided by the San Francisco Foundation, the Zellerbach Family Fund, the Morris Stulsaft Foundation, and the Van Loben Sels Foundation. Partial support for the first author was provided by a NIMH Fellowship in Social Structure, Personality, and Mental Illness, Department of Sociology, University of California.

We are profoundly indebted to our team members—foremost to Mary Tall Shattuck, Ph.D., who shared the work with families during the intervention period. We hold many warm memories of mutual support and stimulating strategy conferences and cotherapy and co-mediation sessions in which her insights about children and her skills as mediator were a special contribution. Thanks to Sharon Mayes, Ph.D., for her assistance in analyzing the intervention data, and to Jamie Edmunds, Ph.D., for her part in collecting and analyzing the follow-up data. Finally, and most important, we are grateful for the ongoing support and guidance of Judith S. Wallerstein, Ph.D., who acted as consultant to the project from its inception.

We appreciate the referrals from, and the collegial consultations with, the staffs of Family Court Services in San Francisco, San Mateo, Marin, and Alameda counties. Last, we salute the families with whom we worked, who allowed us to participate in their struggles, disappointments, and dreams. Together we explored the pathways to the resolution of their divorce and to the reconstitution of their family ties.

Parts of this work have been published elsewhere in somewhat different form. This preface and chapters 1 and 9 include excerpts from L. E. G. Campbell and J. R. Johnston, "Impasse-Directed Mediation with High-Conflict Families in Custody Disputes," *Behavioral Sciences and the Law*, 4:217–241 (1986); copyright © 1986 by John Wiley & Sons, Inc., reprinted by permission of John Wiley & Sons, Inc. Most of chapter 2 was published as "Tribal Warfare: The Involvement of Extended Kin and Significant Others in Custody and Access Disputes," *Conciliation Courts Review*, 24: 1–16 (1986). Most of chapter 7 originally appeared in J. R. Johnston, L. E. G. Campbell, and S. Mayes, "Latency Children in Post-Separation and Divorce Disputes," *Journal of the American Academy of Child Psychiatry*, 24 (1985): 563–574, © by American Academy of Child and Adolescent Psychiatry. Excerpts from "Instability in the Networks of Divorced and Disputing Families," in E. J. Lawler & B. Markovsky eds., *Advances in Group Processes: Theory and Research*, 4: 243–369 (1987), appear in chapters 6 and 7. Finally, a version of chapter 10 appeared as "Multifamily Mediation: The Use of Groups to Resolve Custody Disputes," *Mediation Quarterly*, 14–15: 137–162 (1986–1987). We express our appreciation to these journals for allowing this material to be reprinted.

JANET R. JOHNSTON
Menlo Park, California
LINDA E. G. CAMPBELL
Berkeley, California
January 1988

CHAPTER 1

The Divorce-Transition Impasse

How the Families Present

Martin, a tall, young, dark-complected man, sauntered into the office and sat down with an air of studied nonchalance that belied his intense anxiety and anger. His broad-brimmed hat jammed on his unruly hair, shading his eyes, somehow attested to his guardedness, defiance, and great skepticism of the futility of the endeavor. He had been sent by the local family court to resolve the dispute over the custody of his seven-year-old daughter, Sally, in counseling and mediation.

The counselor was quickly informed that he and Judith, his divorcing wife, had been in hot disagreement over child rearing for two years, most of their post-separation period. A year before, they had sought therapy for six months, but it had proved useless. Invariably, after each session, they had had a terrible fight. Furthermore, the therapist knew nothing about children, and Martin resented her bungling attempts to talk to his child.

He then presented a long list of allegations about the mother's inadequate care and neglect of Sally. Foremost was his concern about the child's unstable living conditions. He claimed that Judith had lived with eleven different roommates in seven different apartments since their separation. Sally's baby-sitters were also changed frequently; his daughter was left for long hours in child care, sometimes from early morning until late in the evening, while Judith was working, going to classes or pursuing a social life. He believed that the child was around a lot of undesirable people, many of whom took drugs and were not discreet about their sexual behavior. He was afraid his child could be influenced to take drugs or that she would be molested by one of them. He strongly objected to the way in which his ex-wife disciplined Sally. She had hit the child a number of times,

1

and he considered this totally unnecessary because Sally was most responsive if one reasoned with her. He concluded by saying that if Judith did this again, he would not be responsible for his actions; he would probably punch her out!

About three months earlier, he had "reached the end of his rope" when Sally phoned him, crying that her mother had smacked her again. Believing he had a good case for sole custody, he resolved to see a lawyer and go to court. During the months he prepared himself for trial, he shared his plans with the child and told her to keep them secret from her mother until the papers were served. Moreover, he confessed to Sally that he had some fears that the judge might be one who favored mothers and that he might lose the case. If this happened, he tried to reassure her that he would take care of the situation in his own way, suggesting that both of them could "disappear together."

Martin explained to the counselor that he had heard terrible stories about how courts and state authorities were lax and unconcerned about serious charges of child neglect, and he did not intend his daughter to suffer the consequences of such bureaucratic inertia. He felt, however, that he should give "due process" a chance, and so he went to court expecting a hearing before the judge. He was dismayed to find himself diverted to mediation. During the brief mandatory mediation session at the court, he became more angry and pessimistic about the outcome and felt even more frustrated when it was recommended that he and his ex-wife become involved in an extended period of counseling and mediation in order to resolve their differences.

Judith became increasingly agitated and morally indignant as she sat listening to Martin's allegations of her neglect and abuse. Although this pale young woman was poorly dressed and presented as anxious, defensive, and rather disorganized, she also managed to convey some dignity and elicited some respect for her struggle to survive and provide a home as an unskilled worker and single mother in the sprawling metropolis. She countered Martin's claims by arguing that he did not understand how difficult it was to find affordable accommodation on her wages; she had to share facilities where and when these became available. She countered his accusations about her child-rearing methods by expressing her concern that he was far too emotionally dependent on the child and needed Sally for his own companionship. He had become the child's "great protector," arriving to rescue Sally whenever she did not like her discipline. She claimed that Sally needed to tolerate the sitting arrangements. She claimed that at least she was providing a better role model for her daughter by working regularly, whereas the father was a "perennial graduate student" who did not work regularly. Judith justified the "very few occasions" she had smacked Sally for bad behavior (for example, for being out on the street at night with her friends). In fact, she was quite articulate about her child-rearing philosophy, describing herself as a stricter and more appropriate authority, whereas the father tried to be the child's "best friend." He was interfering in her management of the child, undercutting her authority, and encouraging Sally to be rude and disobedient to her. The demand to appear in court had come as a total shock; she was terrified that everyone would believe the lies he told about her and that she would lose her child. She felt she was fighting for the only thing in her life that was worth living for. Martin was dangerous and manipulative. He was potentially violent. The counselor should know that he had threatened to kill her during their separation; had, indeed, attacked her twice; and had had to be restrained by companions.

Both parents agreed that Sally had become very distressed by their mounting hostilities and was very fearful of the court decision. She very much wanted to talk to the judge herself. Before the day in court, the mother found her hiding in the closet, crying and fretting about the outcome, fearing that she would be taken away from her father. In addition, she was resisting attending school and complained of stomachaches, began wetting her bed, and had become particularly sassy toward her mother. They both agreed the counselor should interview her alone.

Sally was a pretty, dark-haired child with large eyes in a pale face. Although an attractive array of toys were spread out before her in the playroom, she sat rigidly on the chair, her hands clenched. After explaining her role and the confidentiality of the interview in a simple direct manner, the counselor asked her about her parents' arguments and fights. Sally's voice was tight and her staccato phrases punctuated the silence of the playroom.

Sally: I know more about it than you think. My Dad talks a lot.

Counselor: He talks to you a lot? Would you like to tell me what you talk about?

Sally (beginning slowly and becoming increasingly anxious): I'll tell you the whole story. You see, I was with my Mom a lot and then I was with my Dad. When I was with my Mom, I only saw her a bit. I stayed with the baby-sitter. For four, five hours. Sometimes at nights too. I missed my Dad. It was a long time. I went out on the street to look for my Dad.

Counselor: And what happened when your Mom found you on the street?

Sally (indignantly): She hit me! She's not supposed to hit me. I told my Dad on her!

Counselor: I can see you are mad and upset about this. Can you tell your Mom and Dad how you feel?

Sally: It's like sinking in the quicksand. My Dad, he's calm. My Mom talks different. I talk like my Dad. We talk a lot. I didn't know that until he tells me these things.

Counselor: You and your Dad talk calmly together and he tells you these things. Your Mom talks differently?

Sally: Yes, she gets all heated up. And then she cries. I give her Timmy [the cat] to cool her down.

Counselor: You give her the pussycat to calm her down. So this is how they argue about you. It's like you're in a tug of war?

Sally (relieved to be understood): Yes. And I don't want to be the rope! Let someone else be the rope!

Counselor (warmly empathizing with these feelings): Yes. . . . And so your parents went to court to see the judge. What happened there?

Sally (becoming increasingly agitated): I don't know.

Counselor: What did you think might happen there?

Sally: I've heard scary stories. . . . It's a bad condition. . . .

Counselor: Some kids worry a lot about the judge. They think that perhaps they won't get to see their Mom or Dad anymore. And sometimes they are scared that someone is going to jail.

Sally: I know. It's scary.

Martin, Judith, and Sally were one of eighty divorcing families we saw in our special divorce-counseling, mediation, and research project. They, like the others, were involved in particularly intense and entrenched disputes over the care of their child. Their complaints and allegations, like those of the others, reflected the plethora of concerns that divorcing parents bring to the mediator and to the court. They, like the others to varying degrees, came to our service unwillingly—angry, defensive, frustrated, and quite desperate. Their child, Sally, although more articulate than most, typifies the anxiety, confusion, fears, and emotional and behavioral symptomatology in many of these children.

Our counseling and mediation service for divorcing families grew in parallel with the development and implementation of mandatory mediation in the California courts (McIsaac, 1981, 1983). In a groundbreaking attempt to avoid the escalation and compounding of family disputes, often a consequence of traditional adversarial court procedures, in 1981, California instituted a law requiring divorcing parents who are disputing the custody and care of their children to attempt to mediate their differences. They usually do so with the help of mediators within family court services. This constitutes a revolutionary approach to family disputes in the courts, requiring new teamwork between legal and mental health professionals. The rationale for mediation is based on the premise that divorcing parents need to be empowered to make their own decisions at the time of marital dissolution and that with the guidance of a skilled mediator, families can be helped to reorganize in ways that are mutually more satisfactory and suited to the individual member's needs. The family courts in the San Francisco Bay Area typically provide a very brief (one to three sessions), focused, problem-solving mediation with divorcing couples disputing custody and access arrangements for their children. Those couples who are unable to reach agreement, or who are still disputing despite a mediated settlement or court order, are often referred for more extensive help. Our service was viewed as a backup to the court's efforts and was seen as a further attempt to provide continued counseling and mediation in order to forestall or prevent further litigation, the court staff being committed to the concept of families determining their own arrangements. Alternatively, following a court evaluation and recommendation or judicial decision, judges referred the family for counseling to help implement the court order.

A large proportion of those referred frankly did not want to be involved. Typically, they did not seek mental health services for their personal problems and so were unlike the majority of clients seen in private practice. More frequently, one partner wanted to attend and the other did not. However, since it was obligatory that both parents participate and also agree that their children be seen, there was often difficulty in countering one or the other's initial resistance and engaging them in counseling. They appeared afraid of being evaluated and found wanting as a parent, were worried that their opponent would "present a better front" than they, or feared being coerced into giving in on the issue in dispute. In actuality, they came because it was advised or court ordered, because their attorney suggested it would "look good for them in court if they made this effort," or because it provided a way of forstalling a change in the status quo threatened by an imminent court decision. On the other hand, a smaller proportion of these families was relieved to find an alternative to the adversarial proceedings of the court and attorneys to talk out their problems. They also acknowledged that they could not afford costly litigation. Almost one-third of the couples were already divorced, so that the requests to the court were to modify existing custody and visitation decrees. In general, these involved the more difficult and longer-lasting family conflicts. The other two-thirds were in the process of obtaining a divorce and were having considerable difficulty reaching initial agreements about the post-divorce living arrangements for their children.

Both the initial intake interviews with parents and the Content of Conflict checklist they completed, clearly showed that custody was the main issue of contention. Two-thirds of families were in legal dispute over child custody and access; the other third was disputing visitation. The legal designation of the dispute, however, was misleading in that it encompassed a wide variety of presenting issues and represented, to varying degrees, a strategic maneuver to have other problems resolved.

Characteristic of most parents was a pervading sense of distrust or unease about the other parent's capacity to care for the child, together with complaints that the other parent refused to listen, talk, share, or coordinate plans for the children. Many alleged outright neglect. Inadequate supervision, poor quality food, poor hygiene, not ensuring the child had sufficient sleep, and unwillingness to provide help for school emergencies were all common issues. These parents blamed the former spouse for the child's frequent colds and illnesses, for minor accidents, or for not attending to injuries or illnesses with proper concern. Some parents were criticized for being too permissive, lenient, and unstructured; others were viewed as too rigid, uncompromising, cold, and insensitive. There were accusations of not teaching the child the "right moral standards," exposing the child to undesirable people, allowing the child to witness a parent's drinking or drug taking, allowing the child to see adult movies containing violence and sexually explicit material, and fears that the child was witnessing the parent's sexual intimacy with a new lover. A number actually believed the other parent was a morally corrupt or mentally ill person from whom their child needed to be protected.

In six cases there were serious allegations of sexual molestation and physical abuse, all of which had been previously investigated or were in the process of being investigated by child protective service workers and mental health agencies specializing in such problems. Although in none of the cases was any adequate substantiating evidence of abuse found, the cloud of suspicion continued to hang over the accused parent, and this distrust was shared to varying degrees by others.

Second, the child's difficult behavior (temper tantrums, withdrawal, sleep disturbances, bed-wetting, lying, and so on) were sources of disagreement for many. Typically, the transition times (prior to going on visits and returning home) were difficult for the children, and in a large proportion of cases the custodial parent blamed the former spouse for the child's behavioral and emotional disturbances, alleging that the visits upset the child.

Disputes over access arrangements were third on the agenda of disputed issues for the sample as a whole. Most of these families were embroiled in a battle over the absolute amount of time they were able to spend with their child, with one parent continually pressuring for more access and the other resisting. Some complained that the other parent blocked access by scheduling activities for the child during their time with the child, refused access if child support was not paid, made false claims that the child was too ill to visit, and the like. Six parents had stolen and secreted their children from the ex-spouse for extended periods of time. A greater number were fearful of a potential kidnapping.

Many were constantly fighting about the details of the visit; for example, the exact time the child was to be picked up or dropped off. They were incensed by the child's arriving home late, tired, or hungry or without the clothes and toys with which he or she was sent. Miscommunication about plans, sudden changes in the arrangements, or the child's refusal to go on the visit triggered renewed conflict. Fixed visiting arrangements and long commutes were a constant source of discord for those parents who had other commitments or difficulty organizing their lives and following routines.

The fourth most frequent category of complaints was that the ex-spouse or stepparent was speaking disparagingly about them in front of the child, influencing the child against them, and encouraging the child to disobey and disrespect them. The more extreme accusations were that the child was being "brainwashed" by lies and stories or that the child's mind was being "poisoned" by the other parent.

It is of particular interest that disputes over financial settlements (property and spousal and child support awards and their regular payment) were of least concern to this particular sample of divorcing parents. In fact, there was more agreement than disagreement over money matters. Hence, these entrenched custody disputes did not seem to be a strategy in the fight over the ownership of the home and ongoing financial support. However, where there were negotiations over the property settlement, requests for modification of support, and contempt hearing for nonpayment of support, these clearly intensified parents' anger and sense of injustice and precipitated further disputes over the child.

Conflict Tactics

How did the parents dispute? First, since we accepted referrals only from public mediators or judges in the local family courts, all of these families were, by definition, litigating. In fact, one-half had had repeated litigations over child custody and access in the past (ranging from two court appearances to three full court trials with numerous appearances). Outside the court, the dispute took various forms. It ranged from resistance to the settlement of divorce matters, fear and avoidance of each other—along with refusals to communicate, pervasive distrust, and bitter acrimony—to angry confrontations, including threats and explosive violence.

Physical aggression had occurred between three-fourths of the parents during the preceding twelve months, as measured by the Straus Conflict Tactics Scale (Straus, 1979). More than four-fifths had been violent in the past. On the average, parents were physically aggressive toward one another once per month, and their children were present on two-thirds of these occasions. For most, these were more moderate acts of pushing, shoving, slapping, biting, spitting, and throwing objects. However, for seven families, it involved violent, dangerous fighting with death threats, brandishing of weapons (guns and knives), and bodily injury, together with destruction of furniture and personal possessions. In several families (like that of Martin and Judith) the violence was not ongoing; rather, one or two violent episodes had occurred during the separation period, casting an ominous shadow of fear and mistrust over the postdivorce parental relationship. Unleashed fury and hysterical rages occurred, with five women screaming and hitting their ex-husbands, ramming or sideswiping their cars, or shredding the men's clothes. In each of these cases, the man did not reciprocate but tried to ward off the attack. In another six cases, it was the men who were desperate and brutal during the separation and their wives very afraid. Many of the most dangerous incidents of violence, however, did not occur between the parents themselves; rather, they occurred between the mother's new boyfriend (or husband) and her former spouse. Herein lay the potential for tragedy, as testified by the high incidence of family-related homicides.

The most common form of active disputing, however, was verbal abuse: insulting, belittling, demeaning interchanges that occurred on the average once per week, often on the telephone or at the time of transfer of the child from one home to the other. Usually one parent would make nagging, badgering demands or needling insults. In response the other either tried to avoid conflict (by physically retreating or hanging up the phone) or became enraged and countered with cynical remarks, bitter verbal attacks and denigration. It is important to note that this rate of verbal and physical aggression is significantly higher than that reported in studies of noncourt populations of divorcing families (Gonzalez, Krantz, and Johnston 1984; Hansen, 1983), among whom the Straus Conflict Tactics Scale was also used.

These active and dramatic fights should be placed in the context of the ongoing relationship between the divorcing spouses. The norm was to maintain an icy, defensive silence, and for long periods couples refused to speak with each other at all and instead passed all messages through the children or some other intermediary. It is an intriguing clinical phenomenon that many of these couples who had once been lovers and friends, who had shared many years and children together, now found eye contact intolerable and the sound of each other's voice unbearable. They could not even remain in the same room without fleeing or experiencing overwhelming anxiety, fear, and anger. In only a very small subgroup of families could parents routinely discuss their differences rationally in each other's presence. On the average, parents reported they spoke to each other without physical or verbal aggression about once every two weeks. Their fighting outnumbered their rational talks by two to one. In fact, given their assiduous avoidance of each other, most contact erupted into conflict.

Duration of Disputes

The majority of divorcing couples are in conflict at the time of separation as they separate emotionally, negotiate property and financial settlements, and make plans for the custody and care of their children. In fact, it has been suggested that there is an eighteen-to-twenty- four month period of postseparation adjustment involving personal and interpersonal turmoil for the divorcing couple (Hetherington, Cox, and Cox, 1982; Wallerstein and Kelly, 1980). Following that time, many ex-spouses have been able to develop and maintain cooperative relationships with respect to their children (Ahrons, 1981). The fact that the postdivorce disputes in our sample were particularly lengthy ones is demonstrated by the fact that less than one third of the parents had been separated within the previous twelve months and almost half had been separated more than two years. Despite the considerable length of the time since separation, only 29 percent had managed to obtain a final divorce decree, which seems to reflect the amount of ambivalence and conflict involved and the difficulty of achieving a divorce settlement of both financial and child matters. The dispute over the child had a mean duration of seventeen months (range: one month to eight years). For many of the younger children this comprised a significant proportion of their lives. In addition, the entrenched nature of the disputes is indicated by the fact that all the divorcing couples were in court, all had already participated in attorney negotiations and brief mandatory mediation, yet all remained in conflict.

However, not all were chronic or ongoing disputes; some were episodic. Precipitating factors to intermittent disputes fell into several categories. Most legal disputes were triggered by the necessity of making a legal settlement on financial and child issues before the final divorce decree could be granted. Outside the court, the primary trigger to a renewed dispute was the upset caused by the actual separation or the leaving of one of the parties. Involvement of a new lover and remarriage of a parent, developmental changes in the child (for example, entry into adolescence), or the request by a parent to relocate to another geographical area with the child were significant life events that set in motion many postdivorce fights. Finally, symptomatic or disturbed behavior in the child activated a number of disputes. However, in all of these cases, as we shall discuss further, these factors were only precursors or triggers to the germination and eruption of these disputes. The social and psychological environment of the divorcing family relations was fertile ground for conflict. Before discussing these underlying factors which motivate, maintain and entrench disputes however, it is important to understand the socioeconomic milieu and hence set the context of our findings by briefly describing the salient demographic characteristics of our study's population.

The Study's Population

Our theoretical views and the interventions presented in this book are based on our broader clinical experience with hundreds of divorcing families since the commencement of our service in 1976, as well as on a wide range of research literature in this and related fields. The specific statistical findings reported here, however, are from a special research study of eighty families seen from 1982 to 1984. A two-year follow-up was completed from 1984 to 1986. There were 100 children in the sample, ages six months to twelve years. Fifty were boys and fifty were girls. Two-thirds were only children, reflecting the fact they were a scarce resource or precious commodity to be shared by the two sides of the divorced family. Only two families had more than two children.

When first seen in our service, the parents had been separated on the average two years, three months (range 0–10 years) after a mean marriage duration of 6.7 years (range 1 month–22 years). Five couples (6 percent) had never been married to each other. The average

age of the fathers was 36.6 years (range 22–61 years) and of the mothers, 33.2 years (range 19–51 years).

The families reflected the major racial and ethnic groups in California: 64 percent white, 13 percent Hispanic (Mexican, Central and South American); 8 percent black; 8 percent Asian (Japanese, Chinese, Indonesian) and 7 percent other (e.g. Filipino, American and Asian Indian, Iranian). One-third of the sample were ending a mixed-race marriage. In terms of occupational status, 30 percent rated 4 (clerical, sales, and technical workers) on the Hollingshead Seven-Factor Index. The rest were evenly distributed among the remaining six categories, ranging from major professionals to unemployed. Despite this range in occupational status, as a group the parents were low income: Median annual income for fathers was $14,400, and for mothers it was $10,800. This was considered meager in an urban area where the cost of living, especially housing, is extremely high. The employment status of these men and women accounted for some of the low incomes (only 55 percent were employed full time, 13 percent worked part time, and 32 percent were unemployed). This extent of unemployment was the same for men and women. In sum, this group of divorcing parents were of multiethnic origin, were of varied occupational status, and were facing fairly severe economic stress with their divorce transition.

The Divorce-Transition Impasse

The plethora of presenting problems and the degree of intense anger, frustration, and avoidance of the divorcing spouses can make working with families entrenched in postseparation or divorce disputes confusing and overwhelming. Initially, it may not seem possible to unravel the issues, sort fact from fantasy, or help the couple communicate and begin to build a solid agreement that will protect the children from chaos and conflict. Moreover, it is relatively easy to become enmeshed in the system of disputing relations, to become coopted by one side and hence ineffective in dealing with the other party, to become the central anchor that prevents relations erupting into violence or dissolving (hence to feel trapped and helpless in the eye of the storm), or to become impotent in effecting any change in persons who seem committed to having rigid, negative views of each other.

Our approach is to first make a dispute-specific assessment of the family. With each highly conflicted couple in the project we asked the questions: Why is this particular family vulnerable to chronic or intermittent disputes? What prevents them from settling the dispute and making stable postdivorce plans for their children? In response to these questions, we developed the concept of the divorce-transition impasse, which provides a framework for considering what is blocking or preventing a family's resolution of a dispute. Generally, we view the divorced family in the context of its social network as a system in the process of transition. While disputes are normal at the time of divorce and are viewed as part of the process of reconstruction, the inability to resolve a dispute is seen as symptomatic of the family system's resistance to change and indicative of homeostatic mechanisms predominating within the parents, the child, their interaction, or the wider social system. Where there are chronic disputes, the normal trajectory of change and recovery is stymied. These parents are unable to make use of the divorce to resolve issues within or between themselves and are frozen in the transition—psychologically neither married, separated, nor divorced. In effect, the form of the custody dispute becomes their new pattern of relationship. We conceptualize the impasse in terms of a system's homeostasis, resulting from pathological, outdated, or inappropriate norms and expectations between parents, children, and significant others. It can also be generated by defensive and adaptive maneuvers by the individual parents in the service of maintaining or regaining their intrapsychic equilibrium.

Impasses are typically multilayered and multileveled phenomena, with elements of the impasse occurring at three levels: external, interactional, and intrapsychic. In brief, at the external-social level the dispute may be fueled by significant others (extended kin, new partners, or helping professionals) who have formed coalitions or alliances with the divorcing parties and legitimized their claims. At the interactional level the dispute can either be a continuation of a conflictual marital relationship or the product of a traumatic or ambivalent separation between parents. They can also be generated by a child's emotional and behavioral disturbance and coping strategies in response to divorce conflict. At the intrapsychic level disputes may be in the service of managing intolerable feelings engendered by the divorce (humiliation, sadness, helplessness, and guilt) in psychologically vulnerable parents.

In the absence of a useful overarching paradigm that encompasses both social and psychological factors, we need to draw on a number of theoretical perspectives to delineate the factors involved. However, the important point is that family members can be stalemated on any or all three levels, and these factors coalesce and lock the dispute into a mutually and reciprocally reinforcing pattern. Conceptualizing the problem in this manner helps identify focussed, strategic interventions that aim at working through or around the impasse, or working through layers of impasse where necessary. It also guides the development of a clinical counseling and mediation program.

At the external level some custody disputes were initiated and maintained by the involvement of significant others: extended kin, new partners, mental health professionals, the bench, and the bar. With the deterioration of the marriage, separating parents turned to others for practical and emotional support, encouragement, and advice. This support often came with a price—interference, obligations, and counterdemands that provoked stress and fueled disputes. More commonly, hearing only one negatively biased version of the divorce situation, these significant others became outraged and sought to right the wrong and help the "victimized." Not only did they form strong alliances with and fight on behalf of the "aggrieved party," but in so doing they unwittingly confirmed negative, polarized, distorted views of the ex-spouse, setting the stage for long-term disputes over the children. In this way the parents' social networks were incorporated into the dispute and, in turn, the fight was solidified, maintained, and stabilized by these supportive others.

In the case of large kin networks, especially among some ethnic minorities, we found that "tribal warfare" could be generated between opposing kinsmen on behalf of each disputing parent. Where mixed-race marriages were ending, the parent's return to the family of origin created conflicts over the child's religious and cultural heritage that had never previously been at issue. Alternatively, unrelated disputes in the larger kin network were easily displaced onto or incorporated into the custody fight. For instance, difficulties in a new marriage were at times blamed on the ex-spouse. Or long-standing hostilities with grandparents in several cases activated the dispute over the child's custody. In these cases the custody and access suit, though a hot issue, was actually a bogus one because it had become fused or inextricably linked with other earlier unresolved conflicts with kin and significant others.

Because of their advocacy role, attorneys have long been implicated in the escalation of family disputes within the adversarial system. What has been less obvious is the role of other helping professionals in fueling conflict. We found that coalitions with mental health counselors were germane to some particularly entrenched disputes. Some therapists, who saw only one of the parents, encouraged uncompromising stands, reified distorted views of the other parent, and wrote recommendations and even testified on behalf of their client with little or no understanding of the child's needs, the other parent's position, or the couple and family dynamics. In some cases, each parent's mental health counselors squabbled between themselves, taking on the characteristics of the disputing parties.

Yet another potent external instigator of prolonged custody conflicts was the court itself. Judgments from the bench that were basically premature or unwise, based on insufficient data or punitive reactions to an angry, unreasonable parent, set up unstable, unworkable access arrangements. Moreover, the authority and judgment of the court had powerful symbolic meaning to some disputants. Unless great care was taken in interpreting the reason for court decisions, court outcomes functioned to legitimize each spouse's view of the other and hence solidified their positions: The winner became the "good" parent and the loser the "bad." Often the loser felt compelled to fight for acquittal.

At the interactional level, disputes were broadly of two kinds: those that were the legacy of a destructive marital relationship and those that were the product of traumatic and ambivalent separations. In the first case, the quarrels were clearly a continuation of the marital feud, in which over the years the spouses had deftly learned to unhinge each other's defenses and provoke each other's vulnerabilities in a series of stereotyped, mutually destructive transactions. From a psychodynamic perspective, the result could be described as an interlocking complementary or symmetrical psychopathology. From a family systems perspective, it was "mutual crazymaking." In the second case, the events or fact of the separation set in motion the chronic discord between the divorced spouses.

Couples who experienced particularly unexpected, traumatic separations (sudden desertion, humiliating involvement of a lover, uncharacteristic violence) and who fled the marriage with no talking through or explanation, provoked high levels of desperate reactions in their mates, which in turn evoked desperate counterreactions (hysterical outbursts and physical struggles, child and possession snatching, substance abuse, and suicide or homicide threats and attempts). This enormous betrayal of trust and these outrageous reactions and counterreactions formed the basis for the redefinitions spouses naturally began to make of each other at the time of separation. Consequently, a negatively polarized reconstruction of the identity of the ex-spouse was born, often reified by the consensual support of separate family and friends. There was a sense of discovery as to who the ex-spouse *really* was—that is, she or he was in fact "dangerous, crazy, and fundamentally untrustworthy." Without corrective feedback, these new "understandings" set in motion long-term disputes over the children because each parent was now compelled to fight consciously and righteously to protect the children from the "bad, immoral, or neglectful influence" of the other parent. Years later, each spouse might have regained his or her psychological balance, but the negatively reconstructed image of the other remained fixed and frozen, scripting defensive avoidance of each other and periodic quarrels over the children.

Couples who are extremely ambivalent about separation have long been recognized as among those who fail to settle the divorce, and our findings are no exception. One subgroup of ex-spouses seemed to maintain idealized or positively polarized views of each other and were engaged in a never-ending search for ways of holding together their shattered dreams. They were caught in a repeated cycle of mutual engagement progressing toward intimacy, followed by disillusionment and disappointment as their expectations were not realized, then separation and avoidance. The need to plan for the care of their children was painful because it necessitated renewed contact and triggered reengagement. Their idealization of each other seemed connected to their original coming together. These were often highly erotic relationships or the first "earth-shattering" love experience. Some had met each other at highly vulnerable times in their lives (for example, as teenagers or when very ill); others felt they had a special mission to accomplish with respect to each other. These couples could not live together or apart, and so their relationship was constrained by repeated separations and promising reunions, by periods of intimacy and outrage.

At the intrapsychic level, a number of salient psychological conflicts unconsciously motivated child custody disputes and directly hampered parents' capacity for rational decision making and cooperation. The separation experience evokes a well-known series of feelings of humiliation (narcissistic hurt), loss, anger, helplessness, and guilt. Depending on their preexisting character styles and defensive structures, and on their specific early childhoods and more recent traumas, divorcing parents have differing capacities to manage and integrate these divorce-engendered feelings. Most of our high-conflict litigating parents were among the more psychologically vulnerable and were less able to manage these feelings (a large proportion had indicators of personality disorder according to DSM-III ratings). Unresolved feelings and conflicts, derived from traumatic experiences and deprivations in their past, became inextricably confused with the reality task of the divorce, making it more difficult to accomplish. Disputes helped to maintain or restore the delicate psychological balance that had been disrupted by the divorce and its aftermath.

Two broad areas of internal conflict were those engendered by disputants' reactions to the stressors of rejection and loss. With respect to managing the intolerable humiliation of rejection inherent in the separation, parents, to varying degrees, sought custody to restore self-esteem and to have themselves acknowledged as the "good" or "better" parent. Others, more narcissistically wounded, sought to rid themselves of any vestige of blame by proving the other parent "bad." In cases of more extreme psychopathology, parents experienced their spouses' desertion as a total, devastating attack and developed paranoid ideas of betrayal, exploitation, and conspiracy. Their dominant motivation was retaliation and punishment of the offending spouse, and they sought custody through the courts in order to be publicly and legitimately vindicated. Unfortunately, their hostile, aggressive stance and uncompromising views meant their claims were received with little sympathy. Often this public questioning of their rigid stance redoubled their need to fight and increased their paranoia.

Some litigants, vulnerable to loss, could not acknowledge feelings of sadness and mourn the ending of the marriage. Instead they covered grief with anger, warding off sadness by embroiling their spouses in disputes. Vulnerability to loss derived from two dynamics: reactivated trauma of a previous loss (death of a parent or sibling or previous loss of a child by kidnapping, adoption, or abortion) and long-standing difficulties in separation and individuation of self from others, manifested in a dependent, counterdependent, or excessively ambivalent stance toward the ex-spouse. They struggled to protect themselves or their children from the pain of the loss or stalled in mediation by refusing to settle anything that could end the marriage. Fighting and arguing were ways of maintaining contact (albeit of a negative kind). Despite the anger, reconciliation fantasies persisted. Commonly they had difficulty sharing the child on whom they leaned heavily for companionship and solace. In more extreme cases, borderline-functioning parents fought against a sense of abandonment and feelings of nothingness and emptiness that threatened when they were alone.

Helplessness underlies almost all reactions to crisis and trauma. Most parents experienced varying degrees of helplessness and had corresponding needs to actively restore a sense of power and control. Some did this by taking action in court; others became negativistic and oppositional or insisted on making unilateral decisions. For the more disturbed, this defiance took the form of manufacturing their own rules and pathologically lying and disregarding agreements, often contemptuously. Agreement felt like surrender or capitulation. Disagreeing and fighting felt like being in control and dominant.

Of the intrapsychic, interactional, and external elements that motivate disputes and resistances to making divorce settlements, no one element is usually sufficient to maintain chronic conflict. Typically, a family is locked at more than one level. The greater the number of layers or components of the impasse, the more complex and entrenched the dispute. While there are numerous ways in which impasses can be generated and maintained, it is useful to identify some prototypical examples illustrating the three levels of impasse in mutual interaction.

For individuals with vulnerable self-images, traumatic separations are particularly humiliating (intrapsychic level). Their defensive need to recoup self-esteem and see the other parent as defective (for example, morally reprehensible or mentally disturbed) coincides with desperate and outrageous separation behaviors, providing behavioral confirmation of their emerging negative views (interactional level). These parents also tend to gather an army of supportive others who will espouse their cause and testify to their victimization. These affirmations consensually validate the negative reconstruction of the ex-spouse and reconstitute a more positive sense of self. Entering the public arena of the court, the presence of a formal audience, while offering possible vindication, is also potentially threatening to these narcissistically vulnerable parents, because any questioning of their views further attacks self-esteem and redoubles their need to fight (external level).

Separating spouses with paranoid tendencies who jealously guard, harass one another, and threaten violence, often induce their partners to leave the home suddenly and unexpectedly and to conceal their own and the children's whereabouts. These ex-mates are likely secretly to engage the assistance of friends and professionals for protection and to petition authorities for restraining orders. This series of escalating secret maneuvers and withholding of information then becomes reality-based evidence of their ideas of conspiracy and is likely to dramatically increase the paranoid panic and precipitate a catastrophe. Moreover, since most paranoid personalities are also vulnerable to feelings of humiliation and helplessness, an enormous need to take action, to set the record straight, and receive total public vindication is engendered.

A child's stress reaction (to the divorce and parental discord) and symptomatic behavior maintains many long-term disputes between parents with vulnerable self-esteem. While one parent tries to protect the child, proving the other is to blame for the child's problems, in defense the other attempts to prove him- or herself capable of good or better parenting, frequently making flagrant unilateral decisions. In a vicious cycle, the fight that ensues increases the child's disturbed and symptomatic behavior. In many cases, this impasse illustrates that although parents may be appropriately concerned about their child, their attempts to protect the child are ineffective and often compound the problem.

When a partner who is vulnerable to loss and unable to let go of the marriage separates from one who is very guilty about the desertion, the couple may collude in maintaining long-term conflicts so as to delay the final divorce. For one the anger is a defense against sadness and loss, and a means of maintaining contact. For the "guilty" partner, provoking angry outbursts justifies leaving, and the stalling of a settlement reflects the ambivalence and the wish to mitigate the pain caused.

The components of Martin and Judith's impasse evolved gradually over the course of their relationship. These young parents met and married as teenagers to escape from unhappy and conflictual family situations. Martin was in rebellion against pseudomutual family relations in which open conflict and differences were never acknowledged—especially by his mother, who viewed him as the black sheep of his family. Judith was escaping from rigid, critical, and punitive parents.

For the first few years, the marriage was held together by their highly idealized views of each other and the promises of a happier future as a new family unit. However, the economic realities of surviving in the city with no vocational skills and experience, and the early arrival of baby Sally, taxed their capacity to cope. Unable to deal with interpersonal conflict, this socially isolated young man who distrusted others withdrew into himself, privately nurturing his idealized views of his wife and child, expecting the bad times to pass, attending school and working only intermittently. The young mother, feeling very much alone, cut off from her husband, and afraid for their physical survival, took matters into her own hands. She found regular work and began gradually to establish friendships and a social life for herself. The couple seldom talked to one another and did not sleep together. During the next two years, before Martin was even aware the marriage was ending, Judith gradually began to separate emotionally from him. He believed they were living together because they still somehow loved each other; she believed they lived together only because they could not affort separate housing. Since from her viewpoint the marriage had ended, she began to date casually. Besides, Martin did not seem to care! In actuality he was extremely hurt but said nothing, hoping she would "realize what she was missing" and return to him.

The critical event occurred one evening when he arrived home from his college classes to find her asleep with her date. Judith remembered, in retrospect, that he seemed "incredibly stiff and stony," and she was frightened by his expression—"he looked half crazy"—but he spoke briefly to them both and then left. The next night when she came home from work, she found the locks changed and him barricaded behind a window with a gun pointed at her. He told her in a strange, choked voice that she was to get out of his sight and never be seen again! She was extremely frightened and became convinced he was temporarily psychotic. She remembered all the detective stories and spy thrillers that he spent his long evenings reading; she thought of his distrust of people and how he could weave strange and fantastic plots.

Martin was astounded by her insensitivity and stupidity. Defending against the devastating injury to his self-esteem, he sought to understand and make sense of the situation. He believed she had been experimenting with drugs with her newfound friends and assumed that her mind had been affected. He concluded that she had become irrational and mentally deranged. In the months that followed, he began to seriously doubt her capacity to care for their child and sought to rescue and protect Sally from her neglect and mental incompetence. Disputes between them over the child's care erupted into violence twice when he grabbed and shook her. Sally witnessed the struggle, and neighbors intervened to stop him. Feeling abandoned himself by his wife, the father believed the child was similarly experiencing abandonment by her mother. He tried to compensate for the loss, the void, and the rejection by forming a particularly close emotional relationship with Sally, which became mutually dependent. The boundaries between the father's and child's emotional experiences were becoming unclear.

Martin's allegations of Judith's neglect of Sally and his denigration of her reactivated her early experiences with her critical, domineering parents and threatened her very vulnerable self-esteem. In response, she tried to assert and defend herself as a good parent. However, by this time the child had begun to align with the father and to resist the mother whose authority had been discredited. Feeling more threatened, Judith became more strict and punitive with Sally, laying the basis for Martin's charges of physical abuse. Finally, when the dispute entered the courts, the mother became quite distraught and disorganized—so much so that one could indeed have doubted her competence as a parent. She not only seemed desperately afraid of being found wanting as a good parent by the judge (the ultimate parental authority), but was terrified of losing her child. What the court mediator and counselor did not know at the time was that

Judith had given birth to a baby as an unwed teenager and had been compelled by her angry, shamed parents to give it up for adoption. She had never forgotten this baby, and the trauma of its loss was clearly being reactivated in the present custody dispute.

In sum, the core of the dispute in this family was the highly negative, polarized, and somewhat irrational images that each of these individuals had constructed of each other at the time of their separation. This reactivated earlier developmental conflicts with their families of origin. For the father the intrapsychic component lay in his feeling betrayed and abandoned and his concomitant inability to deal with anger and interpersonal conflict without either withdrawing into himself or exploding into violence. For the mother it lay in her extremely vulnerable sense of self-esteem, hypersensitivity to criticism, and previous loss of a baby. Hence, the impasse in this case was primarily at the interactional level but was strongly buttressed by intrapsychic conflicts. There were no significant external-social components, which perhaps made it easier to resolve than many others.

The inability of Martin and Judith to forge a parental alliance and the alignment that was forming between the father and child, splitting the child off from the mother, were typical structural disturbances in the divorced families we saw. We conceived the child's symptomatology to be both the outcome of this structural breakdown and a contributing factor to the family impasse, in that it intensified and entrenched the parental conflict. This assessment provides the basis for the particular intervention that was effected.

In general, the utility of identifying the impasse is that it suggests strategic, focused interventions that aim to resolve or circumvent what is blocking a stable divorce settlement. From a systems viewpoint, it is epistemologically incorrect to specify the primary or basic cause of any dispute. It is not incorrect, however, to use the nodal point of the system "as being that point in the system at which the maximum number of functions essential to its existence converge, and which if modified, effect the maximum change with a minimum expense of energy" (Selvini-Palazzoli et al., 1978, p. 4.). This means that core components of the impasse, if identified and altered, can create radical and dramatic changes. While many mediators ignore the crucial psychological and social dynamics and pursue a rational, problem-solving approach to the specific issues under dispute, many therapists fail to focus on the realities of the situation, and instead try to intervene in the factors that are least amenable to change (for example, the character pathology of one of the parties). A dispute-specific assessment of the family helps determine what issues must be resolved and in what order (visitation, child care, custody, or financial). It suggests what techniques to use (for example, when an insight-oriented intervention is needed versus when reality confrontations and straight bargaining are indicated). Finally, the impasse formulation suggests the format and content of the written agreement (that is, the language use, style, and aspects that must be made legally enforceable). In sum, if the crucial aspects of an impasse are identified and focused interventions made, severely enmeshed and chronic disputes can unravel, sometimes in a most dramatic fashion.

Each intervention needs to be fashioned for the unique family impasse, taking into account the defensive styles of each family member and their interactions. There is not one but many points of entry into the system of disputing relations; however, some are more feasible than others. With respect to Martin and Judith in dispute over Sally, we do not wish to simplify what was a carefully orchestrated intervention that built on the strengths of these parents (their intelligent, loving concern for their child) and the motivational forces within the impasse itself (the need to prove themselves good parents). Nor do we wish to imply that paths to change are straightforward and obstacle-free. However, it will be useful to delineate the principal strategic interventions that seemed to produce the shift necessary for them ultimately to mediate and maintain a fairly effective joint custody arrangement.

Initially, in searching for an effective entry into the impasse, certain routes proved to be dead ends. For example, intervening at the interactional level by providing couple counseling was useless. It was clearly counterproductive to have these parents meet in joint sessions, although they (unlike most others) were agreeable to doing so. Martin had enormous difficulty in managing his covert anger toward Judith. He was guardedly civil and verbally compliant during the sessions but simply could not act on any agreement afterward. His negative views of her were fixed and he felt he could not trust her. Moreover, he could not listen to her explanations or reasoning. When she was anxious and defensive in the session, she became extremely verbose and circular in her thinking. He would in effect stop listening, block her out, and return to his previous interpretation that she had "blown her mind with drugs." Consequently she felt totally negated, diminished, and ignored by him. They both left joint sessions feeling more angry and frustrated than when they arrived.

A shift to individual sessions proved more effective. Here the strategy was to provide some insight into the interactional dynamics of their conflict. This meant reviewing the events of the separation to help each of them understand how differently they had experienced it and that their reactions to each other at the time were to be expected in light of their perspectives. In effect, they were helped to rewrite the story of their separation, fundamentally altering its meaning and putting together a more forgiving picture of what had happened.

Judith was more amenable to this reinterpretation. She expressed concern and some sadness that Martin felt as he did about the marriage but had never been able to tell her. She could better appreciate that the separation was a traumatic experience for him and saw his uncharacteristic violence as more understandable. She began to take a more protective, less defensive stance toward him. Judith also needed a great deal of reassurance about her capacity for good mothering and her importance to the child. Only then could she listen nondefensively to the more legitimate concerns that both Martin and Sally raised about her disciplinary practices and her not listening to the child's concerns.

Martin, on the other hand, was more skeptical about the redefinition of the events of their separation. It was extremely difficult for him to see his wife in any ways other than as a drug addict and a neglectful, abusive mother. (His investment in these negative beliefs probably reflected his defensive need to continue to ward off both the humiliating blow to his self-esteem and cautions against intrapsychic interpretation.) Hence, the effective strategy with him was to focus on his concern for his child and provide specific information on how the conflict between him and Judith was affecting Sally.

During the individual play sessions with Sally, it was evident that she was distressed by the parental fight, conflicted in her loyalties, and desirous of being with both parents. She felt responsible for keeping her mother calm and tried to prevent her from provoking her father's wrath. Mostly she felt very fearful. She was afraid of losing her father or of being separated from him, afraid of hurting his feelings by loving her mother, and particularly afraid of his barely contained aggression. In fact, she expressed a nightmarish fantasy that he would murder her mother! In response to these fears and threats, Sally was merging with Martin, taking on his views of Judith and losing touch with her own individual feelings and wishes. When this was explained to Martin, he was particularly shocked. He—who had always struggled to differentiate his perceptions and feelings from his mother's projections and extricate his identity from his family's pseudomutual relations—prided himself on helping his child become an individual. Once he was able to hear what Sally wanted and needed in the way of conflict-free access to both her parents, he was more prepared to support rather than fight with Judith in providing it. Both parents were then able to meet together and mediate a new coparenting plan. It took a number of months with this new plan in effect (interrupted by one crisis and setback in implementing the agreement) before sufficient trust and respect could be generated and maintained between this couple. The child's pleasure with this new arrangement, and the parents' subsequent success in negotiating changes, gradually reinforced and consolidated the new postdivorce family structure.

CHAPTER 2

Unholy Alliances and Tribal Warfare

The social world of the divorcing couple is often split in two at the time of the separation, as common friends either withdraw in discomfort or take sides with one partner or the other in an attempt to support and help. As the details of this once private and intimate relationship are shared with potentially supportive and sympathetic others, the norms of privacy and exclusivity that surround and protect the marital relationship break down and dissipate. Through long hours of conversation, the history of the marriage is reinterpreted and rationalizations for the separation are sought, formulated, and confirmed. This is essentially a process of making meaning from the unhappy sequence of precipitating events, coming to terms with what went wrong, and trying to establish who is to blame for the failure of the marriage.

Unfortunately, significant others, family, and friends usually hear only one version of the breakup. With information garnered from only one spouse, these others can be drawn into parental disputes, become outraged, and seek to right a wrong and protect the parent from being further "victimized" by the divorcing spouse. Even if others hear two sides of the story, they usually feel that to give support means to reflect and confirm those understandings that are most acceptable and soothing to the spouse's wounded self-esteem. Hence they are likely to participate in constructing negative views of the ex-spouse, blaming him or her for most of the problems. In the absence of corrective feedback, these negative views are amplified and reified, setting the stage for long-term conflict.

A second social dynamic also usually operates. The support of others often comes at a price—criticisms, interference, and obligations to and counter-demands by these others that tend to provoke stress and fuel the dispute. Because divorcing individuals are often required to respond to the needs and conflicts of these others, post-

24

separation conflicts can actually be initiated and maintained by the demands of others. Alternatively, as others become involved, agendas of dispute from the larger social network that have nothing to do with the child can easily become inextricably entwined with custody issues.

The total effect is that, in the absence of socially-agreed-upon customs and etiquette for organizing postdivorce relationships and dealing with conflicts of interest, there is considerable ambiguity. Consequently, the social networks of the spouses are incorporated into the dispute and the dispute is solidified, maintained, and stabilized by the support of others. New partners, extended family and kin, mental health professionals, and lawyers fuel the fight and in some instances take on the dispute as their own. As the conflict escalates and spreads, the primary players may not be the two divorcing partners but all these others who are not party to the stipulations, court order, or legal sanctions.

In identifying the significant others involved in the daily lives of spouses, the first candidates are the people with whom they resided. Approximately one-fourth of both husbands and wives were living with a new partner. Almost another one-third of the women and one-fifth of the men were living with extended kin. These significant others not only shared accommodation but helped with preparing meals, marketing and household chores, babysat and took children to school or medical appointments etc. They were often present at pick-up and drop-off times when the child visited the other parent. In addition to the above, 9 percent of mothers and 5 percent of fathers who did not live with kin relied on grandparents or aunts for daily child care. In sum, more than two-thirds of mothers and almost one-half of fathers had a new partner or kin involved in their daily lives.[1] On one end of the continuum, significant others supported the parent while at the same time nurturing reality testing and moderating tension and anger about the divorce situation. At the other extreme, significant others agitated and provoked stress, fueled the divorce-engendered dispute, and were critical and interfering.[2]

Involvement of New Partners in Disputes

Approximately 40 percent of both spouses were involved with a new partner. These relationships ranged in degree of commitment from casual-dating arrangements (14 percent of total sample) to live-in arrangements (20 percent) and remarriage (6 percent). Overall, relatively few of the new partners played no role in the dispute. While some did not provoke, their presence alone was sufficient to enrage the ex-spouse and activate disputes over the child. Another more substantial group was drawn into the ongoing conflict and did battle on behalf of one parent. The remainder were actually the prime initiators and maintainers of the dispute with the ex-spouse.

It is remarkable that so few—less than one-fifth of the parents' new partners—were uninvolved, neutral, or positively supportive in the parental conflict. We found that those that were uninvolved often had little commitment to the new relationship with the parent or regarded the matter as none of their business. They sought to avoid the situation. A few of these new partners were actively conciliatory and friendly to the ex-spouse, and their overtures were usually accepted. Several mothers felt gratified at the stable presence of a new woman in the ex-husband's life, especially when that person showed warmth and concern for their child.

Among a large majority of families, however, the entry of the new partner had precipitated or escalated the dispute over the child. In one-third of the cases, the mere presence of the mother's new lover, and in two-fifths of the cases the presence (real or imagined) of the father's new lover, provoked the conflict. In almost all of these, this new lover was the person for whom the partner had left the marriage. Interestingly, in this group of cases the new partner understood that he or she presented a threat and tried to avoid the ex-spouse. In fact, several were quite guilty about their role in the breakup. They withdrew, seemed immobilized, or at times were frankly unsupportive in the face of their mates' distress over the custody and access arrangements.

But for the ex-spouses who had been left, the new partner engendered intense feelings of anger, threat, betrayal, and humiliation, and this partially motivated the fight over the child. Some "left" parents attempted to exclude not the other parent but the new partner from the child's life. The new partner was viewed as the devil who had seduced, and the other parent as the unknowing innocent and naive victim of that malevolent influence. By the strategic maneuver of blaming the new partner and preventing his or her access to the child (preferably through court orders), a sense of power could be restored or a sense of helplessness diminished, the blow to self-esteem undone, a somewhat idealized view of the spouse and the marriage preserved, and the reality of the divorce denied. Other parents who had been left tried to repair injured self-esteem by going to court to prove that both the new partner and the other parent were bad influences on the child, and to prove themselves the good one. They sought the court's help in restricting the child's access to the new partner and parent and, where possible, the child was coopted as an ally in support of this position.

☐ Mrs. A., a sophisticated upper-class woman, was humiliated by her husband's departure from the marriage and doubly insulted to learn that the woman he left her for was a salesgirl at an Indian boutique, far beneath her station. She claimed that the new woman's interest in Eastern religions was a pernicious influence on her Christian children. Her eldest son, in support of his mother, refused to visit with and showed much contempt for both the father and his new girlfriend, whom he had never met.

The underlying fear frequently voiced was that this new person, having stolen the affections of their spouse, would also steal the love and loyalty of their children. Images of "setting up a cozy new family unit" and "leaving me out in the cold" abounded. One father, feeling shut off from his children, lamented: "I've been trying to feed them with a tin cup through the bars for years." These parents wanted legal guarantees and protection against the new partner usurping their position with the child or seducing their child as they had seduced the ex-spouse.

☐ Mr. C., normally a placid, sweet, and easygoing man, became uncontrollably enraged, spat on the ground, and threatened violence when he saw his four-year-old daughter kiss her "stepfather" goodbye. Two years ago, Mrs. C. left a companionate marriage after falling in love and having a secret affair with this man, her husband's business partner. Mr. C. was angry and very afraid of losing his daughter as well as his wife and business to this man.

The ex-spouse often showed great concern and curiosity about the new partner. Some of this was reflected in loaded questions. They asked their children to report: "Was she pretty?" "Did she and Daddy fight?" and, more disturbingly, "Don't you think she's got a fat butt? "What size bra does she wear?" In other cases, they raised questions about the influence of this new person on their child. Would he or she be vindictive or protective? Since the other disputant refused to give any information, several custody disputes were brought into court primarily to gain information about the new partner.

☐ After a four-year defacto marriage with a traditional Latin man, Mrs. N., non-Latin and U.S.-born, was shocked when her partner suddenly left and married a woman recently emigrated from his own country. When Mr. N. refused to allow her to meet his new wife, she cut off the three-year-old daughter's access to the father, insisting that he was acting secretly and ashamed of the new marriage. She suspected that he had been entrapped by a strange, foreign woman who, friends reported, was quite ugly, aloof, and withdrawn. She feared for her child's safety. In actuality, friends and the father had tried to protect the mother's esteem. The new wife was a shy, gentle young woman who spoke no English. Mrs. N. was more reassured after meeting the new wife in a counseling session, and she resumed the joint custody arrangement with the father

More than one-fourth of the new partners became actively involved in the dispute that had been ongoing or intermittent between the parents prior to their entry. They were not the primary instigators and their role was not central; rather, the real drama was between the formerly married. In this respect, the new partners served as puppets, pawns, trophies, or merely weapons in the continuing marital dispute. They were induced to play out projected ego-dystonic aspects of one spouse in the dispute against the other.

☐ Mrs. D., who was actually a very controlling, competent woman, played the helpless little girl, inducing her new male lover (whom she employed as her child's nanny) to act the aggressor with the father. He barred the door to the father's entry, and instructed or berated the father about the care of the two-year-old.

☐ Mr. E., a passive-aggressive man who was unable to express anger directly, submitted in the mediation but mobilized his new wife's rage by reporting back to her how victimized he had been. She and his attorney stormed on his behalf.

The tenor and intensity of the dispute often changes as a new partner becomes more committed to and established within the relationship (via marriage or a live-in arrangement). With increased demands for time and consideration, the delicate balance between the divorced spouses is often upset. New partners' express resentment at the "inordinate consideration" given to the ex-spouse regarding access to the children, or they resent the parent's continual upset by and absorption in the quarrels. Very commonly these new partners become angered by the passivity and perceived exploitation of the parent vis-à-vis the ex-spouse. They demand a firmer stand, lay down conditions, or take over the role of spokesperson in the dispute. Sometimes they begin by being conciliatory and trying to mediate, but since they start from the disadvantaged position as new lover and frequently share distorted views of the situation garnered from only one party, they often become enmeshed. Several new husbands sought the role of protector of their wife from the attacks of the ex-spouse. "He can't talk to my wife like that!" Mr. F. declared. Here the issue was one of demarcating territorial boundaries and acknowledging respective status, power, and authority between the two males (new husband and ex-spouse), with the wife and child being the territory or domain of control.

Though the dispute between ex-spouses often exists before the entry of the significant other, the parental fight triggers conflicts within and actions by the new partner. Over time, the dispute is no longer between the parents but between the new partner and the ex-spouse.

☐ Mr. K., a Peruvian man, angrily condemned Mrs. K. as a wife and mother for abandoning him and his child. She was a Filipino woman who guiltily submitted to his allegations to appease him and to punish herself for leaving. Her acquiescence enraged her new partner. Since she would not be more assertive and fight her ex-spouse, he took over. Vulnerable to feeling powerless and demeaned himself, the new partner in turn taunted and ridiculed the father, provoking Mr. K. to take a gun and threaten to kill him.

Finally, in a small proportion of cases—less than one-fifth of our sample—the new partner is the primary instigator and mobilizer of the custody suit: There has been relatively little disagreement between the parents before the new partner arrives on the scene. In several families, the new partners realistically perceived that the child was endangered by a psychotic or disturbed ex-spouse. They raised the consciousness and guilt of a parent who in the past had been passive, ineffectual, disorganized, or immobilized by guilt and ambivalence towards the ex-spouse. Sometimes this concern for the child was overstated. In other cases, the dispute engendered by the new spouse was rooted in difficulties in the new marriage or in intrapsychic vulnerabilities and conflicts within the new partner. In either situation, the ex-spouse became the scapegoat for these problems. Some of the new marriages were predicated on proving that the new partners were the better parents than the ex-spouses.

☐ Mrs. G. (the new wife) was a paranoid woman who had a very vulnerable self-esteem and was quick to perceive personal insults and threats. She met and married Mr. G. two years after his first marriage broke up. On hearing the story of the separation, she perceived the ex-wife's sudden desertion of him and the custody evaluation report that found him a less than adequate father as a humiliation and an offensive insult that she personally assumed as her own. She wanted to right the wrong that had been done to him by agitating for a reevaluation of custody, so that he and she could personally feel acknowledged as acceptable. She tried to prove that the mother was unfit because the child arrived unkempt and poorly dressed. By contrast, she maintained a designer wardrobe for her stepdaughter's alternate weekend visits.

☐ Mrs. H.'s new partner was deprived of all access to his own children from a previous marriage, Mrs. H.'s new partner demanded that she pursue custody of her son (whom she left with the father three years previously). Since she was dependent and feared loss of this new relationship, she complied with his wishes. During the child's visits, she disappeared so that he could play with the boy.

☐ Mrs. J. was an obese, dependent, and psychologically undifferentiated mother who merged with her newfound mentor, a powerful, paranoid woman. This mentor, who had been sexually abused as a child, insisted that Mrs. J.'s four-year-old son was being sexually abused by the father, despite numerous evaluations that yielded no evidence. Together this mother and her teacher entered a folie- à- deux via the construction of this paranoid delusion, which was primarily the new partner's.

Understanding the specific role each new partner takes in the dispute is essential in order to make directive, strategic interventions into the interlocking system of conflictual relations. Inasmuch as most new partners unwittingly provoke or are drawn into the dispute, they can as easily be enlisted in the service of settling it. First, it is often necessary to provide supportive counseling for a concerned stepparent. With more information about the impact of the disputes on the children, or about the ex-spouses' perspectives, or insight into their own role, most of these new partners can soothe and moderate an irate parent and try to reassure the ex-spouse. They are often more rational and realistic about solutions to the disagreements than are the parents. Where possible they should be encouraged to become mediators in the ongoing communication between the parents. Where impossible, they should be encouraged not to intervene. Not only are they witness to the plans made, but the fact that they are included in the counseling and mediation sessions makes them less likely to sabotage the agreements reached and more importantly, fosters their commitment to the plans.

Those new partners who initiate the dispute between the former spouses require more discriminating interventions. First, one needs to evaluate whether the significant other's vulnerabilities or conflicts in the new marriage, which are provoking the dispute, can be shifted with brief counseling or whether a referral for individual or marital counseling is indicated. For some, a brief intervention can provide the significant other with some understanding of the dynamics of the situation and enable him or her to cope with it better:

☐ We interpreted to Mr. H. how he was attempting to undo the loss of his own children by having his new wife regain custody of her boy. While she was supported in taking an appropriate mothering role with her son, he was encouraged to seek appropriate access to his own children. With Mr. K., the counselor clarified the meaning of his wife's submission to her ex-husband's accusations (she accepted them as punishment for leaving, and because she wanted to have the visits go more smoothly for her son). However, the accusations were an insult to his own integrity. While her strategy of submission might not be working, neither was his strategy of provocation by harassing telephone calls, insults, and physical threats. In fact, the stance he was taking was beneath his dignity and was creating a dangerous situation, one in which he could get himself killed.

It is not always wise to include the partner who initiated the dispute in the mediation because attention to bogus issues (displaced from other conflicts) can inflame the dispute by legitimizing their claims. Instead, shifting or diffusing the focus of paranoid preoccupation with the children to some less vulnerable target is important. Where possible, the parent rather than the new partner should be encouraged to assume responsibility for the children.

☐ In the G. case, the stepmother was not included in the mediation. Rather, the mother was reassured and counseled not to
react to the stepmother's complaints about the child's inadequate clothing. Her calm reactions disarmed the stepmother's
need to fight. Failing to get a response, Mrs. G. then became
embroiled in a fight with her mother-in-law, whom she perceived had insulted her.

Involvement of Extended Kin in the Dispute

There are three types of kin involvement in most divorce disputes. A
large proportion of kin (in our sample, two-fifths of mothers' and
three-fifths of fathers') are not involved in any negative way. Another
group of kin (one-fourth of the mothers and one-fifth of the fathers)
takes sides in the ongoing dispute between the parents. The remainder are experienced by the divorcing parent as making cultural
or family demands that can escalate the dispute.

Among those kin who play no role or are a positive conciliatory
influence, most are not informed about the dispute: They are deceased, ill, and elderly or live far away, or relations between the
parent and kin have long since broken down because of mutual disappointment, rejection, or desertion. Several divorcing individuals are
too ashamed or too proud to tell their parents.

☐ Mr. M., an Iranian immigrant, believed his very traditional,
duty-oriented family would not understand his divorce from his
American wife. In Iran, only husbands could choose to divorce
their wives, so he could not explain that his wife had actually
left him. It would imply that as a man he could not control her.
On the other hand, they would not have approved if he had told
them he was leaving her.

However, there are also kin who know a great deal about the dispute but consistently refuse to take sides. They try to maintain contact with both parents and support them equally, or they coolly refuse to support either. (For example, both Mr. and Mrs. Y's parents
refused them financial and emotional support, telling them it was
their own responsibility.) These are often fragile and short-lived declarations of neutrality. Divorcing spouses either become angry at the
lack of support or misconstrue the declarations as supportive of their
position.[3]

When kin are drawn into the dispute and take sides with one parent
against the other, the central disputants are still clearly the couple.

As the marriage disintegrates, the spouses seek help and understanding from their families of origin. Especially in the event of a traumatic separation, they frequently give distorted and polarized versions with few facts and many suppositions, so emerging negative views of the ex-spouse are constructed and reified by grandparents, siblings, and other kin. These kin subsequently become outraged and seek to protect their relative from being victimized by the ex-spouse. They seek justice, restitution, and even revenge on behalf of the spouse with whom they are involved. Long-buried attitudes toward the ex-spouse are expressed or constructed. (Mrs. N.'s father, for example, remembered how he and his family "never liked that man you married but we were only civil for your sake." "It's about time you came to your senses," Mrs. L.'s mother told her.) Such comments reveal the double-edged nature of the support that is given, which carries condemnation in disguise. In the special cases of mixed-race marriages, ethnic differences became polarized, setting the scene for tribal or ethnic feuds between opposing extended families.

Most kin support their own blood relatives against the ex-spouse. But in a small minority, grandparents and siblings side with the ex-spouse against their own. For example, Mrs. N. perceived her own mother's testimony against her in court as a terrible indictment and betrayal. Mr. O. and his new wife were humiliated and enraged by his parents' court testimony that they were abusive to his child. In both these cases, the custody suit had been activated by, and resonated with long-standing splits in, the family of origin. The parents sought to "set the record straight," resulting in repeated litigation and bitter feuding with extended kin who made "cross-alignments." The divorce dispute was compounded by the insult of the kin's reaction and became inexorably fused with long-standing family feuds. The custody dispute itself might end, but without vindication a deeper injury in the larger kin network remained.

In a few cases, the spouse's return to the family of origin (in a literal or symbolic sense) sets in motion or intensifies the disputes over the child. This involves either a passive submission to or an active re-identification with those of the family's cultural values that were in conflict with those of the ex-spouse. A large proportion of low-income parents (especially mothers) need to live with extended kin in order to provide for their children. This economic dependence seems to give the extended family license to intervene in their affairs, and to have considerable input about the care of the children.[4]

Various ethnic groups experience divorce and the disposition of children's custody according to current California laws as an insult to their family values and a fundamental attack on the integrity of their family structure. The problem is complicated when spouses from second-generation ethnic minorities, and those ending a mixed-race marriage, find themselves caught between the values of the minority and the majority culture when making plans for their children.

- ☐ Mr. P., a black father, could not understand why his large family of aunts would not be more appropriate caretakers for his three-year-old daughter than would her white mother, who had to work and use an outside baby-sitter. In his black family culture, it was acceptable practice to live with and be cared for by various relatives. The laws and policies of the courts, however, give priority rights to parents over kin.

- ☐ Mrs. R.'s Hispanic family were appalled at her loss of custody of her two-year-old son to the boy's father, which was occasioned when she fled the marriage. For this family, which believed in the sanctity of motherhood and inalienable rights attached thereto, the court's refusal to give her the child was a terrible indictment of her mothering and a great humiliation to her family. From the court's point of view, the child seemed to be doing very well with the father and it saw no reason to interrupt the status quo.

- ☐ Mrs. T. returned to live with her traditional Filipino family, in which her father was honored as the undisputed head of the household—responsible for making decisions on family affairs, especially those related to the family's dealings with the outside world. He employed his business attorney to obtain her divorce and decreed how and when she was to share the eight-month-old baby with the father. She acted in a dependent manner, thereby calling forth her father's protectiveness and control but, at the same time, she was resentful and felt exploited in this childish role. She submitted to his stringent demands despite the fact that she was willing to be far more cooperative with her ex-spouse.

While some who return to their family of origin for support passively or ambivalently submit to them, others more actively reidentify with their family and ethnic culture or renew their commitment to their religion. Others join churches or cults for the first time. The disintegration of the marriage involves the loss not only of a significant other but of a shared social and emotional reality, which in turn involves a loss or confusion of self-identity, a sense of anomie, or rootlessness. For these reasons, a common theme is a search for roots, for existential meaning, for a sense of self and a sense of connection. Psychological investment in the new identity, or identification with a new other like the "Mother Church," can precipitate disputes where previously there had been none. (For example, Mr. P., a Jewish man, wanted to send his son to Hebrew school for the first time. His ex-wife, who was Christian, refused. Mr. F. wanted to return with his children every summer to the Indian reservation for his tribe's sacred ceremonies. His Mexican wife did not see the necessity. Mrs. L. wanted her child to spend the Chinese New Year with her family. Her ex-spouse was Jewish.) In some cases, this agenda constituted the whole drama of the custody dispute.

☐ Mr. F., an elderly Chinese man, had for years been isolated from his extended family. When his Filipino wife suddenly announced her intention to divorce, he vehemently protested at first. When she stood firm, he spent the next six months courting the favor of his eleven-year-old son, whom he had previously neglected, with the intention of taking custody of him. His daughter was ignored. A horrendous family dispute followed as the family was split in two. Mr. F. explained his reasoning: "When I realized what was happening, when my mind was clearer, I thought about my ethnic background. Since the marriage was gone, I wanted somehow to preserve the family. My son is third in line in the F. family. My oldest brother had three children and one died. My second brother had none. I'm the youngest. It's an Oriental tradition that the family line goes through the male side. . . ."

In intervening, it is critical to be sensitive to the cultural norms and values about family life, divorce, parenthood, child-rearing practices, the position of women, and the psychological meaning of children within ethnic groups which differ from the values of the majority Western culture. We found it important to positively frame these values, to be respectful of the uniqueness of their culture, and to help the parents (in making plans for their children) to preserve the best in both family traditions wherever possible. Plans were made to honor Chinese New Year, Bastille Day, Hanukkah and other celebrations that were important to parents. We emphasized that private ordering through mediation enables this better than does any court-imposed order. Unlike many counselors who report that cultural and religious differences between divorcing spouses are the most resistant to resolution, our experience has been the opposite: They are relatively straightforward issues to mediate. The problem arises when psychological conflicts with respect to self-esteem, helplessness, and loss are camouflaged by the rhetoric of cultural values. To the extent that a parent insists on the child's allegiance to his or her own cultural identity to the exclusion of the ex-spouse's corresponding right, these other agendas are likely to be involved and need to be acknowledged. In these instances, we regard the cultural-religious dispute as a bogus issue, and here we identify the dynamics of the emotional conflict and intervene in that sphere (see chapters 4 and 5). For example, the cultural issue might have an important symbolic meaning for a more basic problem with self-esteem and identity.

Where parents are submitting to family interference, we help them sort out their priorities and establish their authority as parents or their need to distance themselves from their kin. Reassuring them about their own capabilities alleviates some of their dependency needs. When parents are reidentifying, one can affirm the value in this rediscovery and acknowledge their freedom to choose who they want to be now that they are out of the confines of an unhappy marriage. However, the child likewise needs the opportunity to develop his or her own freedom to choose. The undeniable heritage of a mixed-race or religious marriage for their child is that his or her self-identity is tied to both cultural traditions. Denigration of one culture implies denigration of parts of the child. The child needs to know, explore, and be proud of both identities.

Finally, in a small proportion of cases, the custody and access disputes emanate from enmeshment of the divorcing spouses with their extended families. In these situations, the divorcing parents have never separated from their family of origin, and never formed an independent marriage or family unit. Extended family members have contributed to disputes within the marriage, been a major factor in the separation, and continue to interfere with coparenting after the divorce. This can be regarded clinically as pathological enmeshment.[5] Most noticeable is the lack of boundaries in the nuclear family and diffusion of the extended family structure. It is unclear who is the functional parent and authority and who is the child. For instance, grandparents may continue to infantilize or diminish a parent and take control of the child. Sometimes the child assumes inordinate power and authority and everyone submits to his demands, or symptoms of distress. At times it is difficult to distinguish the fight over custody from the general dynamics of the family's conflictual enmeshment with one another. The custody dispute is another content area for the ongoing struggle of family members to differentiate themselves from one another and for their guilt and ambivalence about being separate.

☐ Mrs. G. married to get away from her family. However, when she argued with her husband, they encouraged her to come home to them. On his and her behalf, Mr. G. became involved in many arguments with them. When they separated, Mrs. G. wanted the father to take temporary custody of the child, but her parents threatened to throw her out of the home and cut off financial support. She took the child back and now she and her parents and sisters live together in a household filled with constant tension, screaming, and arguing. Her parents continually criticize her efforts with the child. Her mother, for example, has slapped her in front of the child, telling her she "can't do anything right, not even fix the child's lunch!" Her mother offers to baby-sit so that she can go out and then condemns her for 'leaving the child again'. Mrs. G. is highly ambivalent and guilty about taking a stand with them. She once again would like the father to help more, but her parents continue to interfere. Hence Mr. G. is essentially disputing custody with maternal grandparents over the mother and child's problems in being separate.

☐ Both Mr. and Mrs. F. were young parents. She was a twenty-year-old white American and he a twenty-two-year-old Chinese who was smothered by an overprotective and phobic mother. Mrs. F. couldn't tolerate living in an apartment next to her mother-in-law, who would knock on her door a dozen times a day. After the baby was born, the grandmother was always hovering, advising, and taking over his care. Continual fights and arguments over Mr. F.'s refusal to live separately from his mother resulted in Mrs. F. returning to her family, which became outraged on her behalf and tried to rescue the baby, aged eighteen months, from the clutches of the paternal grandmother. Both young parents abdicated their roles as parents, and both extended families waged the custody fight on their behalf. Though both families were upper middle class, invidious comparisons were made as to whose cultural tradition and child-rearing philosophy (Chinese or American) were superior.

These disputes are among the most difficult to mediate unless the parents are able to gain some autonomy from their respective families. Naturally, this is the primary goal. A short-term therapeutic or counseling intervention with the parents, aimed at showing them their abdication to, and failure to separate from, their family of origin may prepare them to mediate. In this intervention we point out their need to support each other as parents rather than fight with each other, in the service of becoming independent. If parents are unable to assume their own parental authority, then the intervention of choice is to engage strategically those extended kin most amenable to change, and those most influential within the family, in the actual mediation sessions. Acknowledging or authorizing the culturally appropriate mediator (for example, the elder male head of household in Latin families) may be the most appropriate strategy. However, one needs to evaluate who influences whom, because often the titular head is a public spokesman while someone else has the power. In such cases, during the mediation, both formal and informal leaders need to be involved. In these extended-family conferences, the child's needs can become the focus around which a child care plan can be fashioned. Indeed, if grandparents are likely to remain the primary psychological parents, we found they were the more appropriate persons with whom to mediate, with the parents signing their agreement. In one extreme example, the mother was a seriously disturbed schizophrenic, out of touch with reality most of the time. Her brief supervised visits with her daughter were arranged at a conference attended by her attorney, her extended kin (her aunt and her mother), and the child's father. She herself was not present during the mediation.

Contributions of Attorneys and the Court to Prolonging Disputes

In general, we have been fortunate to work with attorneys and court personnel who were attuned to the special issues of divorcing families and aware of the problems inherent in an adversarial practice of family law. The judges, together with the community of family lawyers and family court counselors, had pioneered mediation of custody and visitation disputes and were committed to helping parents take responsibility for ordering their own lives. Many were influential in writing and implementing the mandatory mediation statute in California. These experienced professionals were also aware of the limitations of mediation and appropriately sought to protect and advocate for their clients when necessary, using traditional discovery processes and court trial.

Nevertheless, among some less experienced attorneys and among lawyers intractably wedded to an adversarial stance (usually drawn from other areas of legal practice), we observed a number of procedures and dynamics that invariably intensified parental conflict. First, some take their advocacy role seriously and literally as requiring sustained support of their client's rights and wishes, regardless of the impact on the child in the context of the family.

☐ Following a four-year custody fight and court trial that clearly found the mother wanting in terms of her parenting capacity compared to the father, Mrs. K.'s attorney insisted on pursuing a retrail, subjecting the ten-year-old child to a stressful interview with the judge. In response to the therapist's pleas on behalf of the child, he answered, "I hear your concerns, but my only responsibility is to my client." He then proceeded to argue the case on a technical point, subjecting the family to six more months of costly litigation. The child attempted to maintain tenuous loyalty to both parents, became very confused, and began to lie profusely to both parents, telling each what they wanted to hear. Given that mediation was unable to shift the parents and the attorneys from their position, the intervention of choice in this case was to have the court appoint a lawyer to represent the child.

More commonly it is the series of maneuvers by attorneys as they formulate their clients' positions, orchestrate their clients' claims, and engage in tactical warfare with the other attorneys that outrages both parents and serves to entrench their dispute. First, the attorneys instruct their clients not to communicate with the other spouse, hence cutting off corrective feedback. They further caution parents against making any temporary arrangements, lest they compromise their position, thereby increasing the parents' unwillingness to collaborate. Some advise their clients to take an extreme position in order to have more bargaining maneuverability. Third, they submit a series of motions to the court that attempt to characterize the other spouse in the most unfavorable light. Needing to show evidence of neglect, abuse, physical violence, or emotional or mental incompetence to win their client's case, these moving papers, which are a public record of charges and countercharges, cite unhappy incidents and separation-engendered desperate behaviors of the parties, often out of context. The consequent public shaming, guilt, and fury at being so (mis)represented motivates the other parent's need to set the record straight. Few separating spouses in the midst of this devastating process stop to consider that all of this can emanate from the strange practices and procedures of our adversary system. They invariably see it as emanating from the other spouse.

A number of attorneys lose their professional objectivity and become too emotionally involved with their clients. While some try to rescue their clients and take on the fight as their own personal vendetta or crusade, others become covertly hostile and ambivalent about representing their clients. As will be shown in chapters 4 and 5, the problem is that many high-conflict divorcing parents have characterlike disorders. They have the propensity for forming complex hostile-dependent relations, losing their boundaries, projecting aspects of their own needs and wishes onto others, and playing out their intrapsychic conflicts in the interpersonal world. Untrained or inexperienced persons can easily be caught off guard, lose their distance, and become enmeshed. Overidentifying with their clients' sense of helplessness, they may rush into unnecessary actions or make unreasonable counterdemands (given the likelihood of success in court). Others may take the opposing party's requests as personal challenges to be controlled or fended off, as opposed to being worked with reasonably. These attorneys often appreciate and benefit from some frank, supportive discussion of their countertransference reactions in order to gain some perspective on their roles in the case. With other attorneys, who are more defensive about their role, a more tactful intervention is needed; for example, complimenting them on their struggles to deal with a difficult client and talking about strategies for case management and client control can be helpful.

Finally, the zeal with which some lawyers pursue the case at times has little to do with the client's needs or requests or even the merits of the case. We have seen ambitious attorneys, wishing to make a name for themselves in the legal community, seize on a case because it provided a means to challenge the constitutionality of a new law or the legality of a procedure. For example, one attorney insisted on a trial because he wanted to challenge the confidentiality of the mediation proceedings. Another attorney wanted a trial in order to challenge the court mediator's right to make recommendations without being subject to cross-examination. Several other attorneys insisted on pursuing litigation because of long-standing rivalries with the opposing counsel. In all these cases the motivation to continue the dispute drew its energy primarily from the attorneys themselves but was enmeshed with the client's motivations, embedding the impasse on several levels. The intervention of choice is to help delineate these agendas clearly in the counseling-mediation sessions, directly with both parents and where possible also with the attorneys themselves.

The authority and judgment of the court have powerful symbolic meaning for most people but take on added psychological dimensions for many clients who are emotionally troubled and depend on others for their self-esteem. Not only is the court a public forum where the private marital fight is open to public scrutiny, but it is potentially invested with a divine moral authority and capacity to enforce sanctions if that moral authority is not upheld. In fact, many of the parents we saw had a fairly primitive conception of justice and the role of law. In entering court, they were seeking ultimate judgment of right and wrong, public vindication of the charges leveled at them, and retribution for the moral crimes perpetrated against them. They also had unrealistic hopes that the court could control their ex-spouses' errant behavior and force them to be more responsible and trustworthy in areas in which the court has no jurisdiction.

The modern-day family court, on the other hand, sees itself largely as a forum for principled dispute resolution under the shadow of the law (Mnookin and Kornhauser, 1979). No-fault divorce law and the very general mandate to attend to the "best interests of the child," means the court cannot and will not take a stand on many of the issues in a family dispute. For instance, the life-style and values of the father or the fact that the mother is sleeping with her boyfriend are usually not of concern to the court unless it is shown to be adversely affecting the child. Rather, the court refers these matters to mediation in which a counselor seeks pragmatic ways of resolving the conflict, searching for compromises and solutions that have little to do with legal or moral judgment. The implications of these vastly different conceptions of the role of law are that legal outcomes in court (via recommendation by the court evaluator or decision by the judge) are often not perceived as attempts to resolve disagreements. Instead, they become dramatizations of who is right and who is wrong, and the consequent decisions are seen as the meted punishment. For example, the court may intervene to stabilize a child's living situation immediately after the separation, granting temporary custody to the father until the parents are better able to handle their own affairs. This is interpreted by the father as proof the mother is "unfit." When a child is progressing well, the court may refuse to disrupt the status quo of custody with the mother. The parents interpret this as an indictment of the father's parenting. A substantial financial settlement awarded to the wife may be seen by the angry woman as retribution for the wrongs perpetrated by her "unfaithful and irresponsible" husband. The husband, in turn, may view this settlement as proof his wife could destroy him if given a chance. He henceforth fights her at every turn lest she be given a second opportunity. In general, the more disturbed the parent, the more these meanings are magnified and distorted, sometimes to psychotic proportions.

More careful thought needs to be given to the symbolic meaning of the court interventions and particularly to explanations given for the court's actions. Where possible, the court should explicitly state the legal and pragmatic grounds for the decision that was made. Further it should undo any misinterpretation of that decision by declaring its neutrality on the moral and personal issues at stake; for example, noting that with whom a mother sleeps cannot be considered by the court unless she is exposing her child to her sexuality. These court judgments constitute a permanent public record of inordinate shame and condemnation for some parents, and continued litigation represents an attempt to set the record straight. One father in our study committed suicide when he received the court evaluation recommending once-a-month visitation with his daughter when he was asking for joint custody. This socially isolated, emotionally troubled man, whose entire identity was his fatherhood, clearly interpreted this as a devastating indictment of his worth as a parent.

Other than these basic problems inherent in clients' psychological views of authority, errors in timing and judgment by the court are most potent instigators of continued postseparation conflict. First and foremost, ex parte orders may incite severe conflict between parents. On rare occasions, one parent's attorney is able to persuade the judge to hold a hearing and make a temporary order without the presence of opposing counsel or the other parent. In theory such action should only be taken where there is substantive threat that if the other party were present, he or she might abscond with the child, commit a violent act, and the like. Also in theory, a hearing should follow these temporary orders. This procedure can be abused, and even if appropriately used, can result in what a client perceives as an enormous sense of helplessness and betrayal by the judicial system, leading to increased paranoia and desperate counterreactions including child snatching and serious violence.

More commonly, however, premature or basically unwise judicial action based on inadequate data or an angry punitive response to unreasonable demands sets up fundamentally unstable postdivorce family situations that are prone to continued stress and conflict.

☐ Distraught and made frantic by the stress of the separation, Mrs. D., in an angry outburst in court, criticized the judge for not attending to her financial needs. Reacting angrily to this breach of protocol, the judge gave custody to the father, an inadequate man prone to heavy drinking who had little interest in or capacity to relate to his two adolescent daughters. This action resulted in the mother withdrawing her petition to separate, and the family continued living together in emotional isolation and intermittent outbursts of conflict for two years.

Alternatively, the court's refusal to make a decision, in some cases rereferring the family for mediation even though it is clearly stalemated, can unnecessarily extend the family's period of turmoil and uncertainty. Decisive court action is sometimes a more rapid and effective way to end the fight.

Finally, the court and other public agencies are often not well equipped to deal with the special case of allegations of child abuse and molestation, which are rapidly increasing among high-conflict divorcing families. The involvement of multiple agencies (police, child protective services, hospitals), the lack of coordination between these agencies and between branches of the judicial system (for example, juvenile and family court), and the inadequate training of investigating officers can inflict serious damage on the children involved and on parent-child relationships. Most commonly, the actions of the accusing parents and the investigators so confuse the evaluation as to render the foundation for the charges unknowable. The conflict is hence perpetuated by the lack of clear resolution. Such children are subjected to physical examinations and assaultive interviews with a series of investigating officers trying to establish a case. If they were not molested by the parent in the first place, we consider that they were effectively abused by the system by the time the investigation is complete. Many of these children go for long periods of time without contact with a parent, or with severely limited contact at best. Moreover, their trust in and sense of safety with the accused parent is severely shaken if not destroyed.

The problem of differentiating actual molestation from fantasied abuse and from deliberate use of the accusation as a ploy in the custody dispute is an extremely complex one. Part of the difficulty lies in discriminating the potential for abuse from its actual occurrence, since the family dynamics of cases of proven abuse are similar to the kinds of disturbed parent-child relationships in families that are severely disorganized by divorce disputes. Furthermore, the psychological profiles of the children may appear similar. Our point here is not to state that abuse is more or less likely to have occurred in these families but rather, our purpose is to show that professional

management of the allegations, whether ultimately proven or un-
proven, can be iatrogenic.

Young children who had been kidnaped or secreted from the other
parent could also be traumatized by the legal procedures used to
recover them:

☐ Two-year-old Sherrie was impulsively taken by her mother,
with whom she was closely bonded, to a mountain resort for
five days, cutting off access to her father, the joint custodial
parent. When found by the police, the bewildered child was
removed from her distraught mother and placed in a children's
shelter until her father could arrange to assume full custody (by
court order). In play therapy later, it was clearly evident that
this child had been severely traumatized not by her mother's
secreting her from her father but by the police forcibly separating her from her mother.

How Mental Health Professionals Promote Disputes

Attorneys and the adversarial legal system have been much maligned
for their role in fueling parental hostility and prolonging disputes.
Education in the social, psychological, and child developmental issues involved has more recently revolutionized the practice of family
law, so that fortunately many of the problems of the legal profession's
mismanagement described in the previous section are now relatively
rare. What has received relatively little attention, however, is the role
of mental health professionals in generating or entrenching disputes.

Mental health professionals who undertake individual counseling
and psychotherapy for a separating spouse are usually privy only to
one view of the family problem. Moreover, they are primarily concerned about the intrapsychic adjustment or social functioning of
their client, remaining somewhat ignorant of the family or couple
dynamics. In support of a seemingly powerless, depressed, or abused
spouse, they can encourage an uncompromising, aggressive stance
that results in prolonged disputes over the postdivorce care of children. Or they can encourage avoidance and noncommunication with
the ex-spouse in an effort to support their client's autonomy. They
can also unwittingly endorse their client's distorted views of the divorce situation and consolidate their client's polarized negative image of the ex-spouse.

☐ Mrs. P. was often tearful and emotionally labile, alternately
depressed and angry. At times she was highly self-critical and
had extremely poor self-esteem, denigrating her capacity as a

mother for four-year-old Danny and her worth as a woman. At other times, she was highly critical of, and projected all blame onto, her husband, whom she described as an "aggressive, powerful businessman, a workaholic who was uncaring about her and neglectful of the child."

During their turbulent separation, she sought help from a psychiatrist who at first characterized her as "chronically depressed, suicidal, and rejecting of the child." In an attempt to stabilize her labile emotional states and shifting views of the world (defensive splitting), he quickly helped her consolidate a more positive sense of self-esteem by reinforcing her views that her husband was indeed "ruthless, manipulative, and possibly sociopathic." In actuality he had never met the father. Moreover, in an attempt to help her with her relationship with Danny, he evaluated the child and diagnosed him as "severely emotionally disturbed, needing long-term therapy and special schooling."

The father became extremely defensive and then irate about the psychiatrist's treatment of his child without his consent. He engaged an attorney to write belligerent letters to the psychiatrist, threatening malpractice suits and demanding that he stop treatment. In turn, the psychiatrist became threatened and extremely angry. Both parents reported he had several shouting matches with the father on the telephone and in person. As a result, he became even more entrenched in his position as protector of this "victimized little woman against the bullying, tyrannical husband." He effectively became a substitute mother-husband for Mrs. P. and a substitute father for the child. The costs of his biweekly conjoint therapy sessions with the mother and child were billed to the father!

Consequently Mr. and Mrs. P. disputed intensely over whether or not the child was emotionally disturbed and whether or not he needed special education. Mr. P. and his attorney entered court demanding cessation of the child's treatment. Mrs. P., together with her attorney and buttressed by the psychiatrist's testimony, contested this and demanded the father pay for the treatment and for special schooling.

Among the potentially iatrogenic influences of mental health professionals are verbal and especially written evaluations of the parents during the upheaval of the separation that explain the situation solely in terms of the individual psychopathology of the separating spouses. Psychodiagnostic nosology—such as "paranoid, alcoholic, sociopathic, hysteric—reduces the explanation of the complex marital dynamics to the level of the mental (or moral) capacities of the individual parents, clearly placing all blame and responsibility on one or the other parent. If shared with the divorcing parties or legal counsel, these authoritative declarations of the characters of the divorcing spouses are highly influential in determining the subsequent form and process of the postdivorce family. The relationship between the divorcing spouses is made rigid by these stereotyped labels, and the children are influenced to perceive and act toward their respective parents in accord with these views.

What is most disturbing are the number of instances in which a mental health professional is willing to offer an opinion or even testify in court as to the disposition of issues under dispute (such as custody or visitation) without having seen the other spouse or sometimes even the child. Or a therapist attempts to see the whole family but only after extensive individual counseling with one member, making his or her neutrality questionable. Furthermore, the court in some cases is willing to give credence to such testimony. Other counselors continue to see one party after family counseling breaks down and participate in the polarization of positions and the escalation of the dispute.

☐ Mr. and Mrs. Z. were involved in marital counseling in an attempt to save their marriage. When Mr. Z. refused to participate further, the counselor continued to see Mrs. Z., helping arrange her escape from her potentially violent husband. Together they made plans gradually to remove possessions from the family home without him becoming aware and to leave secretly with the child. Mr. Z. was devastated by her sudden desertion. He felt justifiably furious and betrayed by the therapist.

Undoubtedly, the most entrenched disputes were those between therapists, who supported their clients' conflicting and opposing views.

☐ Mrs. G.'s therapist viewed the father as an inadequate man, unable to relate in any mutual fashion, who felt compelled to destroy all he loved, including his wife and child. His wife needed to understand why she had selected such a man. Mr. G.'s therapist, on the other hand, viewed the father as "capable of warmth and affection" but married to a woman whose hatred for men barred any closeness. He felt, therefore, that the father would be, in the long run, a better parent for the Gs' eight-year-old male offspring.

In conclusion, there is a need to educate the legal and mental health community as to the role of professionals in maintaining the disputes of high-conflict divorcing families. More explicit guidelines are required for ethical conduct in case management with these families. Moreover, there is a need for more effective channels for communicating between the multiple agencies involved and thereby coordinating efforts in helping these vulnerable people.

Spread of Conflict and Coalition Formation

Besides the individual psychological and interactional dynamics of the involvement of new partners, extended kin, and helping professionals in postdivorce disputes over children, there is a larger drama of "tribal warfare" that often takes on a life of its own in entrenched custody disputes.

While there are no important sex differences in the likelihood of a new partner being involved, women are more often economically dependent on their kin than are men, and they are significantly more likely to have kin involved in the dispute. Although initially more people entered the fray on behalf of the wife, we observed a symmetrical escalation of others' involvement, with new partners, kin, friends, and even professionals lining up on behalf of each ex-spouse in a stepwise fashion as the conflict continued. Once the battle lines get drawn, others are likely to be precipitated into alliances that are fairly evenly matched. An appropriate analogy might be the international arms race, involving an escalatory series of moves in order to maintain the balance of power, which actually intensifies the dispute. This phenomenon may be explained by reference to basic sociological theories of social control (Berger, 1988). The marriage breakdown has involved a violation of the spouses' normative expectations of each other, and a great deal of ambiguity about who was at fault. Since each party sees him- or herself as the victim and the other as the violator, he or she tends to call on witnesses or a jury to establish the normative order, to act as a moral authority to decide who is right and who is wrong. Who is called on depends upon their availability, the particular network of previously supportive relations, and the established boundaries between the nuclear family and extended family system. New partners are most likely to be called on.

Older children are usually coopted into alliances. The extended kin of both spouses, and others, are drawn into the conflict, especially where the boundaries between the nuclear and extended family are amorphous. (For example, when Mr. C. brought his whole clan to court, at the next court date, Mrs. C. came with an entourage of friends. Since Mr. W. lived with his very supportive parents and sister, Mrs. W., a European immigrant with no close family and friends, felt intimidated. She entered an alliance with her therapist, who became a powerful ally, fighting the father in court and out.) As predicted by coalition theory (Gamson, 1969), the spouse who feels least powerful usually makes the first move to seek support from others. Once that person is aligned, the other is threatened and seeks corresponding support. The coalitions become formed by a dyadic process of mutual adjustment to each other's relative power and influence.[6]

When the custody dispute between parents incorporates others, it easily becomes entwined with the agendas of the larger group's disputes with each other. It is important to extricate those agendas and refocus on the child.

☐ Mrs. T. was a twenty-two-year-old attractive Mexican American, soft, sweet, vulnerable, and naive. She was ending a violent marriage with Mr. T., a twenty-six-year-old Filipino man who had been involved in drugs until his recent rehabilitation. Mrs. T.'s new boyfriend was a young policeman who obtained mug shots of the father from his police record, which unfortunately were seen by the four-year-old daughter. The father became very angry at this but tried to control himself. The father's brothers, who had been involved in gang activities in the inner-city area, supported the father's cause and angrily provoked the policeman. When these brothers were subsequently arrested for not paying speeding fines, they were convinced it was a vendetta. Dangerous taunts and threats of violence were made by the gang, and counterrepressive measures were taken by the police who now became involved as a group. The young policeman and the father were brought into mediation to discuss all the incidents. First, they acknowledged that the gang and the police had ongoing problems that had nothing to do with the child. They clarified a lot of confusion and misunderstanding, apologized to each other, then made a pact to support each other's efforts with the child, in a stunning series of conciliatory moves that ended the feud.

The drive to seek the support of professionals who wield power by virtue of their status and authority is evident as the dispute enters the arena of the court. Oddly enough, attorneys themselves play a less important role here. Given their institutional role of advocates, they are expected to be biased and hence their support is not pivotal. Their significance in this process lies in their ability to help the parent muster an army of defenders. Mental health professionals, by contrast, are highly prized allies in a custody dispute. Four fathers and seven mothers in our study were in a strong alliance with a therapist who fueled the fight over the child by reifying their client's distorted views and labeling the other parent as disturbed. In each of these cases the therapist saw only one party in the dispute, or saw the other parent only briefly after they were already perceived to be in support of their client. In two memorable cases in which both parents had therapists who were themselves disputing with each other about the family, it became imperative to involve the disputing professionals in a case management conference about the family. This strategy clearly is more effective if implemented early, before respective positions have been firmly established.

The end result of this escalating "tribal warfare" is dramatically illustrated in the following case, in which everyone, especially the children, ultimately lost.

☐ Mrs. J. left her husband after a secret affair with another man when her twin children were three years old. By mutual agreement she kept custody. For the next seven years the children enjoyed summer vacations and brief visits with the father, who flew in from another state on a wave of gifts and excitement. When the mother and her new husband fell on hard times financially, they began a series of suits for increased child support from the wealthy father. Mr. J., who had been greatly humiliated by the separation, found these financial demands the last straw. He hired the best (most aggressive) attorney and filed for custody of the children, now aged ten years. In a bitter, escalating court trial, the mother wrote, and encouraged her children to write, poisonous letters about the father to the judge. The judge became angry and, buttressed by a psychologist's opinion that the children were being turned against the father, he ordered a precipitous change in custody. The close-knit extended family, local community, church, and school became enraged. Fund-raising efforts and letters to newspapers and local politicians all resulted in the formation of an unholy alliance: the community against the outsiders (that is, the father, judge, attorney, and psychologist). The children became celebrities. Despite the father's efforts to woo them, they spent a miserable two years as martyrs living with their father who found himself doing battle with them and the medley of voices in support of them. The mother was saddened and guilty about what had happened. With great bitterness, the father was forced to relinquish custody and withdraw.

Conclusion

When it involves divorce-related problems, "support" from extended kin and significant others is a misleading and fairly simplistic notion. We have observed repeatedly the double-edged nature of support and how, together with practical assistance and emotional encouragement, it often entails criticism and interference. Even when support is given unambiguously during a child custody dispute, it is often given in the context of helping one parent but without the benefit of understanding the whole situation—that is, the mother's, father's, children's, and family's viewpoints. In these cases, it leads to increased tension and escalation of conflict that is ultimately unsupportive and not constructive. Moreover, in the absence of normative or institutional means for resolving conflicts of interest, each parent is likely to engage the "support" of others, so that the conflict escalates, spreads, and incorporates the social networks of the parties. Finally, the child issues can easily be confounded with unrelated agendas or disputes between significant others or among the larger groups, exacerbating the conflict. Again, what is individually supportive may be destructive for the larger social system and often for the children within it.

The important implications of these findings for counseling is to realize that most disputes over custody and visitation that enter court have been of lengthy duration and have gathered an entourage of supporters or cocombatants. With the vision of rescuing a parent or child, one can enter into the middle of this process, easily become entangled or ensnarled in the drama, and be used as a pawn or puppet of the parties, thereby unwittingly contributing to the stalemating of the divorce process. In terms of the mediation implications of these processes, it is not unusual for divorcing parents to make important shifts toward cooperation with each other only to have significant others, not included in the mediation, undo the progress. Extended kin, new partners, and others are shadow parties in the mediation. They are the ones to whom the parents have to account when a settlement is reached. To them, parents must justify their position, their failure to get custody, or the reason for their compromise. This medley of voices or Greek chorus, which only a parent can hear, is manifested during mediation in unreasonable stands, resistance to settling, and failure to abide by agreements made. It is time to consider the role of these significant others in custody and access disputes, to harness the concern of these significant others in the service of settling the conflict or to help parents extricate themselves from the unwanted tyranny of their influence.

CHAPTER 3

Illusions and Delusions Between Divorcing Spouses

Marriage in our society, according to Berger and Kellner (1970), is an existential drama in which two strangers come together and redefine themselves. Throughout the period of courtship and early marriage, intensely intimate and private conversations between the lovers merge their discrepant views of the world, stabilize ambiguous and shifting images, and serve to reconstruct the present and reinterpret their past into new shared meanings. In the process, images of self and the other are typified, objectified, and metamorphosed into stable self-concepts and stable conceptions of the other. Relative amounts of appreciation and value are accorded each partner so that levels of self-esteem are affected and become mutually contingent.

To what extent are self-concept and conception of others emergent products of current important relationships rather than transferences from earlier primary relationships? To what extent are conceptions of self and others negotiated and transformed within intimate relations, and over what period of time, and what other factors influence these redefinitions? These are complex issues. Nevertheless, Berger and Kellner's bold claims of a social construction of reality and identity point to a sociopsychological process that has been somewhat ignored by many clinicians. Furthermore, their argument can be extended: If marriage involves a construction of a significant shared reality and if it stabilizes the reciprocally connected images of self and the other, then divorce involves first, a major destruction of the reality of the marriage; second, a shattering of self-image; and third, a disintegration of the image of the other—the ex-spouse. Much of our thinking about the impact of divorce has centered on the first two ideas, and relatively no attention has been given to the third— that is, the idea that the images of the other are profoundly altered during the separation, and in congruence with this, the history of the marriage is fundamentally reinterpreted.

We believe that both at the time of courtship and marriage (coming together) and at the time of separation and divorce (parting), couples tend to undertake substantial redefinitions of themselves and each other. These constructions or reconstructions of self- and other-identity may be more or less radical and can occur gradually or quite precipitously. They can also involve greater or lesser degrees of distortions of reality. Most successful divorces result from a more gradual evolution of a measured, realistic view of oneself and one's spouse, together with an emotional disengagement from the marital relationship. Among many divorcing couples stuck in the divorce transition, however, the coming together or parting was so dramatic or traumatic, so infused with emotion and meaning, that the images of self and other created during these significant events at these significant times became fixed forever, unyielding to counterevidence and scripting the couples' turbulent relationship through the postdivorce years.

Two types of interactional impasses which are complementary and opposite in a number of intriguing respects, derive from this dynamic. In the first type, the couples maintain highly positive, idealized views of each other. They are enormously ambivalent about the separation and engage in a never-ending search for ways to reconstitute their dreams. To this end, they cycle through repeated, promising reconciliations that dissipate into bitter disappointment and periodic conflict as their illusions are shattered. The need to plan for the care of their children is painful because it necessitates renewed contact and often triggers their reengagement. For the children of these relationships, the divorce is never a finality and their reconciliation fantasies are continually fueled by the parental reinvolvement, yet they are often neglected by their parents, who are absorbed with each other.

In the second type, ex-spouses have developed extremely negative polarized views of each other that are sustained by little or no evidence in current reality. They view each other as "crazy and mentally disturbed" or as "morally reprehensible monsters." What is more, they act on these beliefs: They resist their children's contact with the other parent and fight, consciously and righteously, to protect their children from the bad, immoral, or neglectful caretaking of the other parent. The spouses seem to mirror one another, each in a victim stance, each viewing the other as the persecutor. These couples avoid contact. They refuse to communicate directly and use others (friends, attorneys, or children) as spokespersons in attempts to make plans. For the children of these parents, transitions between parental homes have all the lonely, frightening qualities of venturing between two armed, opposing camps. Their fears are often confirmed by periodic quarrels and even physical fights.

Whereas in our project we have seen primarily either couples staunchly maintaining polarized, negative views or clinging to idealized, positive views, there is much variation on this theme. In an interesting series of cases we could detect features of both types. These were particularly stormy and dramatic relationships in which both highly idealistic and overly devalued views of each other existed side by side. In some situations, one ex-spouse idealized whereas the other ex-spouse had developed strong negative views. In other cases, both ex-spouses alternated between states of idealization and devaluation.

There are psychological explanations for these phenomena. Psychodynamically, negative views of the ex-spouse may represent restitutive defenses, erected in the service of restoring self-esteem or of warding off depression or guilt (chapters 4 and 5). Idealized views may be seen as defensive denial of the loss and disappointment inherent in the reality of the separation. Alternatively, the phenomena are construed as evidence of personality disorder. Object-relations theorists, in particular, consider these kinds of relationships as characteristic of primitively organized, or at best regressed, individuals who are unable to maintain a balanced view of self and other and thus split and project good and bad onto others. The origins of this defensive splitting are believed to be in disturbances in early caregiving relationships (Kernberg, 1967; Kohut, 1977; Mahler, 1971; Masterson, 1981). The behavioral characteristics of the types we have identified may then be seen as emanating from enduring psychological predispositions or vulnerabilities within individuals, which have been developmentally determined and structurally fixed. This formulation suggests a cross-situational potential for relating to people as transference objects from the past.

Whereas it seemed clear that these psychological factors were operative in a number of cases, we were intrigued by the fact that in a significant number of others, the disturbed behavior and polarized views appeared to take their root in separation-related factors and were almost entirely confined to the sphere of the divorce relationship. One criterion for identifying this subgroup is that outside the ex-spousal relations, with others, these same people could think and act in a manner free from severe psychological disturbance. For these reasons we sought a sociopsychological explanation of the phenomena, derived from classical symbolic interactionalism (Mead, 1934; Cooley, 1964) and attribution theory (Heider, 1958; Kelley, 1973; Jones and Davis, 1965) and developed more fully in recent expectation-states theory (Berger, Rosenholtz, and Zelditch, 1980; Johnston, 1985). We view the idealized images as social constructions of reality that are put together at the time of courtship and the negative stereotyped characterizations as being formed at the time of separation.

Idealized Images and Shattered Dreams

Possibly the saddest and most painful situations among divorcing couples at impasse are those in which one or both of the spouses remain powerfully emotionally attached to the other. In these cases, couples continually seek to reengage but find their expectations disappointed and their hopes repeatedly thwarted. Whereas it is fairly normal to reconcile and separate one to three times during the divorce transition, these couples separate numerous times, spanning many years. Others reluctantly admit years after the final separation that they are still haunted by their love for their ex-partner and found they could never really love anyone else. The fixity of their passion and purpose is indeed the essence of great romantic novels and classical tragedy.

Basic to their hopes and dreams are idealized views that they nurture of the other. They maintain a special attachment to and hold a strongly positive view of the other, oblivious to any incongruities that do not support their fantasied wishes about the other or the situation. Despite much evidence to the contrary, they believe their partner does love them, or that she is capable of warm, compassionate mothering, or that he is able to be faithful and responsible but that circumstances or events, or even they themselves, prevented it. They are quick to make situational attributions (the loss of a job, work pressure), justifying their own or the children's abandonment, excusing their spouse's sins of omission and commission. When overwhelming evidence to the contrary shatters their illusions, they can become bitterly disappointed and furiously angry. At these times, overt conflict is renewed, and they will again break off contact with the other spouse. However, later, often with the most minor encouragement, the idealized view is restored and they become once again powerfully re-attached.

☐ Carrie, twenty-two years old, vulnerable, idealistic, and lonely, told of her initial encounter with a very self-absorbed young Asian immigrant. "I met him Thanksgiving 1977. I fell in love with him at first sight when I saw him across the aisles of the supermarket. He is gorgeous, beautiful looking, my ideal! I promised myself I would marry him. Most of the time he was too busy to see me. He always had his nose in a book. I proposed but he made the decision not to marry me. We broke up. He went back to Japan, he didn't even say good-bye, didn't ask me to his farewell party. He came back two years later and called me up to say he missed me. I dropped everything, my job and my boyfriend, and came back to be with him. Then I got pregnant but he wanted me to abort the baby. I left and married another Japanese man to give the baby a father. I was only married twenty-four days when he came back, crying and saying he loved me and wanted to be the father to our baby. I was still in love with him. It was a crazy fantasy, but I had the vision of being his wife and a mother to his child. I got an annulment from the man I had married and so we began to live together again. Only later when he wanted a green card [immigration visa] did he agree to marry me. The marriage was lonely. He was always studying and I had to work to support him. There was no money, sex, time, or labor expended on his part. So I got angry and left him again. But I still love him . . . it's crazy." At the two year follow-up, Carrie and her man had again reconciled.

For those who nurture idealized views, the origin of this impasse seems to lie in the original courtship or coming together of the couple. During a very significant event or period in their lives, they establish a specific and significant attachment, in which each holds a special meaning or position vis-à-vis the other. There are several different though often interrelated patterns. In many cases this relationship has been their first or most significant love experience. A brief history of their courtship often reveals that they met during adolescence or were high school sweethearts, or that they were virgins when they first came together. Their intense, often mutually dependent relationship usually began as a refuge from a barren or conflictual family situation. In fact, some left their families and went into the marriage, using the relationship with the spouse to effect that separation. Many felt they had found a longed-for other who would provide the kind of warmth and closeness not experienced earlier, someone who would help undo or repair the disappointments and deprivations of their own childhood. Hence, the other was imbued with fantasy and hope, both of which moderated their confusion, depression, and loneliness. This early romantic relationship involved a fusing of boundaries of self and other and a definition of themselves that was intimately tied to that of the other. Many describe their marriages in very grandiose terms as having a sense of specialness and oneness. Obviously this is problematic. Later, either both struggle to disentangle from the confining structures of their relationship or one begins to feel limited, even suffocated, and tries to disengage gradually but painfully over a number of years. However, given the infusion of special meaning, one or both are unable to turn psychologically from the other. They cannot tolerate facing the pain, disappointment, and anger that the other (as so many before) has not met and cannot meet their needs. Hence they are drawn back into the hope that the other will "come through." Sometimes these spouses who wish to disengage report lethargy, chronic depression, migraine headaches, identity confusion, and guilt as they oscillate back and forth, finding the relationship intolerable but unable to let go.

For others, the initial attraction is based on overwhelming erotic attraction. They storm and fight constantly about daily living (care of the children, finances, work, being faithful and responsible) but are completely swept away by the sexual gratification within the relationship and what it represents in the way of need satisfaction and nurturance. Several talk about their obsession with the other as though it were an addiction they have little will or capacity to fight.

☐ "He has such beautiful limpid brown eyes, I drown in them. He comes to me so helpless and confused. I just give up my resolve to keep him out of my bed. Then when we make love, nothing else matters," said one young woman who met her man when she was fifteen and in the following ten years had two children with him and experienced at least sixteen separations from him. During this period, this man also lived with another woman with whom he had a child, did not financially support his wife, and took very little interest in his children. At the two-year follow-up, they were again living together, in considerable conflict, and planning to separate.

☐ Katherine, an extraordinarily beautiful young Irishwoman, had recently broken up a long-term relationship when she encountered an older, morose Latino man. His dark depression, cynicism, and working-class background had a mystique that fascinated and distracted her. Unfortunately, their first love-making resulted in a pregnancy, which she aborted. The young Catholic woman could not forgive herself and married him out of guilt, although she had become quickly disenchanted with him. He, on the other hand, became obsessed by her: "I loved her then and I will till the day I die," he declared twelve years later. Her guilt together with his obsessed attraction resulted in repeated ambivalent separations marked by several occasions of drinking and explosive violence on his part.

Some of the initial engagements were motivated by an idealistic, protective stance toward an emotionally troubled individual. Some maternal women have visions of rescuing a disturbed man and, once engaged, are tyrannized by the emotional demands and dependency of their partner. They feel too guilty, frightened, or responsible to break the unspoken contract that they will continue to care for that person. Others met at highly vulnerable times in their lives:

☐ Susan was driving a car with a boyfriend of whom she wished to rid herself, when she had a terrible accident. They were both critically injured. During the weeks in which she was semiconscious and he hung between life and death, in her guilt she promised that if they survived, she would devote her life to him. Eight years later, despite the fact that this man had periodically abandoned her and transmitted a venereal disease to her, she continued to cling to the marriage.

☐ John, a young professional counselor, became intensely involved and committed to his female patient during her life-threatening illness. He rescued her and later could not extricate from their intense but explosive relationship.

An important feature of the lives of those who maintain idealized views is their social isolation. Through choice or circumstance they are loners. Most protect the vicissitudes of their marital relationship from the scrutiny of others, seeing it essentially as a private, exclusive matter. Whereas the overinvolvement of friends and kin can fuel disputes (as described in chapter 2), the lack of involvement of others is also problematic. Normally supportive others challenge illusions and misconceptions and help test reality. These people lack others who can anchor their views of their spouse in a socially defined reality that will support the separation. It is also possible that their cherished dreams are a defense against loneliness.

In sum, these couples or individuals are deeply cathected, sexually bonded, or ideologically committed to one another, and remain so at some level. While their idealized images draw them inexorably together, so do they break them apart. As they engage and move toward intimacy, the reality of the other person intrudes and their expectations are violated. Since the state of emotional-sexual arousal in these couples is very high, the conflicts that follow are intense and explosive, usually triggering another separation. Consequently their relationships are often dramatic and stormy.

We found that these couples had long-standing problems with shared parenting after divorce. Too much contact with each other intensifies the painful cycle. They can be intensely cooperative and intensely combative, and seem to have few ways of communicating without becoming intimate with each other or remaining distant and outraged. They have particular problems separating the parental from the spousal role. Hence, the cyclical postdivorce disputes over the children are usually an extension of their ambivalent relationship and are energized by their smoldering passions. Often the children are drawn into their hopes and disappointments:

☐ Mrs. L., whose hopes were continually dashed by her husband's unavailability, often pushed her daughter into wanting to see her father, unnecessarily highlighting the father's deficits and disappointing the child.

Interventions in Ambivalent Separations

Since—in these cases more than any others—the origin of the impasse lies in the initial courtship and early marriage of the couples, it is important to review their early experiences in detail to gain clarification of (and, if possible, insight into) the reasons for their coming together and the meaning it had for them at the time. It is imperative that this be done separately with each partner, otherwise they can both easily be swept back into that earlier powerful relationship. We help each identify precisely from what they are fleeing (for example, feelings of loneliness, rejection, and abandonment or an unhappy family situation) and what they found special in the relationship with the other at that time (for example, special acknowledgment as a person, a longed-for closeness and intimacy, belongingness, recognition of special talents and capacities). Then we help them carefully extricate the qualities from the relationship and identify them as qualities they now possess and deserve to own personally. For example, "You really found what an enormous capacity you had to love in those early years," or, "You worried then about your ability to care for yourself. Now you know you can." To diminish the considerable sense of obligation the special relationship engenders, concepts of justice or equality of exchange are evoked by talking about what each had gained from the relationship or about the mutual or reciprocal "gifts" they were able to give each other. For example, "You gave him your excitement and adventurous zest for living; he gave you stability and security." Sometimes it proves to be a powerful intervention to have each acknowledge verbally what they gave each other in the relationship and to thank one another. To counter their guilt about leaving an emotionally disturbed partner, we give them permission to free themselves from a destructive situation by evoking their obligations to their children as well as to themselves.

The next strategy is to examine carefully what went wrong in the marriage, where it ceased to nurture them both or stood in the way of their further growth. If this is done properly, it often involves considerable sadness and mourning of the early relationship, which can be interpreted as a natural way of relinquishing the other. On the other hand, there are some dangers in this strategy because the idealized views of the other can easily be nourished—and hopes rekindled—by the nostalgic return to the past. In fact, it is sometimes necessary to point out that what they are giving up was indeed an illusion and not a real person.

From this point on, to counter the idealized views of the other, it is often necessary to challenge and confront their illusions, pointing to the dichotomy between their views and the facts. For example: "You say he has been a wonderful lover, but by your own admission he's never been faithful to you or to any other woman for more than three months in his whole life!" "You keep believing she will change and be a concerned mother to the children. You have waited twelve years, how much longer do you think it will take?" "You are thirty-five. You anticipate living another, perhaps forty years? Are you prepared to devote the next forty years to the memory of this woman who has left you?" "You say you love going on vacations and trips with her, but in fact you have not left home for two years because of her phobias about driving in tunnels or over bridges." Finally, we encourage each to explore other relationships in which their needs might be better met and their dreams better fulfilled. Since many are socially isolated, this is no small endeavor, and they require considerable support in venturing out.

Teaching them how to communicate about their children without becoming emotionally reengaged is especially important. Drawing on the analogy of a business or professional relationship, we encourage them to discuss and coordinate plans for the children in an extremely task-focused manner. Personal comments, innuendos, provocative body language, references to the past, and alluding to a shared private experience are quickly identified as inappropriate to the task at hand. They are shown how to structure their agreements into contract form and encouraged to meet to discuss plans in an appropriate neutral public place (not over a candlelight dinner). Sharing personal information is discouraged and wherever possible, arrangements which require minimal contact between them are promoted. Spouses trying to extricate themselves from an obsessed other are also encouraged to give clear, explicit messages, defining their intentions as simply being civil for the sake of the children, lest any friendliness be misinterpreted.

The Negative Reconstruction of Spousal Identity

- *Mrs. B.:* "When I married him, I thought he was the strong silent type and he seemed gentle. It was all a big front. I mistook his silence for strength. He's really weak. He's no gentleman, he's a drunk. He has no scruples and cares for none except his drinking cronies."

- *Mr. R.:* "I knew she'd been married before and that she'd gone 'out' on her husband. I thought he was the problem. Now 1 realize that it was her. She is two-faced, entirely selfish and runs away from problems. She's a liar. She can't help herself. Every time she opens her mouth, the lies spill out. I can't believe I ever trusted her. She's capable of putting on such an act!"

- *Mrs. K.:* "He's a bastard, a son of a gun! He is ruthless, a sociopath, lacking in conscience, and uncaring about people. Work and money are everything to him. I've always known this, but I married him because I didn't think I was worth anything more."

- *Mrs. F.:* "He is violent and dangerous. He has homicidal tendencies. The children are not safe with him."

These comments are illustrative of the intensely negative, polarized characterizations that many high-conflict divorced couples make of each other. When we arranged to interview the ex-spouse, we were often led to expect a monster. Instead we met an entirely human person, who nevertheless was very angry and frustrated and who similarly characterized the other spouse as "bad" or "mad." At times, we wondered if we were interviewing the right person or talking about the same marriage and divorce! Moreover, we soon found it was extremely difficult to modify the unrealistic, stereotyped negative views that these embittered and embattled ex-spouses held of each other.

Our clinical experience leads us to conclude that the actual experience of separation for some couples was the crucible in which these negative views of each other are brewed and crystallized. Couples who experience particularly traumatic separations are prime candidates for generating negative images. Perceived experiences of being suddenly and unexpectedly left; abandoned after secret plotting and planning; left after a secret love affair with another person; left after uncharacteristic, explosive violence—all are separation modes that are typically traumatic and involve inordinate degrees of humiliation, anger, defeat, guilt, and fear, thus setting the stage for what is to come. A radical reconstruction of the identity of the ex-spouse can occur at the time of a traumatic separation. The desperate reactions and counter-reactions to the crisis are likely to crystallize new negative views of each other which subsequently become autonomous of these origins.

Excerpts from the accounts of each of the above individuals will typify how at least one partner experienced the separation.

☐ *Mrs. B.:* "We never argued and fought. He was a quiet, silent man. I thought I knew him. We had been married twenty-one years. One evening he went out for a packet of cigarettes and never came back."

☐ *Mr. R.:* "I had just returned from an overseas business trip. It was Christmas eve and it was so good to be home! Lillie and I decorated our Christmas tree together. She left in the car. I thought she would be back in half an hour. I waited for hours and then found the tape-recorded message. She said she was leaving, that she didn't love me any more. Later I found out about this other guy."

☐ *Mrs. K.:* "When I was visiting my family for two weeks this summer, he stripped the house of all the furniture and left. Later I found that he had made secret inventories of all our valuable antiques and secretly visited the attorneys and had papers prepared for the divorce. All the time he gave no indication of his intentions."

☐ *Dr. F.:* "I was stressed by work at the hospital. When I came home she was always nagging me, demanding this and that. I restrained myself, was very depressed and morose. One night I couldn't hold it in any longer. She was bugging me about some stupid thing. . . . I hit her . . . hard. It was awful. I felt so bad. That has never happened before or since."

The common feature of these experiences is a major, unexpected assault on one's expected universe, together with absence of open, intimate, corrective, and correcting communication. The couples have often been living together but in separate individual worlds, projecting their own experience onto the other and receiving no feedback as to the form of the other's reality. Avoidance of issues, hiding from the other, and hiding even from oneself are marked features in most of these cases. In some instances, the leaving spouse was not aware of his or her own degree of alienation, or of the intent to separate, until the actual event was triggered by some relatively minor happening. For example, after an argument about the cat, Mr. O. found himself fleeing from his house in his car and realized he could never return. In general, then, the actual separation is experienced by one and sometimes both of the parties as unexpected, shocking, and/or humiliating—as attack or abandonment.

The subsequent handling of events by the parties usually compounds the problem. In general, the period following the actual separation in many of these cases is marked by a lot of desperate, unusual and atypical behavior that seems quite irrational. Hysterical outbursts, suicide attempts, ominous threats of murder, physical struggles, running away, excessive drinking, and flagrant promiscuity occur. Child snatching and possession snatching were not uncommon.

☐ Mrs. P. missed the last bus home from work and decided never to return rather than face her husband's jealous questioning and oppressive dependency. During the next month, Mr. P. became drunk and smashed the family car, kept his daughter out of school to comfort himself, secretly trailed his wife to find if she had a lover, threatened suicide, and then staked out her workplace with the intent of taking her and her coworkers hostage.

Psychologically and interpersonally, these desperate acts make sense. The separation makes one or both of the parties feel a tremendous disruption and loss of their expected reality: loss of oneself, loss of the other, of order and control, of fairness and justice. Such acts, which are direct expressions of rage and panic, are also attempts to recapture a meaningful sense of self and world. They appear to have four functions: to restore the normative order of the marriage (that is, as an expected, socially confirmed reality), to master an out-of-control situation, to restore self-esteem and a meaningful self-identity, and to restore a sense of fairness and justice.

First, at the initial stage of separation, the primary motivating factor is the violation of the normative order of the marriage and the shattering of deeply held expectations. With a breakdown of the structure of the marital relationship, constraints on feelings and impulses are lifted; images, expectations, and roles break loose from their moorings. Fear, despair, and anger erupt in the spouse who is left, giving rise to behaviors that are viewed here as attempts to restore the marriage to its normal state. Hysterical outbursts, suicidal gestures, and uncharacteristic violence are aimed at shocking or frightening the other spouse into resuming the marriage. Some punish the spouse like an errant child.

Second, failing to restore the marriage, the acts take on a symbolic function as one or both of the separating spouses attempt to regain a sense of mastery over what is perceived to be an out-of-control situation or a runaway spouse. They now represent attempts to hold on to or at least control and manage the other—to regain some sense of order. Hence they refuse to leave the house, refuse to share the child, take out legal injunctions or restraining orders on each other, refuse to give or receive financial support, and refuse to compromise or negotiate in mediation sessions.

Third, many of the acts become attempts to restore self-esteem or to reestablish a meaningful self-identity. Frenetic activity, urgent appeals for validation from relatives and friends or promiscuity are efforts to reestablish self-worth, sexual attractiveness, and moral rectitude after the humiliation of rejection. Some men plead with their wives to return and, when unsuccessful, bully or beat them. In these cases, these violent acts seem to be not only attempts to regain mastery but efforts to restore a positive sense of masculinity and potency after deep shaming and realization of their abysmal dependency and vulnerability.

Fourth and last, the desperate acts acquire the quality of righting a wrong, thereby restoring a sense of fairness and justice. Often they have a sense of counterretaliation or retribution. A spouse may have affairs (as the other spouse did), withhold child visitation (in response to the other spouse's withholding of financial support), snatch possessions (mirroring the other spouse's actions). They aim to get even with the other or to receive retribution or compensation for perceived inequities. Children—as well as cars, bank accounts, and other possessions—are snatched back and forth.

The significant point is that these desperate acts, whatever their reason, are unlikely to be attributed to the stressors, vicissitudes, and reactions of the situation. Rather they are likely to form the bases for the redefinitions the spouses have naturally begun to make of each other at this time. What is basically involved is the "fundamental attribution error," in which too much is attributed to the personality and predispositions of the individuals and not enough to the situational constraints and interactional sequence (Ross, 1977). Desperate acts lead to many negative labels, most typically ones like "untrustworthy," "irresponsible," "stupid," "dangerous," "vengeful," "bad," or "crazy." There is a sense of discovery as to who the ex-spouse *really* is. The result is to objectify or reify a stage of the dissolution of the relationship in terms of the individual pathology of the parties and freeze it forever in time. The reconstruction of self-identity and identity of other go hand-in-hand, such that, "If he's crazy, I'm sane," or "If I'm right, she's wrong." Not surprising, then, that these reconstructions take on the nature of a matching, interlocking pathology. Hence the separated spouses appear as symmetrical images of each other (that is, both rageful and vengeful) or presents themselves as complementary opposites (that is, victim and persecutor).[1]

Under the prevailing distressed emotional states of the parties, thinking becomes more concrete, stylized, fragmented and not integrated with other aspects of their understanding. Perceptual narrowing and distortion occur, all of which is conducive to stereotyped thinking, simplistic characterizations and broad generalizations about the other. During such states of emotional distress, the labels become evaluatively polarized and the ex-spouse dehumanized (for example, "slut," "whore," "bastard," "pig," "tramp"). At such times, with scant evidence, they can accuse each other of outrageous deeds: child molestation, neglect and abuse, maniacal violence, and substance abuse.

The invalid characterizations made of one another often have a self-fulfilling prophecy effect because they form the presuppositions or expectations from which any interaction between the couple will proceed. Fear, distrust, and beliefs that the other is dishonest and exploitive condition responses of withdrawal, counterattack, and counterexploitation. In the early stages, these expectations are more tentatively or poorly grounded in circumstantial evidence. As they enter a "testing-out" phase, the couple inadvertently but inevitably set up the other to confirm their emerging views:

☐ Feeling deceived by her husband's affair and sudden breakup of the marriage, Mrs. T. emptied the family home and bank account and left for her mother's. In response, Mr. T. refused to support her or their son. This refusal was taken as further proof of his lack of caring and decency.

In other cases, because the couple is physically separated and the spouses communicate very little with each other directly, they have little opportunity to correct their invalid conceptions. The result is that they become interlocked and enmeshed as they reconfirm in thought and deed their reconstructions of each other.

It is important to realize that, in these cases, parents are genuinely fighting to protect their children from what they believe to be the dangerous and pernicious influence of the other parent. Their specific fears about the other's parenting are closely tied to their own experience in the separation and related attributions about the character of the ex-spouse. If he was abandoned, he believes she will abandon or neglect the children. If he had a secret lover for whom he left, she believes he will betray the children. If he was violent toward her, then he is likely to be physically abusive to the children. If she lied to him, she will lie to the children.

A traumatic separation experience is probably not a sufficient condition for a full-fledged assignment of negative stereotyped attributes to the other spouse. Another essential ingredient is provided by the consensual validation of each spouse's separate social world. Unlike those who have ambivalent separations and who are more socially isolated, these divorcing spouses often seek the help of friends, family, attorneys, and therapists, all of whom play an important role in helping them make sense of the separation. Hence the interactional impasse is buttressed by external alliances, as described in chapter 2. During hours of conversation with others, the history of the marriage is reinterpreted and the "real" character of the ex-spouse emerges or is discovered. One woman who spent much time with supportive friends recounted a dream she had during this time. She dreamed she had to get not one divorce but two: one from her husband and another from a man she did not know. A month earlier this woman had opened a letter expecting it to contain her airplane ticket to join her husband at his new job location. Instead she found his petition for divorce. Her friends, sharing their once-private views, helped her redefine her husband as an "unconscionable SOB."

What are the effects of this process over time? If negative images are generated largely by the separation experience, reified by the social network, and reaffirmed by interactive behaviors congruent with the negative expectations, then these images will become more stable with time and the interactional impasse between the divorced couple more rigid and unamenable to change. Indeed, our clinical observations bear this out. We have seen many couples whose fight with each other smolders for years following the divorce and erupts into periodic fiery encounters whenever contact is made. When communicating with each other, their negative expectations and reactions are activated with little or no provocation. The turn of a phrase, a facial expression, or simply the sound of the other's voice or the sight of the other (regardless of what is said) is sufficient to release a flood of affect and a total assignment of negative meaning. "All he has to do is breathe and I get angry," reported one woman, ever ready to battle. In these cases, every encounter escalates into a confrontation. The couple immediately react to each other in a stereotyped manner, reflective of their negative images. In the tertiary stages, the stereotyped characterizations have been refined to a simplicity that is bizarre. The image of the other spouse is at best a caricature, at worst a monster. "The children's mother is an alcoholic," "My first husband was violent," become shorthand ways of explaining the divorce to themselves and to others. In these situations, the dilemmas for the children, especially the younger ones, are whom to trust, what is safe, and how to make sense of the vastly contradictory views of reality that are communicated through the passions and fears of their opposing parents.

Interventions with Negative Images

In designing interventions for spouses who have experienced traumatic separations, there are three questions to be asked: How recent is the trauma? How distorted are the parties' perceptions of the experience by their defensive needs? What are the roles played by supportive others in their social world? The answers to each of these questions will dictate or modify a differential strategy. Since chapter 2 has dealt with the issue of helper alliances and chapters 4 and 5 will discuss how to assess and intervene with those who are defensively distorting, the important issue to be discussed here is the recency of the separation and how intervention at different points in the postdivorce trajectory requires very different techniques.

First, if at all possible, it is crucial to intervene early after a traumatic separation in order to prevent an escalation of the desperate reactions and counterreactions to the event and to prevent negative views of the other from forming. The optimal time is during the period of denial and disorientation that typically follows the crisis. At this point, clients are likely to be in a state of psychological shock, confusion, or panic. As with any other trauma, the techniques of intervention are basically supportive and ego-restitutive. Clients may even need practical help and direction in managing their lives and coping with the immediate needs of the children. During this time they are usually amenable to guidance, so that gentle restraints can more easily be placed on their propensity to act out. As the initial denial and disbelief give way, there is typically an urgent, almost compulsive, need to repeat over and over the events of the trauma.

Vivid details are reported about the ordinary daily events that led to the discovery of the illicit affair, to the declaration of the intent to divorce, or to the disappearance of the spouse—as if they were etched or burned into memory. Subsequent conversations or confrontations with the other spouse are repeated word for word. This process of coming to terms with the reality of the event goes hand in hand with trying to make some sense of it. Consequently, there is often a search for explanations that interpret the experience as a temporary, reversible problem. Spouses hope the other partner is merely going through some transitory phase (such as menopause or work or financial stress) or that he or she is being influenced by others (for example, the women's movement). When they are unable to justify such behavior as a "passing phase" or to attribute it to other external agents, the search goes deeper; the history of the marriage is reviewed in order to determine what enduring predispositions of the other spouse are responsible.

This process of making meaning may take several months of obsessive rumination. It is important to engage both spouses separately or together to help them develop an appropriately useful account of the failure of their relationship—one that despite the hurt and pain allows the evolution of a balanced and differentiated view of the other, acknowledging and accepting the other's relative strengths and weaknesses and their own self-integrity. It is not essential that both spouses evolve the same explanation for the failed marriage, as if there were only one view of this complex experience. Neither does the explanation have to be brutally realistic and factual; many hurtful details are better left unspoken. However, the explanation or account of the divorce does have to make it feasible for the couple to reconstitute a cooperative parental relationship if at all possible. A case involving a couple relatively free of psychopathology and without other people involved in their dispute illustrates some of these interventions more clearly.

☐ Tom and Jill had been disputing over the custody of their five-year-old son ever since their sudden separation three months previously. Their parting was precipitated by Jill's discovery that her husband had been having a secret affair with her best friend and work colleague, Mary Ann.

Although their marriage had never been particularly sexually exciting, they both described it as a warm, companionable relationship. There had never been any conflict between them. During the preceding five years, Tom, Jill, and Mary Ann had all

worked together in a small business. They had become a very
close-knit group, spending most of their spare time together.
Jill felt particularly gratified by having Mary Ann as a close
female friend. "She taught me gourmet cooking and I showed
her how to bake bread. We talked lots about our intimate relationships with our men". When Tom and Mary Ann found
themselves extremely attracted to each other, out of great concern for hurting Jill, they tried to break off their relationship
but could not. They kept it a secret for several months until Jill
found some love letters they had written each other.

Jill was devasted. Initial shock was quickly followed by enormous rage, and she precipitously ordered her husband out of
the house. He left taking their child, until Jill was in a better
state to care for the boy. During the following months, Jill was
alternately deeply depressed and angry. She lost twenty
pounds, slept poorly, and obsessed constantly about her betrayal by her husband and her best friend. She ruminated bitterly on the many intimate conversations they had previously
enjoyed and on the details of the affair. She wondered if their
captivation with each other might be a passing fancy but, as
time went on, realized the possibility of reconciliation was unlikely. By the time the couple came to us for mediation of the
custody dispute, Jill had begun to reconstruct her perceptions
of the marriage and her husband's identity. "I was fooled in the
marriage. I was passive and I was walked over. I used to admire
Tom's strength and independence. Now I realize he's bossy and
domineering. If things don't go his way, he won't have anything
of it! I was tricked. I trusted them both. He is a liar. He will say
anything to get what he wants. As for her, she's scum—a low-
down, filthy, conniving bitch. She had this planned for years.
She wheedled her way into my confidence and then stole everything—first my husband and now she wants to steal my child!"

It is not surprising that in view of these reconstructions, Jill
took a strong, bullying, nonnegotiable stand with her husband
over the child, insisting on sole custody and limited visitation.
She believed he was constantly tricking and manipulating her
and that he had an ulterior motive for anything he proposed.
Tom, on the other hand, either conceded to her in guilty compensation or tried to see his child surreptitiously, in a way that
would not enrage her further. This confirmed her opinion that
he was indeed basically deceitful.

While fully and deeply empathizing with her anger and her right to be angry at the outrageous situation, the counselor took advantage of her obsessive ruminations to explore why the marriage had broken down. In particular, the possibility of a minor postpartum depression was suggested as the reason for her disinterest in sex since her son's birth. This, together with the fact that she and her husband had explicitly given each other permission to have extramarital sexual liaisons, was identified as a factor that left him feeling she did not need him or find him attractive and hence made him very vulnerable to falling in love with someone else. The complete lack of any conflict in the marriage was also problematic: What had they been doing with the angry feelings that are ubiquitous in close relationships?

Jill was initially resistant to seeing herself as anything but the victim in this situation. The counselor's questioning challenged her right to be intensely angry—feelings that were guarding against considerable loss and sadness. The counselor, resonating with the theme of sadness, talked about the way in which the marriage had broken down as an unnecessary tragedy that could have been averted had they both understood what was happening. Jill began, for the first time, to consider that there might have been preexisting problems in the marriage.

In a separate interview, Tom was generally defensive about his actions and critical of Jill's unreasonable claims to their child. The counselor did not deal with this defensive stance directly; instead she talked about Jill's behavior being the product of the separation. She was feeling enormously betrayed and her anger was a way of keeping her distance and guarding against her painful, loving feelings for him. In response to this, Tom began to cry, at the same time asking angrily if Jill thought she had the corner on misery. He went on to say that he felt extremely confused and sad about what had happened to their marriage; he missed his wife as a good friend and never wanted to hurt her. Later, in a joint session, the couple shared some of these feelings with each other, including apologies. Hence the importance of their past marriage relationship was honored and considerable self-integrity regained. In these ways the counselor helped the couple build a more understanding, forgiving view of each other. This intervention was then extended to deal with Jill's fears that Mary Ann would assume her position as mother of their child, as a prelude to their working out a shared custody agreement.

Unfortunately, with many litigating couples at an impasse, the traumatic separation has occurred many years previously, and their extremely negative views of each other are fixed, confirmed by their social world, and reaffirmed by years of hostile confrontations with one another. Any attempt to challenge these unrealistic views is met with much cynicism and dismissal of the counselor as being naive and as having been "duped" by the other spouse. "You were really taken in by him, weren't you? That man can put on such an act! You don't know what I know!" The counselor is then assailed with endless war stories supporting these views. There is little opportunity to review or reinterpret the separation experience itself, clouded as it is by defensive forgetting and by the construction of an alternative reality. These couples will refuse to meet together outright, or if they do, the mutual hostility is so easily provoked and intense that the intervention is iatrogenic; they become even less amenable to change, and the judgment and effectiveness of the counselor is discredited.

While any short-term intervention seemed ineffective in changing their fixed negative views, we were somewhat gratified to find that over a longer period of time a series of interventions, including periodic checkups and appropriate availability of the counselor to help with episodic crises, gradually stabilized their hostile interactions and allowed more realistic expectations to evolve. In fact, at the two-year follow-up, some of these extremely embattled couples had made moderate progress. They could actually talk together in a civil manner on the telephone and occasionally meet to negotiate simple changes in the child's schedule.

The peace mission usually begins with shuttle diplomacy. The spouses (and their new mates, if relevant) are seen separately and the concerns of each opposing side are laid out. The counselor has to be extremely careful during this phase. On the one hand, each side needs to feel thoroughly understood; on the other, it is important not to agree with and confirm unrealistic views least the counselor later be seen as "having spoken with a forked tongue" or "having betrayed them" when the actual negotiations begin. An explicit statement like, "I understand you believe that . . . .but I don't see it quite that way," is often necessary to differentiate the counselor's perceptions from the parties'.

Building on their concerns, the counselor then engages them in problem-solving, taking a very pragmatic approach. "Given that you consider the child's father dangerous, and given the court says he does have the right to visit his child, how can we set up a plan to make your child safe and you feel less worried?" or "So you find her unreliable and irresponsible; then you need to get smart in dealing with her. . . ." It is important to be very specific about the parent's concerns: "You say he is dangerous. But you are not worried he will neglect the child. He will feed her and care for her safely? He won't abuse her? What you mean by dangerous is that you fear he will talk negatively about you, try to influence her against you by telling her what you believe to be lies. Isn't that so? Let's deal with that problem then."

The next step is to negotiate provisional contracts or trial agreements between opposing sides on smaller, less controversial issues. Subsequent honoring of the contract involves explicit behavioral contradiction of their mutual negative expectations. To the extent that there is compliance with the agreement, there exists a base for continuing to build a more comprehensive agreement and to shift gradually towards more positive perceptions of each other as being more trustworthy. Usually the contracts are kept because both parties are conscious of being monitored, and they sense they are on trial and want to prove that they are not doing anything for which they can be blamed. During this process the counselor continues to interject new specific information or interpretations that counter their unrealistic views. This information can be specific to the person within a given relationship: "I agree that she may not be able to be faithful to a man, but she is able to commit herself and is consistently available to her child." At other times, it may be a relabeling of a person's motivation: "My sense is that this man is afraid of backing down. By your own analysis, he's been dominated all his life by his mother. He feels weak and inadequate with women and tries to compensate for that. He begins every conversation with you in a bullying, demanding, and insulting manner." This reinterpretation of the ex-spouse's obnoxious behavior is likely to call forth a different response from the parent in future interactions, one that is less defensive and less aggressive. Alternatively, the contradictory information can be specific to the situation: "During the separation you did have cause to be alarmed about his mental state. By all accounts, he was distraught and quite irrational. Now he has stabilized. It has been two years. He has remarried. His new wife is a calming influence. She will be there and will ensure the visits go smoothly." The counselor might further clarify: "It's hard for you to really know how he is today since you haven't talked with him for a long time."

The counselor can predict that episodic crises will occur and that

CHAPTER 4

Threats to Self-Esteem and Self-Integrity

While distorted perceptions and interactions between the former spouses, as well as alliances with others, play important roles in most divorce impasses, individual psychological disturbances may be a contributing factor. Thus, it is appropriate to ask to what extent there are psychological disturbances in this special population of divorcing parents, and if there are disturbances, what kinds? How does psychopathology contribute to entrenched postdivorce disputes? These are thorny questions, difficult to answer without considerably more theoretical development and research than presently exists in the literature.

At the outset of our counseling and mediation sessions, clinical assessments were made of the disputants, using DSM-III classifications. Each parent was rated by their counselor and by a second clinical psychologist who read the case record. The most notable finding was the high incidence of Axis II diagnoses: 64 percent were seen as having personality disorders and 27 percent as having personality disorder traits. Men were more often diagnosed as compulsive, paranoid, antisocial, avoidant, schizoid, and passive-aggressive. Women were more often diagnosed as dependent, histrionic, and borderline.[1]

Diagnoses on Axis I of the DSM-III were fewer. Almost one-fourth of the spouses were found to be substance abusers, primarily with alcohol, marijuana and cocaine, although some claimed to have ceased using these drugs. Many more were accused by the ex-spouse of having drug and alcohol problems, without any corroborating evidence. Despite the high incidence of verbal and physical aggression in this sample, only 15 percent were diagnosed as having an intermittent explosive disorder or an impulse-control disorder. This supports our contention that much of the violence was interactionally triggered

74

and sustained and that, in general, it was a feature of the marriage relationship or separation experience, not of ongoing personal psychopathology. Depression and anxiety disorders occurred in one-fifth of the sample. Given the loss and change consequent upon divorce, these incidences appear low and support our clinical interpretations that the ongoing disputes helped ward off depression and provided meaning and structure so as to alleviate some of the anxiety experienced. Only 2 percent of the sample were diagnosed as psychotic. This small percentage reflects the fact that the courts referred most flagrantly psychotic individuals for psychiatric evaluations rather than to our counseling-mediation service.

We have reservations about these diagnostic findings and find it important to make some interpretive qualifications. First, DSM-III ratings of social stress level (on Axis IV) indicated that the majority of these spouses (68 percent) were subject to extreme or severe social stressors, including the divorce, the legal dispute, unemployment, and financial difficulties. On Axis V, 74 percent of the sample were rated as having had moderate to superior levels of adaptive functioning in the past. The critical question, then, is whether their manifestations of psychopathology represented ongoing personality disorder or evidenced a chronic or acute regression in response to severe stressors? Since the disturbed behavior was often observed in the context of extraordinary sociointeractional and system pathology, it was difficult to sort out what was internal and external to the person. For instance, it is difficult to determine the degree of paranoia of a parent who is being accused by an ex-mate or evaluated in a court process that is attempting to determine fault.

Second, spouses presented with puzzling new patterns of behavior that clearly evidence impaired functioning but that do not fall within the well-known personality disorder categories. In particular, their severe decompensation seemed to be situational and relational; that is, it was frequently limited to certain issues (especially symbolically significant ones) and times (pressure of court dates, anniversaries, and holidays) and was confined to the relationship with the ex-spouse and associated persons. Moreover, we observed that a number of seriously emotionally disturbed individuals could effect a separation and disentangle themselves from ongoing disputes in a fairly adept manner, while relatively less disturbed litigants became entrenched in disputes and were unable to put together or sustain a coparenting relationship.

Clearly, reducing the explanation of the discord to individual psychopathology is an oversimplification. A more adequate and useful orientation begins with the premise that high-conflict divorcing parents are, to varying degrees and in special ways, psychologically vulnerable, and that the particular nature of the psychosocial stressor or crisis of divorce interacts with these vulnerabilities to provoke regression and to produce more rigid defensive styles and patterns of behavior that *look* like personality disorders. Our thesis is that separation-engendered conflicts (the humiliation inherent in rejection, the grief associated with loss, and the overall helplessness in response to assaultive life changes that are thrust upon both leaver and left) all resonate with long-standing vulnerabilities in the character structure of these parents, making it more difficult for them to extricate their reactions to the divorce experience from earlier unresolved problems and traumas. The central focus in developing treatment strategies becomes, then, to understand these special vulnerabilities and to design interventions that are maximally restitutive and supportive to divorcing spouses and that avoid unnecessarily disarming their precarious defenses or attacking their coping styles. Divorce involves both rejection and loss and hence provokes vulnerabilities in these two distinct but interrelated areas.

Narcissistic Vulnerability to Disputes

For many divorce involves a threat to their self-esteem and to core elements of their self-image as a spouse or parent. Consequently they need to save face. Whereas some experience the rejection inherent in divorce as a blow to their self-esteem, others experience it as a total humiliating assault on the self. The degree to which individuals feel assaulted depends on the degree of their narcissistic vulnerability— that is, on the strength, and the adequacy of integration of, their preseparation self-identity.

Narcissistically vulnerable divorcing individuals are characterized, to varying degrees, by problems in their capacity to maintain a positive self-image and a clear sense of self-identity, both of which can be easily threatened or injured. Moreover, they need and use others to regulate and enhance their low self-esteem, to confirm an inflated (though fragile) sense of self, and to provide a receptacle for the projected "bad" parts of themselves. In short, they depend on other people to confirm the view of self they wish to maintain.

For the more narcissistically vulnerable, the initiation and continuation of custody disputes may serve as a defense against the sense of failure, rejection, and humiliation engendered by the divorce. Since a successful custody dispute can compensate for, or even repair, an injured self-image, a legal dispute may be waged in the service of restoring threatened self-esteem and identity. The court is an arena in which to master painful feelings of rejection, humiliation, and role loss; to construct redefinitions of the self as good (or the ex-spouse as bad); and to recover a more positive sense of self.

Divorcing spouses with narcissistic vulnerabilities have a spectrum of responses to the perceived threat to self-esteem and self-integrity and develop different strategies for dealing with the threat. These involve different symbolic and defensive uses of the ex-spouse, child, and the court, resulting in different kinds of disputes with varying degrees of resistance to resolution and amenability to mediation. Over time, as individuals respond to the pressures and supports from their environment, it is quite possible for their perceptions and coping strategies to change. In this sense, their narcissistic vulnerability can be seen as ranging on a continuum from mild to severe.

Overall, those who are mildly narcissistically disturbed (45 percent of our sample) suffer primarily from a blow to their low self-esteem or fragile self-image, which they attempt to restore by demanding confirmation of their worthiness from others: they argue and fight to achieve self-validation. Those who are moderately narcissistically disturbed (37 percent of our sample) suffer from a more extensive narcissistic insult. They attempt to repair the assault on self by actively blaming and projecting badness onto the ex-spouse. They not only seek affirmation of their own goodness but also require recognition of the other's faults. Severely narcissistically disturbed spouses (9 percent of our sample) suffer from a severe narcissistic injury. They develop paranoid delusions or fixed ideas about the ex-spouse, whom they perceive as intentionally hurtful, and in response, they counterattack, aggressively attempting to undo the perceived assault by seeking revenge.

Narcissistic Vulnerability: Mildly Disturbed Spouses

On the less vulnerable end of our continuum are parents who have a fairly stable sense of self but who have a special vulnerability in maintaining positive self-esteem. Having difficulty sustaining their own sense of self-worth from internal sources, they turn to others to bolster good feelings about themselves. Most such individuals are characterized by one of two underlying dynamic constellations, basically involving neurotic conflicts.

The first subgroup has low self-esteem and hypersensitivity to feelings of inadequacy, failure, and rejection. They present as somewhat depressed and in pain, consciously experiencing their poor self-image. They make frequent self-deprecating remarks and have a concomitant expectation of and sensitivity to blame and criticism. Because of their already lowered self-esteem, in crisis they are unable to maintain a positive narcissistic balance; hence they turn to others for approval.

> □ Mrs. S. felt rejected by her husband's avoidance and with-drawal during their relationship and by his final departure from the marriage. During the separation, intense feelings of rejection were triggered each time her husband refused to talk with her or give her what she wanted: the return of her bath supplies, an old pillow, an extra diaper. She tearfully in-terpreted each incident as a put-down, became infuriated, and from time to time would erupt into an angry tirade at him. Her husband, she said, reminded her of her own father, whom she described as "tuned out" and never available. Needing mas-culine confirmation, she sought it from attorneys and judges in the courts, to prove that she was good and not deserving of rejection.

The second subgroup has exaggerated views of self and unrealistic expectations of how others "ought" to behave toward them. Their inflated standards make adequate acknowledgment difficult to ob-tain, especially during a crisis. Consequently, they are susceptible to feeling threatened in their self-regard. They present with a mixture of shock, mild indignation, disappointment, frustration. and anger to-ward the ex-spouse.

> □ Mr. R. felt angered by the obstacles his ex-wife put in the way of his seeing his child, and he was morally indignant when she would not let him visit. He felt he was "a wonderful father who had a lot to offer the child." He resented the mother's question-ing his parental abilities and was affronted by her position that she was the superior parent. He felt slighted that she did not see what a swell fellow he was. His psychological agenda in court was to have his importance in the child publicly acknowledged.

> □ Mr. Y., who held to traditional Japanese values, felt that his wife never supported him or gave him the respect a man should have. After the separation, he felt his wife became even more "uncooperative," refusing any contact with him and not "hon-oring" any of his requests. "I don't exist for her. She refuses to talk; never says hello during exchanges; never answers any legal requests." His wife's failure to respect him, coupled with

her accusations that he was irresponsible, triggered in him feelings that he was being dishonored; his ego ideal and male self-esteem were offended. He fought for custody of his sons to prove he was a good father and an honorable man, seeking validation of his masculine ideal of himself.

Whether made vulnerable by a low or an inflated self-esteem, mildly narcissistically disturbed spouses feel dismissed, disrespected, and devalued, and they seek recognition and validation from others. Frequently they want specific acknowledgment of certain aspects of themselves that have been problematic for them in the past, such as being competent, attractive, independent, nurturing, strong, worthy, appropriately masculine (or feminine), or reliable. Hence, the dispute often focuses on these vulnerable areas within their own self-image.

☐ Mr. Y.'s narcissistic vulnerability lay in his sense of himself as a man. He had very much wanted children, and while his wife attended law school, he performed more of a maternal role in the family. Consequently, although he enjoyed parenting and was a good father, his masculinity was threatened; he needed acknowledgment as a man from his wife, which she refused to provide. His masculine ego was additionally made vulnerable because he needed to be seen as a particular kind of father—one who was properly responsible to his family (in ways his own father was not). His wife's accusations that he was irresponsible were therefore especially threatening. His preexisting vulnerability resulted in the need for a particular kind of acknowledgment from his wife that he could not provide for himself.

Many such spouses have reparative fantasies that if the spouse would "only do something" (only validate them), "all would be better"; they would "not be so angry."

☐ Mr. Y. kept waiting for his wife to act decently toward him, to "say hello." "If she'd only do that, things would go smoothly."

☐ Mrs. S.: "If he would just let me into the house and talk to me, we would not have any problems with the visits."

☐ Mr. R.: "All would be okay if she would just acknowledge why I am so angry. If she would appreciate what I can do for our child, I would do anything for her. I would cooperate if it were not for her attitude."

Indeed, many of these parents stubbornly refuse to cooperate until such time as the spouse will confirm them and "behave in the way he should." They will not budge until they are spoken to politely or "shown some understanding," until, in effect, the blow to their self-esteem is redressed. They engage in a series of seemingly petty furies over a few symbolic issues, such as who will get a Chinese teakettle, a rug, or a picture. They resist compromise in the hope of recouping self-worth, often holding out for the "correct" confirming response or action, one that fits with their views of how things should be. Settling their disagreements is often difficult until these underlying narcissistic needs are satisfied or replaced. Nonetheless, unlike those who are moderately or severly disturbed, once these mildly disturbed spouses are acknowledged (once a hello is given or a teakettle offered), they are able to shift into a more flexible stance. If the spouse refuses to respect or openly confirm them, mildly disturbed spouses sometimes turn to the public arena of the court for recognition of their feelings, validation of the rightness of their views, and proof that they are not failures as fathers or mothers, men or women, and do not deserve rejection or belittlement. The custody-visitation issue becomes the contest in which they seek acknowledgment.

Mildly disturbed individuals are not likely of their own accord to become entrenched in disputes. Although their vulnerable self-image provides fertile soil for conflict, it is often the interaction with the ex-spouse and the involvement of others that evokes and prolongs their disputes. Though initially, these people may have needed only minor confirmation—an old rug, a hello, a photo album—as the fight progresses they become more deeply injured, more defensive, and demand greater restitution. Many of them have been married to partners with matching narcissistic problems. Feeling unacknowledged and, in turn, refusing to grant acknowledgment to their ex-mate, they each struggle to maintain their respective self-esteems. Their regressive interactions, characterized by growing animosity and stubborn refusal to support or acknowledge each other, lead to more deeply entrenched disputes.

☐ Both Mr. and Mrs. J. Felt discarded by the other in the breakup of their marriage. A mutual defensive denigration and a stubborn refusal to communicate (until respected) characterized their relations. During the marriage, Mrs. J.'s stance toward him had involved accusations that he was irresponsible and unreliable, complementing Mr. J.'s accusations that she was a nag and did not appreciate his aspirations. With the divorce, she denied him not only as a man but also as a father. She felt he showed no genuine interest in caring for their daughter and was not capable of doing so anyway. In court Mr. J. countered that mother was too bookish and too inhibited to play with, support emotionally, or care lovingly for a child.

Other mildly narcissistically disturbed individuals, especially the self-critical subgroup, have married very aggressively paranoid spouses with severe disturbance. Their already vulnerable self- images are further injured by their exmates' public insinuations and insults and legal accusations of wrongdoing. In fact, the underlying narcissistic vulnerability in these parents is often obscured by their spouses' demeaning attacks.

The need to have their good parenting acknowledged frequently diminishes mildly disturbed parents' ability to parent their children. Efforts to prove to themselves and to their former spouses that they are a good parent interfere with a more balanced, less self-conscious relationship with their child. Their parenting efforts often become exaggerated as, reacting to perceived or expected criticism, they overprotect their children or pressure them to perform, in an effort to highlight their own good caretaking.

☐ Mr. R. felt devalued by his wife's claim that he had nothing to offer his child. He sought to disprove her accusations by showing what a good time he could provide his son, often exhausting his three-year-old in strenuous all-day outings. He would claim of these jam-packed Saturdays that he did more in one day with his little boy than his wife did in the thirteen "dull and boring days" she had with their son.

Other parents transfer some of their need for validation and acknowledgment from their former mate to their child. Their children become significant in buoying their self-esteem. Children, especially the younger ones, have an extraordinary capacity to help parents feel good, to reassure the parent that they are lovable and valuable. These parents become dependent to an exaggerated extent on their children's responses to their efforts. The children are cast in the role of "witness" to their goodness. Signs of dissatisfaction or age-appropriate defiance are taken as a personal rejection and proof of parental inadequacy. As a consequence, these parents put heavy emotional burdens on their children, to constantly reassure them that they are doing enough. In addition to these demands and pressures, parents fail to set clear and reassuring limits. Overanxious for their child's positive validation, they find it difficult to discipline. Their indulgence of their children is seen as proof of their parental love and their status as beloved parent. However, unlike their moderately and severely disturbed counterparts, mildly disturbed parents have the capacity to view their children realistically and—when clarified—can recognize the consequences for their children of their actions, and change them.

Narcissistic Vulnerability: Moderately Disturbed Spouses

In the middle range of our vulnerability spectrum, individuals do not have a well established self-identity and have difficulty maintaining a positive, clear, cohesive, and realistic self-structure. Essentially, these parents function as if they had character disorders with a major vulnerability to loss of an integrated and positive sense of self. By and large, the central sense of self they attempt to maintain involves a grandiosity, a highly exaggerated sense of importance, personal superiority, entitlement, and an entrenched need to see only good in themselves.

Their major defensive and compensatory style is dominated by efforts to maintain this rigidly positive view of themselves. Experiences of self and other that fit in with their highly idealized self-images are claimed; those that do not are vigorously disavowed. To see the self as partly "bad" or the ex-spouse as partly "good" causes them great anxiety and confusion. Their fragile ego organization depends on keeping all sense of badness outside the self—in the other or in the situation.

If the moderately narcissistically disturbed spouse is the one who left the marriage, he or she rarely feels sadness or sorrow in relationship to the other. He or she feels entitled to leave and simply wants to get rid of the spouse, to have the other disappear.

> ☐ Mrs. C., a rather attractive but self-centered woman who was inordinately concerned with her appearance, raided the family home after the separation, stripping it of furniture, glassware, and pictures, which infuriated her husband and daughters. She insisted that she alone had made the house what it was by selecting the furnishings and that she therefore had a right to take whatever she wanted for her own new home. Later, when discussing her daughters' anger at her, she defensively forgot and avoided these events, blaming the father for filling the girls' heads with lies about her.

Many such parents view themselves in such a superior light that they do not feel they should have to develop plans or cooperate with the other parent. Indifferent to the needs or desires of the other, they feel the ex-spouse should capitulate to their demands. They expect special favors and privileges, without assuming reciprocal responsibilities, and they become outraged if they do not get what they want. They look upon any attempts to coordinate the children's schedules as annoying interferences with their own lives. By and large, these parents manifest little overt anger. Rather than actively blame and denigrate, they coolly dismiss from their own minds the reality of their ex-mate's existence. They see only their own good, their own needs, and their own views, and believe that they are the best, the only parent. Clearly, many of these spouses would not be involved in disputes if it were not for their ex-mate, who becomes infuriated by their lack of regard, alienated by their demands, provoked by their self-aggrandizement and presumptuousness, and frequently apprehensive over their lack of care for the children.

- ☐ Mrs. D. perceived herself as a traditional Latin mother who was of central importance to her children. Being a mother, in her eyes, gave her the right to do whatever she wanted with her children. Her "mother's intuition" meant she knew what was best. If she was fulfilled, then the children were fulfilled. As she had no need for the father, she completely rejected his importance to the children, frequently denied him visits, and at times completely terminated his access to them by snatching the children across the state line.

When the narcissistic parents are the ones who are left, they usually have little or no understanding of their spouses' leave-taking. They experience the rejection inherent in the divorce as a narcissistic insult to their basic grandiose view of self. The divorce shatters their illusions of greatness and self-importance and triggers in them an exaggerated sense of shame and humiliation. It is not (as with the mildly disturbed spouse) just one aspect of themselves that has been hurt or disavowed ("I did something wrong"), but their basic sense of themselves feels completely condemned. Such feelings are intolerable.

The primary psychological defense is to rid themselves of these feelings and any vestige of badness. While they need and want affirmation of their idealized self, the primary thrust for many such spouses in the restitution of their demeaned self-image is to prove the other fundamentally at fault. In effect, they construct a negative image of the ex-spouse as a defense against viewing themselves in a negative light. The idealized view of self and the devalued view of the other are reciprocally and dynamically connected. They cling tenaciously to their view of the other as monstrous, destructive, and dangerous, unable to recognize the part they each play in their problems. Some need to be seen as responsible, nurturing, and morally superior, in contrast to an irresponsible, unavailable, and morally inferior ex-spouse.

☐ Mr. G., a high-ranking government official, presented in a supercilious manner. He refused to give his ex-wife any information about their child when with him or answer any of her questions, calls, or letters. In his words, he was not going to "report to her," since he viewed any compliance or even communication with her about their child as an insulting submission and loss of his sense of autonomy. He sought custody to prove he was the better parent, who could "provide a more wholesome home." He refused to follow the medical regime that his wife (a nurse) had helped set up for his son's epilepsy, seeing it as an insult to his competency. This refusal led to his son having a seizure, which resulted in a serious accident, while riding a bike.

☐ Mrs. A.'s wife left him (and returned to her own family) while he was recuperating from a back injury that left him unemployed, on disability, and unsure of his future. With great bravado, Mr. A. took a very condescending attitude toward his wife, who he said was "incompetent, unable to care for their child or live independently." He projected his own sense of weakness and inadequacy onto her, not recognizing any of these qualities in himself, and argued for no less than a fifty-fifty time share of his daughter.

Those with moderate narcissistic vulnerability become threatened when the other does not respond as represented in their views. Real differences or qualitities in self and spouse, inconsistent with their projections, are disregarded, often creating more unrealistic images. Similarly, challenges to their views are met with great anxiety, increased resistance, and strong representations of their beliefs. When, for example, mediation or court proceedings do not go their way, or when other points of view are investigated, they become disruptive and panicked, insisting angrily, "You're not looking at what is best for my daughter. You're not getting at the real issue" (the real issue being the "badness" of their spouse).

Once the unwanted, incompatible affects are projected onto the spouse, or into the external situation, these spouses still cannot resolve the dispute and let the spouse go, because they would then have to reown the negative feelings and aspects they have worked so hard to project or externalize. Hence, they need to continue the fight to ensure the psychological presence of the spouse as a repository for their own devalued parts. To resolve the fight would in effect open them up to further injury, for they would be left without the external containers that keep their rejected "bad" qualities outside the self. Additionally, letting the other go means letting go of the good parts of the spouse they had claimed for themselves. They therefore remain tied to the other, and to the crisis and conflict.

Moreover, these parents often attempt to evoke qualities in the spouse that confirm their projective fantasies, or they try to create situations in the real world that will put pressure on the spouse to behave in a manner that conforms to their projective fantasies.

☐ Mr. S., who perceived himself as loving in contrast to his ungiving and unnurturing wife, would offer her, on Thursday evening, an opportunity for an extra visit with their child on Friday. When she was unable to accept his offer on such short notice, Mr. S. took this as proof of her lack of love and rejection of the boy.

Such parents almost always enter court with the conviction that they will "win"; their grandiosity and basic sense of entitlement interferes with a realistic appraisal of what is likely to occur. The court is viewed as an arena of vindication and the judge-mediator as an authority who will justify the parent's position (and perhaps provide approval and narcissistic sustenance). Moreover, the public nature of the court gratifies their exhibitionistic wishes. They often insist on an immediate judgment in their favor with respect to custody or changes in visitation, and are unable to work step by step toward achieving these aims.

☐ Mrs. Z., following her hospitalization for and recuperation from a suicide attempt, wanted an immediate resumption of her visits with her daughter. She felt insulted by the suggestion that she needed to rebuild the relationship with her daughter and found working with her ex-husband humiliating, a sign that she was inferior. She felt she should not have to "prove herself."

A "win" in court protects their positive sense of self and the "vindicating" judge is often idealized. A judge who does not rule in their favor is negatively construed; seen as incompetent, biased, or misled;

and treated with contempt. The losing parent often seeks another judge, blames or fires the attorney for the lack of success in court, and accuses the court worker–mediator of favoritism.

Since these moderately disturbed persons' disputes with their ex-mates are often primarily intrapsychically motivated, their spouses can do little to offset their need for conflict. As it is their mates come with their own set of psychological problems. In the cases in which both spouses are moderately narcissistically disturbed, the interactional impasses, involving a mixture of reality and fantasy about each other, and result in very enmeshed bitter narcissistic struggles. Their perceptions of each other contain components of projection that–given their mutual provocation–are difficult to disentangle from their real-life experience of one another. Each spouse, sensitive to insult, has an intense need actively to place the other in the wrong. They externalize and project blame and create fights and situations to prove each other inadequate.

☐ Mr. and Mrs. H. had a mutually demeaning relationship, characterized by escalating, vituperative personal assaults. He would call her names; she would call him names. He would make allegations; she countered with allegations against him. He verbally sniped at her; she retaliated with castrating barbs. She had a need to keep him in the role of a "sadistic brute" who could not control himself, and would provoke him to behave as such (by failing to have their daughter where he expected the girl to be). He, in turn, needed to see her as a "conniving bitch" and tried to avoid her control (by failing to return her calls or tell her where and when he was going to visit). He refused to talk to her because she was a "liar who couldn't be trusted." She refused to talk with him because "he gets me so upset."

In other cases, where such spouses are married to mildly narcissistically disturbed individuals, disputes are entrenched by the latters failure to correct the former's projections. Faced with condemnation from the more disturbed spouse, the mildly disturbed parent withdraws into a protective shell, passively resists (becoming ever more devious and manipulative), or resigns from the battle feeling an overwhelming futility.

Children, for such parents, are narcissistic extensions of themselves, appendages similar to their body parts. They have limited ability to recognize and respond to their children beyond their own wishes and needs. They discuss their children with little empathy or sense of the child's separateness. Indeed, they gauge their child's feelings by their own: "My child is Okay because I am Okay." In the custody dispute, they are outraged if someone suggests the child not be with them; they feel they are fighting to prevent the extreme injustice of being separated from a part of their own being.

In accord with their own overvalued sense of self, these parents hold an idealized, often stereotyped, view of their children and their relationship with their children. All the problems in the child (as in the parent) are often denied or seen as the fault of the other parent.

□ Mr. J. saw Bobby as "the most wonderful, the most sensitive child—there's nothing wrong with him. I have no problems with my son, in fact, we have a fantastically close relationship; the boy feels my feelings. It is beautiful. I talk with my son, but I don't show him any of my negative feelings. I show him only love. I don't have to tell my son about his mother; he knows about her. He knows she's a bad mother. He knows who cares about him. The only problem Bobby has is with his mother, who deserted him."

Hence, such parents have difficulty engaging or making real contact with their children because the children's feelings and needs, like those of the ex-spouse, are distorted along the particular lines the parent needs to draw to confirm their entrenched views. In effect, the children became what Kohut (1977) has termed "self-objects." Consequently these parents are unobservant and frequently impervious to the children's needs or worries. They are often so focused on proving a point that they ignore their children.

□ Following a dispute with his ex-wife over Debby's attendance at a private school and her involvement in afternoon activities, Mr. G., with little regard for his ten-year-old's interests and without considering her feelings, refused to watch her play soccer and rarely visited her school.

In their need to reject their former spouse, these parents do not recognize the child's attachment to the other parent. From their perspective, they and the child are one: "I want him out of our lives"; "She left us." By placing value only on their own relationship with the child, they fail to acknowledge the total life of the child. They pursue their own interests with the child, more or less disregarding the other parent, thereby fragmenting the child's world.

Many such parents perceive the child as a judge who has the power to undo the narcissistic wound. The child is thus courted and wooed away from the other parent. A few parents do not feel loved unless the child actively disfavors the ex-mate. Any display of warmth toward such a parent, or expression of negativity toward the other parent, is triumphantly seized upon as evidence of the child's preference and total agreement with this parent's point of view. The child is thereby given implicit permission to reject or mistreat the other parent. In general, they perceive the child as existing for their benefit.

□   Mrs. D., whose daughters refused to see her, stipulated, "I want to see the children, but only on my terms." She was angry at the girls for "their lack of understanding" and emphasized to them how much they were hurting her. She did not see their own intense needs, or their sadness and anger in response to her leaving them.

Finally, as a consequence of these parents' inability to see their children as separate entities, and because of their need for their children's approval, they often fail to protect their children from spousal acrimony. They air their grievances and denigrate their ex-mate to the children. The children, in turn, respond to these tensions and parental pressures with symptomatic behaviors or with behaviors they feel their parents need (such as telling stories), all of which further entrench the dispute.

Narcissistic Vulnerability: Seriously Disturbed Spouses

In the most vulnerable range of our spectrum are parents with either serious paranoid disturbances, or those who have fairly well circumscribed paranoid delusions or fixed ideas about their ex-mates. What these spouses have in common with moderately disturbed ones is a grandiose sense of self and a paramount need to keep the bad external to themselves and to maintain good internal representations. The two types are differentiated by the higher degree of distrust and animosity these parents feel towards their ex-mates, by their belief that their former spouses intend to and could harm or exploit them and their children, and by their more urgent need actively to counter the hostility, danger, and victimization they perceive and anticipate from their ex-mates. Hence, these spouses generally have more actively aggressive, suspicious, accusatory stances vis-à-vis their ex-mates. With often frightening intensity, they collect evidence and build their cases, intending to prove that their ex-mates are "drug addicts," "neglectful or abusive," "predators," or "sociopaths." They write bullying letters; make frantic, ominous phone calls; leave death threats; and pressure their attorneys to act more aggressively, often with little or no concern for the consequences to others. Under conditions of a very traumatic separation or a sustained challenge to their narcissism (for example, the rejection inherent in ongoing conflict), moderately disturbed spouses can decompensate into the more paranoid disorders of this group.

Severely disturbed spouses experience their separation and divorce as a deeply humiliating attack and injury. Feeling vulnerable and intentionally weakened by assault, they respond defensively with an immediate desire to counterattack and seek revenge, a desire that often becomes a central obsession in their lives. In these cases, the revenge motif is the overriding motivation rather than a desire to increase a good sense of self or the desire to prove the other spouse bad. They seek retribution, not simply a righting of the wrong that has been done to them. More than a container for their bad traits the other spouse becomes a dangerous, aggressive, persecutory figure.

By and large, these spouses are socially isolated and often secretive. Retreating into fantasy, they develop florid delusions or ideas about their ex-mates. As they piece together, in their memory, the rubble of their marriage, they begin to rewrite history. This reconstruction justifies the feeling that they have been wronged, duped, and betrayed, probably intentionally.

☐ *Mr. J.:* "Her loving femininity was all a sham. She's absolutely evil and . . . untrustworthy. When I first met her, she played a sweet, innocent, feminine, dependent child, but when no one was looking, she turned diabolical. It was all an act."

☐ *Mrs. S.:* "[He] is an unsavory, unscrupulous, opportunistic, amoral cad whose appearances are deceiving. He makes a great appearance. He has a lot of education. But appearances are deceiving. He's a swine. He can't distinguish right from wrong. He has no morality or values."

Almost all focus on the exploitation they believe they have experienced. In their version of the breakup, they are blameless. While many are unable to acknowledge how devastated they feel, some remarks suggest their sense of degradation.

☐ *Mrs. F.:* "There was nothing wrong with the marriage. It was fine. He decided he didn't want to be married, another woman came along, and so off he went."

☐ *Mr. L.:* "I gave her everything . . . backed her up with every penny, and she took everything until there was nothing left and then spit me out like a piece of dead weight."

Seeing themselves as having finally caught on to the grand malevolent schemes against them, these spouses feel they must now make the right moves to protect themselves against further exploitation. Expecting trickery and deceit, they are watchful and guarded toward their ex-spouse and all his or her allies. Everyone is perceived as taking sides either with or against them. Frequently they refuse to meet with the ex-spouse lest they reexpose themselves to the dangers of being exploited or injured. Mrs. H. said: "It's not worth talking to him directly. He never delivers. If you give him half a chance he would take again." Consequently, she rejected all her ex-husband's ideas, proposals, and offers—suspicious of their meaning—and refused to talk with him without the protection of her attorney. Her extreme sense of moral injustice and her feelings of being cheated made her keep a constant vigil of self-defense.

Because they feel wronged, they feel justified in seeking revenge and retaliation. Simply, they maintain a policy of preemptive attack—that is, attack before being attacked. Many feel little conscious shame for their assaultive behaviors; they can kidnap their children or violently attack their ex-spouse while simultaneously maintaining their sense of justification, righteousness, and superiority. Their counterattacks are perceived as self- or child protections. In their views, they are forced to protect themselves from the other's malevolence. Moreover, they derive a good deal of relief from this aggressive activity, which is at once a source of protection and of comfort, as it restores their sense of self-determination, control, and power. Revenge is a powerful antidote to intolerably painful feelings of rejection and helplessness.

In court, such parents seek revenge by depriving the other parent of access or by interfering with the other parent's relationship with their children. They can be ruthless in their attempts to "get custody no matter what" and to "nail to the wall" their ex-spouse and his or her allies. Custody litigation frequently occurs in the context of vengeful behaviors, as angry parents act out their rage by ramming their ex-spouses' cars, wrecking their furniture, and destroying irreplaceable personal treasures.

Other such parents may deny or mask their desire for revenge and counterattack. They enter court ostensibly to protect or rescue their child from the demonic influence of the other parent. They label the other parent as not merely unnecessary (as moderately disturbed parents did), but as actively dangerous to the child. They truly perceive their child to be in grave danger and view themselves as the child's "savior" and "great protector." As one father proclaimed to the counselor, "You and I are the only ones in the world to save my son." The grandiosity that salvages their sense of self is apparent in these reconstructions. Focused on the "welfare of the children," they enter court requesting custody and accusing the other parent of child abuse, neglect, improper conduct, often with little to substantiate their allegations. Dynamically, ego-dystonic parts of themselves are projected onto the spouse and the child. Typically, they project their anger and fury onto the spouse and identify their own helplessness in their children. Their internal conflicts are then dealt with externally.

□ Mr. X., a persistent and intensely aggressive man whose wife left following one of his violent attacks on her, went to court seeking custody because he believed she was abusing his child. He had a tremendous need to control his wife's "aggression," this being his aggression projected onto her, and at the same time to project his own feelings of vulnerability onto the child.

Some parents need to protect their children from what they perceive the spouse as having done to them during the separation. They believe the spouse will abandon, reject, be unreliable, or exploit their children. One mother who had kidnapped her sons refused to allow the father any access to the boys, for fear he might in turn steal them from her. Another mother, who had subjected her children to a barrage of angry denunciations of their father, wanted visitations discontinued because she did not want the children to be confused by the father's tirades against her. Given their view of themselves as "great protectors," many such parents feel a need to make a strong stand against their ex-mates.

Litigation can become a way of life for these parents, as it fuels their fixed ideas or paranoid delusions and offers them "legitimized vindication." They can get even and at the same time redress their narcissistic injury. Winning the custody battle proves them "right." If the judge decides in their favor, it justifies their negative view of the ex-spouse and their conspiracy theories. If the judge does not decide in their favor, he or she is seen as another conspirator or persecutor. They dismiss this judgment and continue the fight in another court. The latter is most often the result, since these parents' disturbance is usually evident, and their ability to parent adequately is therefore clearly suspect.

Finally, there is a small group of these parents whose need to counterattack (or seek revenge and protection) stems less from feeling humiliated and rejected than from a perceived attack on their parental role. The narcissistic injury they feel is not to their spousal but to their parental role. These parents, by and large, define themselves these are usually caused by misunderstandings and regressions to old expectations of one another. Each spouse should underscore that trust takes time to rebuild, especially when it has been so thoroughly demolished. Over the months that follow, the counselor should also point out when episodic crises occur less often and if they are less intense and more easily resolved when they do occur. Hence it is most important to remind these divorced couples of the *nonoccurrence and weakening* of conflict over time since such evidence of improvement is unlikely to be noticed. In sum, this serious, interactive engagement with both of the disputing ex-spouses, separately and together, helping them solve the problem and take care of their concerns for their child, enables redefinitions to be made, carefully supported by behavioral confirmation. Gradually, over time, more realistic images of each other can evolve and emerge.

almost totally in terms of being a parent and need the children to complete an image of themselves. Parenting is the only area in which they feel they function as an adult, and it is the role around which they have organized a positive sense of self. The potential loss of the child feels like an attack on this central sense of self and leaves them with tremendous fears of being a nonparent without identity.

☐ Permanently disabled and unable to work, Mr. Y. defined himself almost entirely as a "good parent." He came to the initial counseling session armed with three books full of photos of himself and his daughter as well as declarations and documents from friends attesting to his parenting skills. This man was totally absorbed in demonstrating to the court that he was open, loving, sensitive, and nurturing. He felt he was on trial. When the court evaluator recommended that sole custody be granted to his wife and limited visits awarded to him, feeling utterly rejected and totally disaffirmed, he committed suicide. The court evaluation destroyed his only claim to adulthood and hence a positive view of himself.

☐ Mrs. Z., a mother, of dull-normal intelligence and on welfare, had channeled all her limited energies and ability into providing therapy and schooling for her two children, both of whom had learning disabilities. The girls were clearly the center of her life; she organized not only her days but her identity around their care. Being a parent conferred on her an adult status and sense of confidence. When threatened with a temporary loss of the children during visits with their father, she was threatened with the dissolution of her adulthood. Feeling attacked, she defended and retaliated by kidnapping the children.

The spouses of such parents commonly share the psychological makeup and behavior of the mildly narcissistically disturbed: They are dependent, acquiescent, insecure, passive individuals. Frightened by the wrath of, and exasperated by and tired of the suspiciousness and jealousies of the narcissistic-paranoid mate, the dependent spouse during the breakup often begins to sneak around, hiding outside contacts. Finding it more and more difficult to circumvent the paranoia, they become more secretive and terrified of being discovered and punished—in many cases a legitimate fear. This has the effect, however, of fueling the fire, as the paranoid spouse fantasies of betrayal find some evidence in the spouse's behavior. Further, during the separation process, the ex-mates withdraw and avoid confrontations, thereby failing to correct the narcissistic distortions and accusations of the severly disturbed spouse. While more capable than their spouse of considering their children's feelings, these less disturbed parents, bewildered and overwhelmed by the fury and aggression of their former partners, find it very difficult to negotiate with their mates on the children's behalf.

The parents who actively seek revenge usually involve their children directly in their attempts to punish the ex-spouse and redress perceived injustices and attacks. They enlist their children as allies and coconspirators, press them into espionage activities, and in other ways use them as weapons or instruments of their anger, with little understanding or concern for the impact on the children. Mr. F. threatened never to see his children again if his wife left him. Mr. P. refused to visit his son, to spite his ex-wife: "I'm not going to be used as her baby-sitter." While for some, parenting remained intact (usually individuals with more focused delusions about their ex-spouses), most are barely cognisant of the children's feelings or emotional needs.

□ Mrs. E., whose husband left her for a "younger model," sought to ally her two sons against their father. She continually gave the children the message that their father had failed them (in contrast to her support). She freely provided them with her view of their father (he was an "irresponsible cad"), and her perspective on the breakup (he "didn't want to be responsible"). She kept the children well informed of what their father was not doing financially (he is "trying to cheat us"), and adamantly refused to allow the father any holiday family visits. She expected and demanded the children's loyalty and had little understanding of how depressed, confused, and forlorn they were.

These parents customarily view their children as being either totally on their side or as having been turned against them by the other parent. To ward off the latter possibility, many such parents do not allow contact with the other parent, certain that their ex-spouse will "contaminate," "infiltrate," or "brainwash" the child's mind. They keep the children away from the other parent sometimes out of a conscious fear that the children will be malevolently seduced from them, or out of a less conscious concern that the children will see and prefer the other.

□ Mr. W. refused to allow his girls any access to their mother outside of their agreement and would not allow any contact with anyone associated with their mother. Hence, he withdrew his daughters from their school and volleyball team . . . on learning that his ex-wife's new stepson would be attending the same school and league.

Such parents are often unable to tolerate any of their children's feelings (loyalty, love, concern, guilt) for the other parent. Sensing these, they feel endangered and become suspicious that the child has "gone over to the other side." Now seeing the child as a copersecutor, they can become vindictive and precipitously reject the child. Even the child's entry into an alliance is not always sufficient to assuage the parent's suspicions and assure caretaking.

Severely disturbed parents who are intensely focused on rescuing their children from the pernicious influence of the other parent tend to deny the children's problems. What difficulties they do acknowledge they attribute to the ex-spouse's pathology and thus make an added reason to decrease access. All too often, they try to involve their children in their delusions about their ex-mate, often utterly undermining the child's sense of reality.

☐ During most visits, Mr. 0.—who believed his ex-wife was abusing their daughter—undressed her and checked her body for bruises. He continually questioned the child about the mother's abuse and demanded that the child's gymnastic teacher do the same. Again and again he tried to make his daughter admit to things that had never happened, which was greatly confusing to her.

What is most significant is that although these parents request custody, their focus is on being a rescuer, not on being a parent. Generally they maintained little involvement with their children, rarely ask for extra time, and are often erratic and capricious in their visitation.

Differential Interventions with Narcissistic Issues

In intervening with narcissistically vulnerable disputants, it is important to remember that, although the dispute is often precipitated by the parents' vulnerable self-esteem, it is frequently perpetuated in interactional cycles by the reactions of others, such as the ex-spouse, court workers, or relatives. In fact, the role of others may be pivotal in determining whether and what kind of ongoing dispute occurs. When, for example, a parent's angry, blaming stance is met with retaliatory strategies by the ex-mate, a battle of pride may ensue.

Alternatively, when the angry blaming is met by the ex-mate's dependent acquiescence or inflexible withdrawal, the parent's narcissistic view of the situation—and the blame—may remain unchallenged.

As parents enter the legal arena, it is relatively easy for court workers and lawyers either to ameliorate or further entrench the dispute. The parent's self-esteem, already temporarily lowered, may become even more threatened as the court suit, with its evaluative processes and adversarial orientation, gets under way. On the other hand, family, friends, therapists, children, and court workers may become potential enhancers of self-esteem and alleviators of insult. Clients obtain a great deal of narcissistic gratification from attorneys who "fight for" them, and from relatives and friends who "believe in" them. While the wishes of significant others may be experienced as supportive, they may also serve to escalate the conflict. As the adversarial climate inside and outside the court increases, the parent's need to defend may rigidify his or her position. Fighting over custody may then come to serve both the external purpose of pleasing significant others who are new or renewed sources of narcissistic gratification, and the internal purpose of restoring or protecting self-esteem and self-image.

The point of departure for intervening with all narcissistically vulnerable parents is to help them save face. This involves repairing their wounded self-esteem and preventing further attacks on their sense of self-worth and self-integrity, lessening their need to be acknowledged and proved right in court. Sensitivity to parents' continuing narcissistic vulnerability and the adoption of a neutral, respectful, nonjudgmental stance is essential. Generally, restoration of self-esteem requires the counselor's active, positive, genuinely supportive orientation toward the vulnerable parent. The counselor demonstrates respect for the parents by mirroring their real capacities, highlighting their specific strengths, reminding them of their accomplishments, crediting their good intentions, and actively focusing on and reinforcing positive behavior (while tactfully avoiding labeling, blaming, or invidious comparisons). This stance often assuages the narcissistic hurt and, in addition, helps parents discover the skills and capacities within themselves. Indeed, successful mediation, especially for deeply mortified severely disturbed parents, often hinges on the respect shown them. Carefully and seriously considering and even investigating the parents' allegations is often pivotal in gaining their trust. It is only in a context of respect and a careful appraisal of their claims that the counselor-mediator is able to provide (and these parents to accept) a reality check on their projections.

Another overall strategy is to redirect spouses away from the need for their spouses' approval—an unlikely source of confirmation—to new sources of appreciation. (Mr. Y., for example, was able to redress the blow to his self-esteem engendered by his wife's disparagements by becoming involved with other women, who appreciated and admired him.) Looking within spouses' social networks for other sources of support, we encourage them to seek out family, friends, and other adults, and help them develop an expanded support system. We find the supportive milieu of a group to be especially useful in providing positive feedback, understanding, and acceptance to spouses who feel devalued and mortified by the divorce. Similarly, we encourage them to focus again on their hobbies and special interests and attempt to provide them with new arenas and channels, such as their work, for building self-esteem. In particular, we encourage spouses to pursue their talents (in art, music, writing, and so on), for both the pleasures and narcissistic gratification to be gained. We also facilitate their completion of some of the practical tasks of the divorce (finding child care, housing, employment) and highlight their sense of mastery and self-sufficiency. These efforts help to undo the narcissistic injury, dilute the intensity of the conflict, and divert their focus from the ex-spouse and from their attempts to enhance self-esteem through a custody dispute.

Without careful diagnoses, however, disputes easily become entrenched. Differential diagnoses of the spouses, narcissistic vulnerabilities are essential for intervention. Each diagnosis determines the degree and kind of support offered, the utility of dynamic explorations, the possibility of leveraging concern for children, the kind of interventions to make with their significant others, and the need for reality confrontation.

Support and acknowledgment are vitally important in the restoration of mildly disturbed parents' vulnerable self-image. Unlike the other two types, these parents are able to turn to others for support, thereby finding new sources to repair self-esteem. They are also able to utilize counseling wherein each parent's motivation and role in the destructive interaction and impasses are explored. Such parents are able to tolerate such exploration and hence are amenable to clarifications and interpretations of their defenses and their ways of using the ex-spouse and the dispute to recoup self-esteem; therefore it is possible for them to achieve insight.

□ Hence, with Mrs. S., we clarified that her ex-husband's withdrawal was not a put-down and rejection of her. She felt easily injured by perceived criticism because her ex-husband's behavior recapitulated her own father's unresponsiveness, which made her feel insignificant. We then reviewed the patterns of her communication with her ex-spouse, action by action, clarifying and redefining his behavior: "He tunes you out partially in response to or in anticipation of your angry explosions, which remind him of his own mother's hysterical outbursts. Seeing his mother in you, he retreats, refusing to be a victim of a woman's rantings. His withdrawal is a disacknowledgement only in terms of his need to protect himself, once again, from feeling flooded and helpless." With this intervention, Mrs. S. was able more calmly to approach and respond to her ex-husband.

With help, these parents are able to develop a balanced picture of the divorce as the failure of a relationship resulting from problems in the marriage, not in themselves. This more rational reassessment helps to dissipate their feelings of rejection. Finally, their capacity to view their children realistically and their wish to view themselves as good parents means that their concern for their children can be appealed to and used as leverage for change. Highlighting the children's experiences and perspectives, therefore, usually suffices to bring about the change in their outlook.

☐ We explained to Mr. R. that his action-packed weekends were too tiring for his three-year-old. While he had the potential of becoming a "wonderful" father, he needed first to learn about the developmental needs and capabilities of his child.

The use of these same techniques with moderately and severely disturbed spouses can bring about an escalation of the dispute and is hence contraindicated. Moderately disturbed people tend to overgeneralize support, seeing acknowledgment as confirmation of their world views. Such "legitimization" often hardens their positions. Counselors need to be specific and concrete in their acknowledgment, clearly and tactfully detailing what they are and are not saying. Emphasizing that their role is that of helpers and not of judges is necessary ("Do I look like a judge?").

It is important to remember here that the counseling service is not long-term therapy aimed at resolving the parents' narcissistic problems but is rather a short-term intervention aimed at moving spouses through a crisis situation or impasse and developing a mediated agreement. Moderately disturbed spouses are seldom able to utilize dynamic counseling or insight-oriented clarifications. Such interventions frequently foster major ego regressions and panic. For most such spouses, any suggestion that they are contributing to a problem, or any examination of their dynamics, only increases their anxieties and rigidities and results in indignation, categorical denial, projection, splitting ("I'm good, she's bad"), with a concomitant polarization of their position that brings about their devaluation of and possible flight from mediation.

> ☐ One father who maintained a rigid, condescending attitude toward his ex-wife was unable to tolerate anything but the counselor mirroring his own position. When asked about a recent altercation with his ex-spouse in which he was extremely provocative, he furiously declared with much agitation, "I don't want any more excuses. She has to be reliable! My son needs better mothering! She has to start being responsible!"

If therapeutically mishandled, moderately disturbed spouses can become severely disturbed. Although a deeper understanding of their narcissistic needs and problems is not always possible, some of them are able to utilize an intellectual formulation of their own dynamics, especially when blame is placed outside themselves (onto their past, an external other, or onto the normalcy of their feelings). An understanding of the interactional nature of the dispute and the complementarity of the spouses' behaviors places the blame on the relationship itself, reduces self-other blaming, and relieves the individuals' sense of shame, thereby partially mitigating their need to prove the other guilty.

By and large, however, alternative strategies of intervention are aimed not at shifting the spouses' underlying narcissistic conflicts but at directly changing the spouses' motivations, attitudes, and behaviors. To foster cooperation, parents are asked whether their strategies are working to produce the results they desire. Encouraging them to define their goals and, with some, directly suggesting how to achieve their goals by demonstrating the benefits of taking certain actions (deemed by the counselor as important in protecting the children) support and guide their behavior. Interventions take into account and utilize the spouses' defensive narcissistic structure to reach counseling-mediation goals.

> ☐ We taught one mother, who viewed herself as a lioness protecting her cubs against a predator, to fight cleverly and teach her children how to cope with their father, rather than to pursue her unsuccessful strategy of proving to the court that her ex-husband was totally unfit to visit.

Finally, these parents have little capacity to understand their children's perspectives; therefore, clarification of the children's needs and problems (as was done with mildly disturbed parents) does not suffice. The counselors demonstrate more clearly and concretely to moderately disturbed parents the hurtful effects of the parental fights on the children. For some, however, such interpretations result not in improved parenting but in a blaming the other parent for the problems. Here, interventions that realistically link the children's suffering with the parent's own suffering allow the counselor to use the parents' own needs more strategically as leverage for change.

☐ Mr. Q. frequently left in a huff without his son on Friday nights following a dispute with his ex-spouse. The counselor focused on his son's intense disappointment and feelings of rejection and talked about the child's burden of caring for his distraught mother following his departure. Additionally, we reminded Mr. Q. of his stated goal of wanting a "healthy boy and a close father-son relationship." If he wanted to achieve this goal, he needed to take control of the situation and make the interchanges smoother and conflict-free. In this way he could demonstrate to the boy his caring, despite his antipathy toward the boy's mother.

With severely disturbed parents, the counselor has to take great care in giving support and acknowledgment, as both tend to be perceived as either seductive (increasing parents' suspicions and fears of entrapment and deception) or as siding with their world view and supporting their private wishes. If the counselor evidences any acceptance of the other parent's views or later does not behave as an ally, these parents feel completely betrayed and are furious. An attitude of detachment in the counselor, on the other hand, is interpreted as a preference for the ex-spouse. For these parents, one is either for them or against them; hence the counselor has a very small window of trust within which to operate. Paradoxical interventions, which begin with the counselor not expecting trust or the possibility of change, often successfully generate a "working alliance." Clarification and insight are virtually impossible with this group, except for certain well—integrated paranoid parents whose delusions about their ex-spouses are fairly circumscribed. Psychodynamic explorations of their underlying dynamics are threatening to these parents, who feel accused, belittled, morally outraged, and exposed; such maneuvers precipitate in them defensiveness, devaluation of the counseling-mediation, increased suspiciousness, delusional projections, or even uncontrollable rage. A strong, immediate, ego-supportive role is immediately necessary to restore their functioning.

☐ One man broke into a sweat and threatened to kill his wife when his contribution to their conflict was broached. "I have had it! Next time I am going to shoot her! I just want to live in peace and quiet. I've been talking, but no one has been listening!" Realizing the extreme gravity of this threat, given this man's rage, the counselors immediately responded by taking responsibility for the situation that he found intolerable. They agreed to call an emergency meeting of the attorneys, help him obtain a restraining order against her provocations, warn his ex-wife that he had reached his limit, and then persuaded him to rid himself of his gun.

In situations that pose less of an extreme and immediate threat, strategic attempts to shift their views of reality by relabeling and reframing behaviors are sometimes successful. For example, a clear relabeling of the ex-spouse's motivation, which reduces negative attribution and salvages the parent's self-esteem, is at times effective: "She keeps fighting because she can't let you go." "He's been extremely dependent on you in the marriage, and this is his way of managing without you." Similarly, presenting the other spouse as wanting acknowledgment, feeling like a failure, or as deeply hurt by rejection, diminishes these spouses' fears and need for retaliation. Likewise, a relabeling of their own motivation can sometimes redirect the intensity of the dispute. For example, we told a deeply shamed, paranoid father, who was adamantly resisting cooperation, that he was an honorable man with extremely high standards for himself and others who was very disappointed when others couldn't live up to those standards. He did not want to dishonor himself in his response to other's failures. Highlighting the children's needs and experiences or concretely articulating them often does not suffice to persuade these severely disturbed parents to act in their children's best interests. A stronger child-advocacy stance is required, wherein the counselor directly confronts parents with specific examples of the children's sufferings. Again, it is important not to impute any blame but rather to emphasize that the children are in an intolerable, "no-win" situation. Specific recommendations are made by the counselor, for example: "I understand how you feel and feel pained by your pain, but I cannot professionally recommend joint custody at this time. There is too much hostility and distrust between you and your ex-wife. Your daughter is already suffering and would suffer more if she split her time between the two of you."

Given the rigidity of some of the more disturbed views and the ego functioning of moderately and severely disturbed parents, their resistance to counseling-mediation, and their inability to make internal shifts, our strategy of choice is to circumvent the narcissistically vulnerable parents and intervene directly with their former partners (who are usually not as troubled as they), or their extended support systems. The counselor helps the ex-mate recognize the parent's special vulnerabilities (sensitivities, feelings of humiliation, fears of being criticized, need to prove themselves good), provides them with a formulation of what triggers their paranoia and elucidates better ways of coping with the narcissistically injured parent. Hence, the passive-dependent mates of these spouses who, out of fear of harassment, withhold information from their spouses, are advised of the importance of setting realistic limits and of clarity and directness in communicating with their spouses. In particular, the counselor encourages the former spouses not to do anything that might justify the parents' distorted perceptions (overreact or respond in kind). Without reality confirmation, their projective defenses become less effective, which increases the likelihood of their spouses' recognizing their own contributions to the conflicts, or at least of their seeking other containers for their painful, unwanted aspects of self. In effect, the spouse's good behavoir defensively disarms the narcissistically vulnerable parent. Enlisting the support of significant others whom they do trust, and who can modulate their anger and views, also provides leverage for change.

Lastly, firmly entrenched moderately and severely disturbed spouses often require a direct attempt at modifying their unrealistic expectations and magical wishes. In one of our final attempts to help parents develop their own solutions, the counselor-mediator orients and confronts severely disturbed spouses with the realities of their situation—the reality of their divorce, their ex-mate, and the law, as described further in chapters 9 and 10. Legal consultations that focus the spouse on the realities of the court and what can be done legally may help correct their fantasies of restitution and revenge. Confronting the problems of the most entrenched spouses often brings us to the limits of our counseling-mediation model, which is independent of court. For the severely entrenched, potentially violent spouses, interventions that rely more heavily on the authority of the court are necessary.

CHAPTER 5

Loss, Attachment, and Separation

Divorce always involves loss. It is normal to feel sad and pained at the loss of a loved one. In fact, descriptions of divorce in terms of loss and the recovery process as one akin to mourning permeate the literature on divorce (Bohannon, 1970; Kaslow, 1979–81; Kessler, 1975; Rice and Rice, 1986; Weiss, 1976; Wisemann, 1975). While everyone experiences loss, some are unable to tolerate its pain. Many spouses we saw had specific underlying vulnerabilities to loss and conflicts around attachment and separation. In general, two types of dynamics derived from these vulnerabilities are implicated in prolonged or entrenched divorce disputes.

In the first type of dynamic, the spouse experiences a reactivated trauma associated with a specific loss in the past. This includes loss of a child (through kidnapping, death, abortion, or adoption) or separation from one's own parents, sibling, or family (as a consequence of divorce, death, war, and forced migration). The separation from the spouse reawakens these as-yet-unmastered losses and the intense emotions that surround them. In this way the earlier loss becomes psychologically interwoven with the divorce, making the present loss more difficult to resolve. The second type derives from long-standing personality problems in separation and individuation of the spouse from his or her own primary caregivers. Because of early, oft-repeated experiences of severe deprivation, abandonment, neglect, and abuse, or by contrast, extreme indulgence and overprotectiveness, these people are excessively dependent or prone to fuse their identity with others. The present divorce, therefore, is experienced as another abandonment, a severe threat to their survival, and frequently as a loss of a sense of themselves. The ongoing disputes with the ex-spouse represent their often-conflicted struggle to separate and exist as a separate individual.

Common to both types, reactivated loss and separation-individua-

102

tion conflicts, is the defensive use of disputes over custody and visitation to ward off the painful sense of loss, sadness, and loneliness experienced in the divorce. To varying extents, these parents are unable to tolerate and accept the pain of the loss of separation from the spouse or child. Hence they are unable to mourn, grieve, and let go of the child, the spouse, or the marriage itself. This is manifested in different kinds of disputes.

Some try to prevent the actual loss from occurring by prolonging or clinging to the marriage. They do anything to set up roadblocks to the end of the marriage, refusing to settle anything, including plans for their children. Others, feeling helpless, try to control the speed of the divorce and use mediation and counseling to put off the impending inevitable loss.

Some try to deny the loss by refusing to acknowledge the full reality of the separation.

☐ Mr. I. continued as usual, painting the family home, fixing the car, and gardening, despite the fact that he had been evicted from the house. He expected his wife to continue to provide him meals and plan the children's activities during his visits. He pretended there was no loss, that he could go on as before, walk into the house when he liked, and even have intercourse with his wife from time to time.

Rather than deny the reality of the loss or resist its occurrence, other parents try to ward off and defend against the feelings of loss by denigrating the spouse and rationalizing that the marriage was not worth it. For example, Mrs. M. defended against the sadness of her spouse's abandonment when she became pregnant by claiming that she and her baby son did not need him. "He was all fun and games, incapable of taking care of or being responsible for a child." To have acknowledged his importance, she would have had to face her own hurt.

Simultaneously, many cover their sadness over the loss with anger. We will not belabor how anger is an antidote to loss, as the divorce literature is replete with how individuals ward off pain and grief in varied ways, including embroiling their spouses in legal disputes. Fighting is also a means of maintaining contact and fending off loneliness. The custody dispute allows parents to live out the fantasy that they are still together in some way. Many parents we saw despite volcanic eruptions in the mediator's office, waited for one another at the elevator or in the parking lot. Reconciliation fantasies, also in the service of avoiding loss, often persist side by side with the disputants' continued hostilities.

In an attempt to ward off loss, parents often turn to their children as replacements for the spouse. They became emotionally dependent and lean on their children to soften the loss, using the children as companions or confidantes. The intensity of their need for the child as surrogate parent or spouse increases with the stress of the divorce and with the severity of parent's own vulnerabilities. Some parents use their children as a bridge to the ex-spouse, for example, by insisting on increased visits or being present at the child's exchange to ensure their own (not the child's) contact with their ex-mate. Other parents, over-identify to varying degrees with their children and project their intolerance of sadness and fears of being alone onto the children. They then seek to protect their children from these distressful emotions and consciously view the custody suit as a means of doing so. In the end, the child's distress and their own loneliness is ameliorated in this flurry of protective activity.

However, though there are common dynamics, there are also important distinctions between the two main types of intrapsychic conflict—reactivated loss and separation-individuation problems. It is useful to describe the different ways in which each is manifested in post-divorce discord and in the defensive use of the child in order to derive differential prognosis for treatment and intervention strategies.

Reactivated Trauma of Loss

There are parents who are basically intact, with less severe intrapsychic difficulties, who have a specific difficulty in mourning the loss of a real, psychologically separate loved one. Consequently they cannot let go of the spouse, the marriage, or the family and also have great difficulty in allowing their child to leave, even for visits. Their vulnerability derives from a specific (circumscribed) trauma around loss that is reactivated and confused with the present divorce situation.

   ☐ Mrs. C. lost her mother during her early adolescence. She described her as "warm and wonderful," and she choked back tears to preserve a severe, controlled, angry expression whenever she spoke of her mother's death. Now she was divorcing a husband whom she described bitterly as having once been "outgoing, warm, and loving" toward her but who proved "undependable." They had been trying to separate for the past two years and were locked in a fight-to-the-death struggle over custody of their daughter. Mrs. C. showed no grief or sorrow at the separation, only intense bitterness and cold anger toward her "irresponsible" husband. She insisted that he would, likewise, be unreliable for her daughter. It was clear that her unresolved grief at her mother's death, experienced as abandonment, had been reawakened and she heavily defended against these intense feelings.

Parents who have previously lost a child are often enormously fearful of losing another in a custody battle. For example, some mothers especially feared the loss because they had been forced as unwed teenagers to give up a baby for adoption.

☐ Mrs. M. explained tearfully, "The reason I wanted this baby so bad is because I had one at sixteen and my parents persuaded me to give her up. I've spent twelve years crying over it and haven't stopped yet." The thought of losing her daughter to her ex-husband who might want to return to his homeland overseas was now unbearable.

☐ Mrs. S. had lost her first baby through a sudden, inexplicable crib death. She now wanted to be in total control of her new baby's physical environment. Any slight fever or illness in the child activated overwhelming concerns for the child's survival, and she would cancel the father's visits. She also spent an inordinate proportion of her small salary for a trained nurse's aide who would care for the child in her home, and then wanted the father to help with this expense.

☐ Mrs. N.'s firstborn, a daughter, had been kidnapped by her first husband and she had not seen her since. Terrified that she would lose her second child, she allowed her second husband to bully and harass her because of his threats not to return her son after visits. Neither could she take action to protect her son from this sadistic man.

☐ During her adolescence Mrs. K. had lost three siblings on three separate occasions, two in car accidents. She was now very fearful of letting her husband, who was a truck driver, take her two sons on visits. She held on to the boys as if they were her brothers and found it very hard to believe that he would take good care of them.

Past grieving associated with past miscarriages, abortions, or difficulties in becoming pregnant is often reactivated in the present cus-

tody suit. Two-thirds of the children of our sample were only children, and many parents had lost the opportunity for more children
through sterilization, physical illness, or age. For others who were
immigrants, especially those who were in this country as refugees
from war and political oppression, the child represented their only
accessible blood relative, their only real family. In all of these situations, the previous loss had not been worked through and the mourning was not complete. These parents made specific demands based on
fears associated with the past trauma, and they held on to their children tightly so as to ward off potential further loss. Despite the often
dramatic nature of their past trauma, most were not aware of their
sadness over the previous loss and the fact that they were experiencing this again with the second child.

Other parents seek to protect their children from specific loss experiences—such as painful parental divorce, desertion, or deprivation
in their own childhood. This frequently leads them to demand particular kinds of custody arrangements.

☐ Mr. G., a rather passive man, painfully recalled, "I watched my
   mother go through three husbands. I never wanted to marry or
   have children for fear they would end up like me . . . and not
   know who their father was." He was reluctant to divorce and be
   unavailable to his daughter. He persisted with surprising intensity, given his passive style, in his demands for extensive access
   to his daughter, and despite no support from his working-class
   peers.

☐ After his father's death, Mr. B. was raised by a series of relatives
   who gave him little time and attention. His mother was always
   busy working and involved in her own concerns. The divorce
   from his wife recapitulated his early sense of abandonment by
   his mother and intense feelings of not being wanted anywhere.
   He projected these onto his child and insisted on sole custody to
   protect his daughter from being neglected by his spouse. Mrs.
   B. was actually very warm and available to her daughter and
   wanted the father very much involved in the child's life. She
   offered joint custody. Mr. B. rejected this outright, stating that
   he would not allow his child to be "shuffled back and forth and
   not belong anywhere like I [did] as a child."

☐ As a child Mr. K. was the victim of a long-term visitation dispute following his parents' divorce. His mother actively kept
   him from visits with his father, punished him for expressing

preference for his dad, and finally rejected him when, as a teenager he went to live with his father. Only several months later, his father died of a heart attack, dashing his hopes for a long-term reconciliation with his idealized father. In his own divorce, Mr. K. was convinced that his wife, as his mother had, was keeping his sons from seeing him. When he arrived at irregular times to pick up the boys, he believed her refusal to cooperate was evidence of her attempts to prevent the visits. He was convinced that she was trying to turn the boys against him.

Interventions with Reactivated Traumas

In general, there is a reasonably good prognosis for resolution of custody and visitation disputes motivated by specific traumatic losses in the past, using counseling and therapy techniques. This subgroup is experiencing the loss of an objective other, not a projected part of themselves or an idealized other. They also have the capacity to view their children more objectively and to make distinctions as to where their own anxieties end and where their children's begin. Basically, their psychological development is sufficient to be able to simultaneously examine both their own feelings and different views without major regression. Hence, with help they can work through repressed or displaced conflicts.

The overall goal is to help these parents mourn and work through loss and accompanying feelings. This is done by providing insight into the dynamics of the conflict, helping them to distinguish earlier loss from the present one, and by supporting their expression of grief. This latter process involves confronting denial and helping them move through sadness, depression, and anger to acceptance, detachment, and on to forming new relationships. These interventions with reactivated trauma warrant further explication and illustration.

☐ With Mrs. C., who lost her mother during early adolescence, the counselor spent one session having her recall this earlier time in detail, and having her explore her overwhelming feelings of abandonment and her angry adolescent resentment, as well as the pressure her European father put on her to "keep a stiff upper lip" and not to demonstrate unseemly emotion in public. As she teared in response to these memories, the counselor gently connected the early experience with her current bitter feelings that her husband had failed to support her when she needed him most, and showed her how her cold anger and biting sarcasm were similar to the ways she had dealt with her mother's death. For the first time, Mrs. C. began to soften in her attitude towards her spouse.

☐ With Mrs. S., who had lost her first baby through a tragic crib death, we focused on her inordinate and excessive fear for the second child's physical safety. We explained how she was trying to "prevent the unpreventable," the potential loss of this child, because she was still trying to protect herself, and undo, the unbearable loss of her previous daughter.

☐ For Mr. B., who was raised by a series of relatives, none of whom cared about him, we explored his early feelings of being unwanted and shuffled around. In particular, we focused on his disappointment with his mother, whom he had idealized and excused. The more anger he was able to express toward her, the more he was able to differentiate her from his wife. He was then able to acknowledge his spouse as a good, available mother for his child, and he relinquished his claim for sole custody.

☐ With Mr. K., who was a child of a divorce and convinced that his ex-spouse was keeping him from his sons, we clarified all the ways in which his ex-wife supported his relationship with his sons. We then had her meet with him directly to reassure him and work out a shared parenting agreement. Since his ex-wife was the one who had lost three brothers, we clarified to both of them how she held on to her children through fear of losing them, also, in a traumatic accident.

Sometimes these interventions do not stimulate a real understanding and working through of grief. They remain only cognitive explanations for parents who are skeptical or brush off the interpretations as irrelevant or meaningless. However, their ongoing expressions of denial, anger, and disappointment with the ex-spouse allow the counselor numerous opportunities to make the connections between the present and the past. One man, after describing his utter desolation when his wife left, was asked if he had ever experienced this in his life before. Without thinking he immediately answered, "Yes, I was three when my mother left me. I remember . . . I was standing all alone in a room which was big and empty. I felt so lost!"

As the loss is properly acknowledged and connected to its appropriate source, we support and encourage the experiencing of intense feeling. The parent is given a temporal framework of the expectable feelings and tasks of the mourning process, and we emphasize the importance of going through this without skipping a phase. With those stuck in the denial phase, we gently and firmly point out the reality of the divorce and their wish not to give up the ghost of the marriage. However, the present losses consequent upon the divorce are framed as relative, and different from the more devastating experiences of total loss in the death or desertion they had previously experienced. For instance, it is pointed out that they will continue to parent their children after divorce and will have a different kind of family, perhaps an extended or binuclear family. Even for those who are parenting long distance, we demonstrate ways of staying close to their children and being important to them.

Those stuck in the phase of protest and anger are given ample permission to express their disappointment and frustration. We frame their anger as having a function in allowing them to separate. However, we clearly give a time frame as well as appropriate places for the expression of these feelings and help them move on to active mourning—for their dashed hopes and dreams, for their ideal, traditional family, for the lost time and opportunity with their children as well as for their ex-spouse. Considerable support and empathy is necessary to help them sustain the sadness that ensues. Finally, we help them detach and restructure their lives, giving them permission and support in their exploration of new relationships and renewal of old friendships.

Separation-Individuation Conflicts

Among those involved in long-term, entrenched divorce disputes, we found a much larger group of parents for whom dependency and separation-individuation conflicts are the key underlying issues. To varying degrees, these parents have not mastered the developmental task of psychological separation from primary caretakers and have, in their marriages, replicated these disturbed primary relationships with their spouses. Object-relations theorists (for example Mahler, 1971; Kernberg, 1967; Masterson, 1981) have described these people in times of disturbances in their "self-object relationships." For them, others do not fully exist and have never existed as separate persons, but to varying extents, are perceived as projected fragments or reconstitutions of their inner psychological needs.

The actual histories of these people are sometimes difficult to piece together because they are replete with fantasied reconstructions of the past, in which others—especially their parents—have been idealized or devalued. However, from their own and their spouses' re-

ports we find, not only specific losses to which they are now responding, but more ongoing failures in their relationships with primary
caretakers, who by and large were ungratifying, unsupportive, and
frequently abandoning. Many are the children of severe alcoholics or
mentally ill parents. They have been subject to a variety of caretakers, repeated foster home placement, a succession of fathers, or
recurring incidences of neglect and abuse.

☐ Mrs. T. was abused by father as a preschooler. Her parents were
   estranged from one another. After her mother died when she
   was five years old, she was kidnaped from maternal relatives by
   her father, who subsequently abandoned her in an orphanage
   two years later. When she was nine years old, she was adopted
   by parents who "didn't get along." For most of her childhood
   she had no one on whom to rely. Fending off a major abandonment depression, she clung to her spouse. When he was not
   available she depended completely on her boyfriend. When he
   left, she turned to her three-year-old child.

Interestingly, some are the children of extremely overprotective.
indulgent, and controlling parents on whom they continue to depend.

☐ Mr. L., an only child of elderly parents, was often ill as a young-
   ster and confined to bed. He was overprotected and pampered
   by a domineering mother, and never developed a relationship
   with his father. He married a woman who became the primary
   caretaker not only for the children but for him. He was passive,
   ineffectual, and often absent as a father. When his wife had a
   serious accident, requiring his help, he could not respond. She
   left the marriage and he became severely depressed. He clung
   to both his wife and his elderly mother.

With the divorce, these persons do not experience sadness over the
loss of a psychologically separate other, as do those with a reactivated trauma, but in varying degrees and levels of conscious awareness, they experience panic or intense feelings of being abandoned,
deserted, and cut off, never to be reconnected. They feel insignificant.
overwhelmingly helpless, and unable to survive on their own. In extreme cases, they feel empty, hollow, without form and substance.
Strong, disturbing images of fading into nothingness, withering
away, or dying abound.
   The custody disputes, therefore, serve the function of defending
against the severing of a crucial or symbiotic attachment, or the
psychological death of themselves. In general there are three differ-

ent ways in which they respond to their inner desperation and extreme separation anxiety. First, some remain diffusely dependent or actively cling to the spouse or child and will not allow the divorce or the visits. Second, some defend against the threat of abandonment and emptiness by a pseudo-autonomous, counterdependent stance, aggressively protecting themselves and their children, refusing to capitulate to anything lest they lose part of themselves. Thirdly others are markedly conflicted about attachment and separation and oscillate from dependency to counterdependency. This is manifested in abrupt, contradictory shifts. At times they are compliant, at other times, over the same issues, they are resistant and negative. It is useful to elaborate on each of these dependent, counterdependent, and oscillating states.

Dependency

The parents in this group basically maintain a dependent attachment to the spouse or child. Some diffusely dependent individuals refuse to acknowledge the separation as permanent. They continue to wear their wedding rings, introduce themselves as a spouse, send flowers and presents on anniversaries, enter the home without permission, and try to engage their ex-partner in long personal discussions. Despite ample evidence that there is no chance of reconciliation, they continue to fantasize getting back together. One man maintained a patient vigil, awaiting reconciliation, despite the message from his wife that she would "prefer a slow, painful, laborious torture."

In general, these people are characterized by emotional and social isolation. Though some appear outwardly friendly, they have little capacity to initiate or maintain mutually gratifying intimate relations with other adults. They are also socially isolated and, out of loneliness, stay involved with their spouse. During the actual marriage, these persons shared few real pleasures or emotional interchanges with their spouse. Often they had separate interests (spectator sports, repairing cars, attending business meetings, maintaining the house and garden). They hold a kind of fantasy about their marriage and spouse, and despite much expressed dissatisfaction by their partners and a clear absence of intimacy in the marriage, they nevertheless continue to believe that their partner feels the same attachment and commitment to them. In this respect their psychological profile is likely to correspond to that of people who cherish idealized images of the other, as disucssed in chapter 3.

□ Mr. A. talked about his fourteen-year marriage as though it were an extended honeymoon, and he was shocked by his wife's announcement that it was over. He had no idea that there was "trouble in paradise," as he felt their relationship was "idyllic."

As the marriage and family dissolve, they continue their attachment to their spouse in the same way, experiencing intimacy at a distance. They stay involved with the spouse on a fantasy level and continue the same emotionally distant, vague, pseudo-mutual pattern of relating, assuming they are very much a part of the family, to the chagrin and fury of the separating spouse. These spouses do not express much anger directly, rather they are passively aggressive:

☐ Mr. A. took a morally superior view, seeing his wife as pathetic. "Frankly, my daughter and I feel sorrow and pity for my wife, who is underweight and seems to be floundering. I hope she can get it together." His anger was submerged in patronizing and condescending concern.

☐ Mr. K. was ingratiating and obsequious. Despite his wife's intense, clearly expressed wish to get him out of her life, he phoned her frequently. He asked her advice on numerous trivial matters—for example, what present to buy his daughter—and expressed humble gratitude for her help and hurt puzzlement at her frustrated anger.

Others infuriate their spouses by forgetting to do things when and as they promised. They bring the children home late or forget to pick them up on time. They lose toys, clothes, or schoolbooks on the visits, or take their children on the kind of outings that drive the spouse into a frenzy of anxiety. At choice moments (for exmaple, when the other is ready to leave), they provoke a fight to keep the attachment, albeit negative.

These passive-aggressive maneuvers keep the dispute, the relationship with the spouse, and hence themselves emotionally alive. If the spouse does not return or remain involved with them, these dependent persons sometimes try far more active strategies to sustain the relationship. They lavish gifts, beg to resume the marriage, or become withholding—bargaining their resources (money and children)—or when really desperate, blackmail by threatening harm.

☐ Mr. L. lost thirty-two pounds and could not sleep. He was totally obsessed with his wife's leaving and fantasied reconciliation. He threw himself at her feet, clinging to her. He sent flowers, left love notes, and chased her van when she came to see the children in order to talk to her, hoping she "might come round." He entered mediation planning to use this forum to reconcile. When his efforts failed, he became extremely angry and vindictive, using threats of legal measures to restrain her, vowing to leave her financially destitute. He felt that if he punished her for abandoning him and their daughters, she might come back.

By and large, these parents have little understanding of the children's needs separate from their own and use the children in a number of ways to gratify their own needs. Depending on the sex and age of the child, this may lead to incipient pathologies in the parent-child relationship. For example, some men substitute their early-adolescent daughters for their spouses so that the child becomes the new fantasy object. This leads to disturbing, diffusely sexualized relationships between father and daughter.

☐ Rather than maintain a fantasy attachment to his wife, Mr. A. turned to his twelve-year-old daughter and developed a mutually affectionate, adoring, seductive romantic relationship with her. The daughter would cook the meals, and nightly the father and daughter would eat dinner by candlelight and then cuddle in bed watching TV. His relationship with his daughter undid his feelings of abandonment and provided a feeling of connection and emotional support. His only complaint was that he felt helpless in disciplining his daughter, a feeling that came from his unwillingness to exert any authority lest she withdraw. His only form of discipline was to cajole or sweet-talk her into doing special favors for him. Additionally, he protected himself from feeling abandoned by projecting his feelings onto her. He saw the abandonment as happening to her, not to himself. He saw her as having lived in a world of bliss and being unprepared for the separation. "Just a few weeks ago her life was serene and now it is in shambles. My wife left the house bare, and it was a trauma for Jane to find things gone." To add some stability for the child, he went out and bought her as much as he could. His daughter did not experience the father's actions as supportive but as pressures to hold paradise together.

Typically, grade-school children are used for emotional support: These children essentially become peers and parents to their mothers and fathers, monitoring and guarding the vital signs of their parents' well-being. Their constant presence is required to stave off loneliness and emptiness.[1]

☐ "My husband left and Peter is all I have left, and now he's trying to take him too!" Mrs. R. cried. Claiming that she was "slowly dying inside, a plant without roots and water," Mrs. R. depended on eight-year-old Peter for her survival. She became depressed and extremely panicky when he was not in the house and often asked him to sleep with her. She could not permit him to spend more than one night away from her, so that visits to his father were constrained by her needs.

Mothers of very young children may transfer their symbiotic needs from the spouse to the child in an effort to create the illusion of a union that will never be broken. Hence they cannot allow the child to separate and individuate from them.

☐ Mrs. W. had a very deprived early history. Her mother was an alcoholic, and she spent extensive time in an orphanage and foster home. She married her boss, a father figure, and became very dependent on him. When her husband lost his job, she became enraged about his inability to support her and the marriage ended. She became completely centered around her preschool son. His toys were placed in every room of the house including hers and the bathroom. She enmeshed him in her own conflicts and felt his every need and anxiety. She was as afraid for his physical safety and survival as she was for her own. Both of them experienced severe separation anxieties from one another when he left for school and when he visited his father.

In all of the cases described above, the children felt highly valued and necessary to the parent's survival. They also felt burdened by the emotional demands and worried about failing to sustain the parent. However, not all parents transfer their emotional dependency onto their children. Many children of parents with dependent personalities are used merely as bridges to reach the ex-spouse, as instruments to effect reconciliation, weapons to punish an errant mate, or simply as a toy to be played with for a while, for diversion and amusement. These children are important mainly in terms of the parents' relationship with the spouse. At other times, preoccupied with their own needs, they give little attention to the children, who are consequently forgotten, ignored, or abruptly left. Despite the dispute over the child, these parents can leave the children unattended for long hours. The children feel inconsequential, unwanted, rejected, and that they do not exist by any right of their own.

Counterdependency

In contrast to parents who are diffusely or actively dependent, others fend off underlying dependency needs and intense fears of merging with another by developing a pseudo-autonomous stance. They attempt to present themselves as being extremely independent, actively in control of their lives, and totally self-sufficient. They are rigid and dictatorial in their thinking and refuse to compromise, comply, or cooperate. They reject their ex-spouse's proposals or suggestions outright. "I won't let him influence me one iota." They become furious at any implication that their ex-spouse or anyone else "is going to tell [them] what to do." In fact, they often want nothing to do with the ex-spouse; they are reluctant to talk or to meet. In short, they want their spouse out of their own and the children's lives. This tough, angry stance frames the dispute. Their dependency and lack of clear boundaries of self are belied by their intense oppositionalism. Their sense of self is so brittle that they are compelled to remain coldly rigid and distant and to react to any request with a categorical no. They hold on to their position tightly lest they waver, collapse, and lose their own separateness. On those few occasions when their defenses partially or temporarily collapse, these parents experience overwhelming confusion and panic.

Most of these counterdependent parents are women, who historically report intense dependent relationships with early caretakers from whom it was difficult to separate. The marriage was often conceived as a way of breaking these ties and leaving home but quickly became a reenactment of earlier unresolved individuation conflicts—that is, they replaced their dependency on their mothers with dependency on their spouses. During the marriage they felt they had been too passive, molding themselves submissively to their partner's wishes and expectations. The divorce represents to the parent, and indeed often is, a positive step forward in the individuation process. However, they pursue their separateness with a rigidity and aggressiveness that is provocative and frustrating. They are not able to accomplish the final major step in the individuation process: They cannot say yes, cooperate, or compromise without feeling submergence of self. They have not yet learned how to work with others.

☐ Mrs. H. grew up "loving my mother but hating how she raised us. She made all of us children very dependent on her. She loved our dependency and fed on it." Mrs. H. left home to marry her childhood sweetheart when she was twenty-three years old. She became extremely dependent on her husband. "I looked up him. I was pleased by his telling me what to do. In the early years I was a doormat. I allowed myself to be swallowed up by him. Originally I liked being a slave. I let him sap every bit of my energy for twenty-five years." However, when she began to grow, her husband did not like the change and put pressure on her to comply with his needs and expectations. She felt oppressed and depressed. As the relationship deteriorated, she cried out for help but he turned away from her, saying, "In life you have to walk the valley alone." At this point she began to defend against her feelings of dependency on him, "though it took me a long time to believe that I had the possibility of getting out." Their relationship ended in legal divorce but extended into a six-year child custody dispute.

In attempting to counter her dependent wishes and perceived fear of being engulfed by him, she claimed she did not want "him running my life nor my life revolving around his." Hence she would make unilateral decisions with respect to her son. For instance, she changed schools and moved thirty miles away without even informing him. She dictated his access arrangements and constantly interfered with his plans when it suited her needs. She misperceived his requests and concerns as evidence that he was trying to undercut her authority (her independence). When he wished to discuss where his son would go to school and his concern for the child's hygiene and clothes, she felt he was trying to "impose his values" on her and the child. When he made reasonable requests, for example, to increase a visit by one hour in order to return from a weekend camping trip in nonpeak traffic, she imagined he was trying to control her and categorically refused. Despite her protestations that she wanted to "get him off [her] back," this woman remained overly focused on her ex-husband's opinions. For example, when he told her he liked her new boyfriend, her response was, "How dare you say this to me!" She was defending against her feelings that she depended on him for evaluation or cared what he thought. Her underlying dependency could hence be seen in her counterdependent actions and her complaints about him. (If truly separate, she could have ignored her spouse and moved on). In mediation, when her ex-husband became conciliatory, she became more oppositional. When an attempt was made to establish a shared custody agreement that would involve them talking regularly and making mutual decisions, she first agreed and then experienced overwhelming panic and fear of being submerged in the old relationship again. She withdrew her agreement and reinstated her stubborn, oppositional stance. Similarly, when a plan involving very minor changes in the current schedule was proposed, Mrs. H. rejected it, becoming progressively more vehement that her ex-husband was a "psychopath" to whom she would never submit. Each time her concerns were addressed and a new plan that logically eliminated her previous objections was presented, she found another reason why the plan would not work. Despite her continued rejection of proposals. she blamed her ex-spouse for the lack of settlement and insisted on returning to court.

Unfortunately, these counterdependent or pseudo-autonomous parents tend to repeat the separation-individuation conflicts with their children. Consequently, the parents' relationship with their children is often characterized by a harsh belligerence and cool distancing, especially as the child enters adolescence. Generally, they need to have their child merged with them. In part, this means having their child physically near. Though demanding closeness, when with the child they often have considerable difficulty being available and providing warmth and nurturance. In part, they need to have their child's views and feelings merged with their own and have difficulty tolerating their child's separate individual needs or personal strivings, as well as concern, love for, and loyalty to the other parent. Because of their wish to be rid of their spouse, they are often rigid in their belief that the spouse is not important to the child. Indeed, they want to get the ex-spouse out of their life and the child also. To this end they attempt to elicit the child's support of their views and at times force the child's expression of preference. Dynamically, they tend to see the child either as themselves (especially their vulnerable, dependent aspects) or as their ex-spouse. Their perceptions of the child as their ex-mate often result in their fighting with the child as a substitute spouse. When, for example, the child rebels against the parent's demands, he or she is perceived not as having legitimate requests but as being manipulated, controlled by, or aligned with the other parent.

☐ Mrs. H. was very distrustful of her eleven-year-old son's motives and felt the child was trying to manipulate and walk all over her (much like her husband). She often saw the child as "sneaky and a liar," much again like her "manipulating ex-husband." Father and son were fused in her mind, and she would not submit to either. When the child talked back she saw this as a reflection of her husband. The son reported, "My mother gets mad when she thinks she hear dad's voice." Mrs. H. acknowledged this. "he's voicing his father, his father is pushing me through him."

On the other hand, when they overidentify with their child, they see their vulnerable aspects in the child and act as if the child indeed has these same vulnerabilities. Children are, by and large, good receptacles for these parents' split-off dependency needs because they are, in fact, dependent.

☐ Mrs. H. imagined that her husband was dominating and "trapping" her son, much as he had once oppressed her in marriage. She was alarmed when she saw her son "do what I have done" and became furious at her child for "not standing up to him." Her own submissiveness was deposited onto the son. She was intent on protecting her child-self from the husband's domination and resisted her ex-spouse by pressuring her son not to submit to his father.

Oscillating Dependency

Some disputants reveal elements of both the dependent and counterdependent types. They demonstrate marked instability in behavior, feelings, and attitudes towards themselves and others in abrupt, radical shifts in preferences regarding custody arrangements and corresponding feelings about their ex-spouse and child, which make resolution frustratingly difficult.

☐ Mrs. O. clung to various contradictory demands. She wanted the father always to be available by telephone. Then she decided this was unrealistic but later insisted on it again. She would sometimes call and ask him to help her out with household chores or pick up their son at school. At other times, she would call to forbid him to go near the school, scream at him to get out of her house, and threaten to call the police.

Like Mrs. O., over time or even within a session, these parents switch between an expressed wish for closeness and dependency and an angry pseudo-independence. Rather than an unrelenting negativity, a categorical no of the counterdependent type, these parents flip between yes and no and appear markedly unstable in their attitudes and behavior. The basic issue is a marked separation-individuation conflict that is externalized, acted out, and manifested in these mutually contradictory stances. This involves not merely an obsessive or indecisive rumination, a going back and forth in one's mind, recognizing alternatives but remaining indecisive. In these cases, the contradictory states are segregated so that when one is operating, the other is split off and dissociated. The person is unaware and therefore unable to integrate their opposing views or contradictory feelings into a total realistic picture. These segregated views and accompanying emotions contribute to their psychological impasse to accepting the divorce and resolving the access disputes. They are unable to examine their disparate views. As they begin to contemplate one side of their ambivalence, intolerable feelings are evoked (either fear of abandonment or merging), they despair and retreat to the opposite side of their conflicted wishes, evoking once-again untenable feelings. Typically, parents manifesting these patterns of behavior have borderline personality disorders. Often they split off and project unacceptable feelings onto others in their social world and then struggled in conflictual relations with those others. At times this is the psychological basis of the splits and tremendous conflicts engendered in their surrounding social environments.

These parents cannot tolerate closeness or being alone. They cannot allow intimacy lest they merge; they cannot allow distance lest they feel abandoned. During their marriage they cling and distance, moving back and forth, in and out of the relationship. They can neither engage nor let go and are at an impasse in their own intrapsychic growth, which has resulted in the impasse with their spouse. The process is repeated in the marital dissolution in which they cannot tolerate settling or not settling. In mediation they are willing to negotiate one day and feel furious and betrayed the next. Settling their custody dispute is tantamount to giving up part of themselves. As they move toward an agreement, they begin to feel anxious, incomplete, empty and stranded. As they move away from settlement, their equilibrium is re-established, but they are left with unresolved real life tasks.

> ☐ Mrs. O. had great difficulty coming to closure on her final agreement. She would first agree on a plan but then kept asking for sundry addenda and limitations to the contract, which made the agreement increasingly vague, punitive, and unworkable. This plan would be scratched, a new, opposite one developed, and the process would begin again.

These borderline parents usually become intensely involved with one of the counselors-mediators in a rapid transference that illustrates their underlying disorder. They are friendly, talkative, gracious at one moment; screaming, and stubborn the next. They immediately entangle the counselor-mediator in the same ambivalence, desire for loyalty, and fear of engulfment that characterizes their other relationships. At times, they express the wish to let the spouse go, as they want to agree (merge) with the idealized counselor, and thus move towards a settlement. Then as they become aware of this merging, they become terrified of engulfment and loss of self, they split off these feelings, flipping into a contradictory stance. The counselor is often precipitously deidealized and they return to the defense of refusing to settle.

☐ At times Mr. S. expressed a wish for a close, continuing visiting arrangement; at other times he would abruptly cut off contact with his daughter for months at a time at any perceived rejection, disappointment, or hurt, then suddenly reappear and expect to resume the relationship as though nothing had happened. At times Mr. S. idealized the counselor as an expert and perceived her as having authority and judgment over him, promising to "go along with anything she said." Then he would defy any perceived judgment and abruptly walk off in a huff, refusing to continue the session, upset over not being able to manage the problem on his own. Over the course of mediation, he fired the counselor on four occasions, charging her with bias, but would come back again each time apologizing and requesting to continue.

Marked instability in attitudes and behavior characterize their relationship with the child as with the spouse. These parents repeat with their children the same wish-fears of closeness and alternately hold onto and distance themselves from their children. As part of their lack of separation from their children, these borderline parents often expose their children to the family mayhem. Seemingly unaware of the child's presence (even when holding the child), they can be extremely volatile, at one moment bestowing affection and the next, erupting into a screaming tirade and becoming physically abusive.

☐ Mr. A. waxed poetic about the wonders of parenting and his children's "infinite capacity to love and forgive." At other times, he became tense, morose and irritable and neglected them or became harshly punitive. In fact, one night he severely beat his son for not living up to his expectations and lost custody.

Treatment Interventions with Separation-Individuation Conflicts

Overall, the aim is to help these parents separate by making them less frightened and overwhelmed by the real and symbolic loss of the marriage and spouse. We attempt to modify or circumvent the psychological conflicts (around separation and individuation), feelings (of loneliness and emptiness), and fears (of abandonment and merging) which block their capacity to separate. It is important in intervening to attempt some shifts in the dynamics of the conflict, if at all possible. This involves working simultaneously on a number of fronts:

1. Developing a clear understanding of their underlying fears of separation and, where appropriate, the historical antecedents of these fears; this can moderate their fears and thereby increase their ability to tolerate loss;

2. Supporting their sense of independence and feelings of separateness, competence, and hope; this helps to sustain their fragile sense of self and their capacity to handle the separation;

3. Helping them understand their relationship with their child vis-à-vis their fears and conflicts and to help them more appropriately nurture and protect their children;

4. Intervening with significant others who can help moderate their sense of loss and neediness and stabilize their perceptions of themselves and others.

Some parents can make good use of clarification as to why their marriage did not work and insight into how early experiences with their primary caregivers was repeated in the marriage and the divorce. Understanding why it is difficult to let go helps differentiate the unrealistic from realistic fears, making the process of desengaging more manageable and more enduring.

☐ During her marriage, Mrs. R. was excessively dependent on her husband. She followed him dutifully across the country but then fretted for her family of origin. Many times she experienced states of panic in which she would need to contact her mother and father because she had ominous fears that something had happened to them. When her marriage failed, partly due to her excessive dependency needs, she became deeply depressed and distraught about her own survival. She clung to her husband and child and kept reporting that if left alone she was going to die. In exploring the origin of these fears, Mrs. R.

revealed she had been her parents' second child. Her older sister had died as a toddler prior to her birth. In reaction to her sister's death, her parents had been extremely overprotective of her and fearful of her survival apart from them. From the time she was a toddler, they infantalized her to such a degree that she never felt safe without them or without a parent substitute, her husband. In intervening, we made this interpretation to Mrs. R. and showed her how she had been made to feel helpless and unrealistically worried about her own survival apart from others all her life.

With those who are counterdependent, the divorce can be readily acknowledged as an important step in their growth towards a healthy independence. Their strivings to be self-sufficient are applauded. At the same time, the way in which they construe their ex-spouses' actions as attempts to control them and sabotage their autonomy and, in turn, their own stubbornness and oppositionalism are pointed out as evidence of their continued dependency, albeit a negative one on their mate. Until they can give and take and work mutually, they are defined as not being truly independent. These clarifications are usually strong motivation for them to work further on their individuation.

However, insight and clarification of the dynamcs are of limited use with many of these clients because they are extremely anxious and often easily incapacitated by overwhelming feelings of abandonment. Rather than resulting in insight and resolution, interpretations—especially for those who oscillate from dependency to counterdependency—may make their fears more real and frightening. For these people, a special intervention that provides an explanatory map or intellectual formulation of their own or the situational dynamics facilitates their overall understanding of the nature of their conflicts in a way that allows them to keep a cognitive distance and a feeling of separateness. Further, placing information about their own behavior in the context of their interaction with their spouse also makes interpretations less threatening and more palatable. Finally, laying out an explanatory map helps ambivalently dependent parents organize a more integrated sense of reality and provides a more realistic framework from which to plan and predict the likely outcomes of their actions.

Supportive interventions are probably the most useful with those who have separation and individuation conflicts. Here, their capacities to cope with the separation are supported by helping them organize more of a life of their own psychologically (acknowledging their feelings of independence and self-sufficiency), practically (increasing their ability to restructure their lives in real ways), and socially (developing a network of supportive others to replenish the loss). First, we help parents feel less needy, less dependent on others for security or for a sense of self, and less despairing by challenging their fears and unrealistic beliefs about themselves. For example, the counselor asked Mrs. R., "Why have you been so dependent on him? You are a smart, witty, competent woman who has obtained an accounting degree in two years! When are you going to give him up and find a more admiring, caring other?"

We acknowledge and build on clients' strengths by underscoring the discrepeancy between their actual abilities and successes and their lack of confidence and fear of failure. Even for those who deny their neediness, we agree they are coping well and give them much credit for marshaling their resources and valiantly holding their family together. The marital loss is redefined as offering an opportunity for change and personal growth, a chance to develop new identities and more satisfying intimate relationships. For those who are angry and frustrated by the lack of support from an ex-spouse who is clearly incapable of providing it, we verify the other's limitations and encourage them to expect nothing so as not to be repeatedly disappointed: "If he gives you something, regard it as a windfall, an unexpected gift." In all cases, we support their efforts to be alone and to provide for their own emotional gratification and financial security. To this practical end, they are given factual information on how to find legal assistance, housing, child care, and employment. They are referred to community resources to learn to manage finances or to provide them with educational and vocational alternatives. They are introduced to others who are struggling with similar issues, especially support groups for single parents. They are encouraged to establish a network of friends and colleagues, and to pursue new or old interests. In effect, the counseling involves helping them prepare for a more independent life.

☐ Mr. J.'s intolerable loneliness was offset by seeing his brother more frequently, going to church regularly, where he joined a Bible study group, and entering counseling. He coped by finding these supportive others.

☐ Mrs. L.'s daily life was dreary (working at a boring job, coming home, watching TV, and sleeping). The boredom and loneliness were punctuated by dramatic fights she had with her ex-spouse, during which time she rammed his car and shredded his clothing. She was encouraged to take up her artwork again, a talent she had not used during her marriage. This had the double value of making her less involved with her husband and providing a better model for her daughter, who was also chronically bored and isolated.

In this regard, it is important to remember that what they fear losing is, in part, a fantasy or a distortion of the other and, in this sense, a part of themselves. To the extent that the ex-spouse is a projection of their own wishes and needs and does not exist for them as a real, separate person, he or she may be easily replaceable. In fact, if the other is not too enmeshed in their fantasy, these parents can rather rapidly transfer their dependency to others—new lovers, friends, spiritual leaders, family of origin, as well as their children. In the same way, therapists or divorce groups may be used as transitional objects in the separation process. Hence, a custody dispute motivated by separation-individuation conflicts can evaporate fairly quickly if another person or group assumes a supportive function for the parent. Alternatively, it can reappear again if the parent loses that support; for example, if he or she breaks up with the new lover.

Many interventions are directed toward helping parents understand the effects of their actions on their children and improving their capacity to parent. With those parents who cling to their children, we show how they are replacing their spouse with the child. As a consequence, their children often feel overburdened and excessively worried and have difficulty separating from them when the parents go to work or when they themselves go to school play with peers. These observations offer the parents feedback along with encouragement to maintain their parental authority and primary nurturing role. We help parents differentiate the children's fears and worries from their own. For example, with those counterdependent parents who believe the child is being dominated and controlled by the other parent, we point out how, the child is in fact enjoying the visits and learning to manage the relationship with the other parent. When they become angry at the child's individual need or expressed wish to see the other parent, we point out how their child is trying to separate and be an individual, similar to their own struggles to be independent. They are encouraged to respond warmly and supportively to these strivings, much as they wanted their parents to be toward them in the past.

☐ We differentiated Mrs. H.'s feelings from those of her son. "You feel you have to get John away from his dad. It is you who needs to get away, he is not you. He can distance himself from his father and is not trapped and at his mercy. He knows his father responds to reasoned arguments and so he offers him explanations, thereby avoiding conflict." Mrs. H. was also encouraged to allow her son "to stake out his own territory, to be a little boy and make a few mistakes. He experiences your protection as you hanging on and wishing him not to grow up." We also advised Mrs. H. to talk with her ex-husband because "John needs a model of someone who can be appropriately assertive. When you refuse to talk with Mr. H., it places John in the middle of the conflict, and the child feels he needs to defend his father. This in turn leads you to believe that your son is speaking for his father and assuming his views."

With those who are intensely ambivalent about dependency and markedly erratic in their demands, counseling and mediation need to be more strategic. These individuals, who are typically borderline personalities, cannot tolerate insight or clarification of their intrapsychic dynamics, nor can they easily be supported by a warm, empathic counselor. Often they perceive the mediator to be depriving them of what they need and want. Alternatively, they fear engulfment and are likely to distance themselves by rejecting the counselor and refusing to reach a settlement. Paradoxical interventions, where the counselor takes on and argues for one side of their ambivalent views and feelings, can sometimes provoke the other side, allowing them to be maneuvered toward a settlement. Reality-testing, by continually juxtaposing the different strengths and weaknesses of a particular action or agreement, mitigates their tendency to split and only perceive one aspect at one time. Finally, it is often wise to break the agreement into small parts, and develop the final settlement one piece at a time. In this way they are not overwhelmed and can hold out by refusing to settle on other issues. It is to be expected that such parents will agree on all but one small issue, which they may need to have resolved by the court. In this situation, it is especially important that they return to their attorneys and the court with all the issues they have agreed on in place and those they still need to resolve clearly delineated. This latter strategy prevents their disrupting and rescinding all progress made.

Last, it is important to be alert to the tendency of these parents to project their various contradictory states onto others, and hence play out their ambivalences externally by having their attorneys, therapists, family members, and others take on various disputing roles. In this case, it is important to bring these significant others together and mediate a settlement with the larger network, which will in turn constrain the parent.

☐ After seven years of postdivorce conflict, Mr. and Mrs. C.'s final agreement was worked out by seven professionals (two attorneys, three therapists, a school psychologist, and a mediator). Until this meeting, all these professionals had been kept separate and disputing with one another by the parents, both borderline personalities, who informed each of only subparts of their ambivalent wishes and views. This was a psychologically fitting conclusion for parents who had projected aspects of themselves onto others. They were now bound by their larger social systems to keep the agreement in place.

CHAPTER 6

How the Preschool Child Responds

They said, "Let's get a divorce!" and they lived happily sad ever after
—Jennifer, five years old

Since marriages have been ending earlier in divorce, almost half the children of divorce are preschoolers at the time of parental separation (Furstenberg et al., 1983). Little is known about the impact of the breakdown of the family before the child is able to conceptually grasp and experience what family relationships involve. How much do children understand what is happening, what intuitive meanings do they infer from overt expression of parental conflict and from caretaking parents' anger and distress? What resources do they have for coping with family stress and how do they defend themselves? What are their special developmental vulnerabilities?

The fifty-six preschoolers in our study of families litigating custody and visitation had been given relatively frequent and continuing contact with both parents, by court recommendation or judicial order. One-fourth of the couples had joint physical custody, usually a split-week schedule. Almost two-thirds of the mothers had sole physical custody, while only a small group of fathers (one-eighth) had this arrangement. The children spent on the average 29.1 hours per week with the other parent (range 1–84 hours) and were making an average of 2.4 transitions each week between parental homes (range 1–10 transitions). Three-fourths had at least once-a-week contact, one-fifth had alternate weekends, and the small remainder had no regular contact with the other parent.

Reactions to Transitions Between Parents

The preschool children were multisymptomatic during transitions from one parent's home to the other. These symptoms were a major issue in the parental conflict and often a reason for the next fight. At least one parent (usually the principal custodian) found the child extremely difficult or distressed before or after visits, and cited the child's disturbed behavior as reasons for limiting or eliminating the contact with the other parent, who was seen as an inadequate caretaker. The other parent countered by claiming that the complaints were untrue or exaggerated (rationalizations for reluctance to share the child) or by blaming the first parent for inducing the child to behave in a disturbed manner.

☐ When Mrs. A. found her three-year-old daughter curled up on the sofa, sucking her thumb, and talking in a regressed manner after the visit, she concluded that her ex-husband had been talking "baby-talk" to the child, and she cited this as evidence of his inappropriate fathering. Mr. A. felt his daughter "was upset because she had to interrupt the wonderful time we were having together and return to mother."

After observing the children and receiving detailed weekly reports from parents and others (such as teachers and relatives), we became convinced there was validity to the claims that these preschoolers were distressed. They had a plethora of dramatic emotional, behavioral, and somatic responses, many of which seemed contradictory. For example, a child would be happy, even wildly excited about the visit, but would resist and cling when it came time to leave. Or they could be compliant and mature about leaving but return regressed, babyish, and difficult to manage. After a seemingly smooth and uneventful visit, they awoke in the night screaming with terror or wet or soiled the bed.

☐ Three-year-old Cedric wet his pants when his mother told him to prepare for his father's weekly visit. He said he did not want to go. Ten minutes later, after he changed his pants, he said he did want to go. His five-year-old sister, Jill, bit her lip until it bled. She became extremely upset because she could not find a picture she had painted for her father, and yelled angrily at her mother to help her. When the father arrived, she clung to her mother and refused to leave.

Separation anxieties were characteristic of three-fourths of the two- to three-year-olds and three-fifths of the four- to five-year-olds (see Table 6.1). They cried and clung to whichever parent they were leaving, so they protested departing for the visits and resisted return-

Table 6.1   Child's Reactions to Transitions Between Parents*

| Type of Reaction | Number and Percentage of Children in Each Category of Reaction | | |
	(2–3 yrs) n = 23	(4–5 yrs) n = 25	Total N = 48
Quiet/withdrawn	9 (39%)	13 (52%)	22 (46%)
Tension/apprehension (hyperactive, highly excited)	16 (70%)	18 (72%)	34 (71%)
Resistance (protests, separation problems, clings and cries)	17 (74%)	15 (60%)	32 (67%)
Somatic symptoms			
Physical illness	8 (35%)	8 (32%)	16 (33%)
Sleep disturbances	11 (48%)	7 (28%)	18 (37%)
Regression (wetting, soiling, babyishness)	13 (57%)	15 (60%)	28 (58%)
Aggressive/difficult (tantrums, opposition-al)	14 (61%)	14 (56%)	28 (58%)
Happy/positive	13 (57%)	15 (60%)	28 (58%)

*Data are taken from a checklist of twenty-one child reactions to transitions between parents for visitation or time sharing of the child in shared custody, reported by both parents to the counselor.

ing. Several were preoccupied with the question of who was to pick them up from nursery school each day, asking this question of teachers over and over again. They seemed to be searching for structure and reassurance. Their tension and apprehension was not manifested in behavioral constriction, as it was for many of the older children. Instead, they were more often actively and acutely upset, wildly excited, hyperactive, or difficult to control. Regressed behavior (wanting to sleep with the parent and bed-wetting) and infantile aggression (oppositional demandingness and tantrums) were reported for almost three fifths of the children. Somatic symptoms (stomachaches, constipation, asthma, allergies, frequent colds and flu) were reported for one-third of both the early and late preschoolers. Half of the two-to three-year-olds and one-fourth of the four- to five-year-olds had nightmares following visits. In cases where we could discern the content of their frightening dreams, we found they were associated with fears of separation and abandonment or worry about the well-being of the parent they were leaving. Remarkably, despite all the distress, parents also reported that three-fifths of these children also had positive responses: They were often happy, warm, and loving before and after visits. In general, the difficult, symptomatic behavior differed from their usual adjustment.

☐ On returning to her father's home, Elsie, ordinarily an adventuresome and outgoing three-year-old, became timid and passive. She began to speak in a whisper and refused to go on the swings in the park.

Parents reported that it took hours and sometimes one or two days for the children to settle after the visits, and for their normal behavior to be restored. Many of those who made frequent changes were continually distressed. By contrast, a few had little or no difficulty with the transitions, especially preschoolers who had an older sibling accompanying them.

The parents' inability to communicate and coordinate with each other made it extremely difficult for them to ease the child's distress at transitions. They often did not prepare the child for leaving or returning (they were too angry or ambivalent about the visits, or dreaded being alone without the child). They fought over possession of the child's transitional objects (favorite blanket or toys) and sometimes even completely changed the child from one set of clothes to another at the time of transfer. Some grabbed the child and ran, to avoid painful contact with the former spouse or his or her lover or to avoid an angry confrontation. Some wrested the child from each other's grasp. The child's attempts to maintain contact with or talk about the absent parent were ignored or responded to with anxiety or anger.

☐ Two-year-old Kate put a photo of her mother in the diaper bag. Finding it there, the father assumed the mother had packed it. "She doesn't want a picture of your ugly mug," he said as he threw it out on the pavement.

Parents complained that their two- to three-year-olds arrived back from visits "exhausted, hollow-eyed, dirty, and unmanageable." They had no idea where they had been, whom they had seen, what they had eaten, whether they had napped, and sometimes even whether prescribed medication had been administered. Furthermore, as the children desperately clung to the departing parent, they found it difficult to soothe and reassure their children as to if and when they would see that parent again.

In sum, a number of factors contribute to the child's upset at transitions apart from parents' claims of inadequate caretaking. At each transition, the child struggles with a renewed threat of loss or abandonment, without much preparation or reassurance. Second, the transfer frequently becomes the forum for another incident of verbal or physical conflict between parents, which the children find frightening and distressing. Third, the children are required to make adjustments to very different parenting styles, household schedules, and child care routines, all of which are seldom eased or coordinated. Finally, some of these children seem to find change per se difficult, and their parents are in dispute partly in response to their distress.

Attitudes and Behavior of the Children
Toward Their Disputing Parents

Most of these preschool children had the capacity to attach to both parents, and reactions of anxiety, clinging, or anger toward parents in response to observable fights was only temporary. Hence, they showed acute distress reactions and confusion at transitions in the presence of both disputing parents, but then settled into a relatively warm and accepting relationship when alone with each parent. Although none of the children were making strong preference for one parent to the exclusion of the other, almost one-fifth of the sample, mostly four- to five-year-old boys, had a consistent mild preference for one parent, usually the mother. They appear more secure and at ease with this parent, and more insecure, afraid but compliant, in the presence of the other. Two three-year-old girls were bonded to neither parent. One had substituted her grandmother as her primary attachment, the other was angry, cynical, and rejecting toward her parents, both of whom had abandoned her for long periods of time.

In general, there is no indication that these younger children are more protected than their older counterparts from witnessing the fights, nor are girls more protected than boys. In fact, only two children were completely shielded from any overt sign of the dispute. Though parents usually gave lip service to not fighting in front of the children, it was evident that in their fearful and angry confrontations they were often unaware of the child, or exploded despite the child's presence. Alternatively, they cut short an angry exchange by abruptly leaving the scene, and sometimes their children who had been packed and awaiting the visit. Many parents denied the impact of the fighting on the child. One father noted, "Bobby loves police cars. It doesn't bother him at all that they are called [to quell the fights]."

Most commonly, preschoolers are bystanders to the parental conflict, witnessing the anger, insults and aggression. They are also passive weapons in the dispute; for example, used as bargaining chips in negotiations, and intermittently kept from visits if child support was not paid. Six children had been secreted from the other parent for lengthy periods of time. Perhaps more important, they are exposed to the aftermath of the dispute. They are often left in the care of an emotionally distraught or fuming angry parent. Few parents, unlike those of the older school-age children, talk persuasively to gain the preschool child as an ally, or use them to pass messages, spy, harass or denigrate the other parent. Where this occurs, the child is likely to be relatively older (about five) or the parent is likely to be psychotic. On the other hand, the children are seldom provided with any explanation about the issues under dispute or given sensible information that would help them integrate their two worlds. Many children receive contradictory information. No coherent account is given for the dramatic conflict, and often even visitation schedules are not explained. Children are uniformly considered too young to understand. They are left, instead, to piece together what they have witnessed with bits of overheard conversation, along with their fears and fantasies.

Preschool children's cognitive understanding of conflict partly determines their reactions, attitudes, and behavior towards their disputing parents. (Selman, 1980.) Among the younger group (two to four years), their capacity to take a perspective in social relations is limited to making concrete and observable distinctions between people, with little awareness that others have distinct, different, or continuing subjective or internal feelings other than those overtly demonstrated. Further, their egocentricity is evident in that they assume that others perceive, feel and think like themselves. With respect to conflict, these children seem to believe it exists only if overtly demonstrated in some physical observable manner, for example, by yelling or hitting. Without such evidence, they believe conflict no longer exists. Hence they have little sense of their parents' continuing animosity toward each other, nor do they understand the dispute inherent in parents' avoidance and withholding.

For these reasons, the children experience tension and stress when they are in the physical presence of both parents who are expressing overt hostility to one another. The predominant response is submissive distress: three-fourths of our preschoolers cried, clung, became 'frozen', anxious, panicked, or immediately regressed when witnessing parental hostility. Typically, they cling to one parent and resist going to the other. Two-fifths of the children at times become aggressive, willful, and contrary as if they are identifying with or mimicking the parents' anger (see Table 6.2). Though these behaviors sometimes resemble an elementary alliance, their temporary character is demonstrated by their disappearance as soon as one parent leaves and the child is alone with the previously rejected parent. Moreover, on those occasions when the parents converse amicably,

Table 6.2   Preschooler's Observable Response
             to Witnessing Parental Disputes*

Type of Response	Number and Percentage of Children in Each Category of Response		
	(2–3 yrs) n = 23	(4–5 yrs) n = 25	Total N = 48
Submissive distress	18 (78%)	18 (72%)	36 (75%)
Aggressive distress	8 (35%)	10 (40%)	18 (37%)
Avoidance	1 (04%)	8 (32%)	9 (19%)
Attempts to control	4 (17%)	10 (40%)	14 (29%)
Takes position/co-opted	0	4 (04%)	4 (08%)
Excitement/pleasure	0	1 (04%)	1 (02%)

*Data are taken from a checklist of twenty-five reactions to witnessing/hearing parental fights, reported by both parents to the counselor.

the child immediately responds warmly to both, appearing delighted at the truce. Despite the great reluctance to go on visits or to return home (evidenced by clinging, whining, or crying), there is a fairly good adaptation once the transition is effected, and the children usually adjust to each parent's home environment.

Preschool children also respond with anxiety and behavioral problems to the parent's tension, agitation, and depression following the fights. Not understanding that their mother or father is upset because of the parental conflict, these children can easily attribute the parent's distressed behavior to their own actions and blame themselves (for example, for being too noisy or making demands). The younger ones experience the parent's tension and hostility almost directly with little or no cognitive mediation. Hence they are barometers of the parent's affective state and are diffusely reactive to the tension level. In this way they experience the conflict even when it is not overt.

Compared to girls, boys showed a more limited repertoire of responses and were more lost in the affect. They were primarily submissively distressed or became aggressive. By contrast, the girls, who were similarly distressed and likely to be aggressive, were more verbal and made more attempts to control the fights. They acted to distract the parents from their disputes by diverting attention to themselves or by having a mishap. Some tried to prevent the dispute. For example, K. stood between her parents, put her hands up, and yelled "Stop." T. tried to have her parents say "Hi" and kiss each other. E. tried desperately to have her father leave the day-care center before her mother arrived. H. gestured behind her mother's back. urging her father not to say anything.

Very young children's hyperresponsiveness to change and overt expression of hostility and other fluctuating levels of anxiety implies they have little cognitive conception of the system of relationships in the family as a whole in any enduring sense. These children react to parts of the system as they become immediate, seek secure relationships in the immediate family situation, and seem unaware of the parents' continuing internal or private angry feelings toward one another. In sum, two- to three-year-old children typically have temporary reactions during observable fights and accept both parents at other times (see Table 6.3).

By contrast, as the child grows older (four to seven years), subjective internal feeling states are recognized in others and acknowledged as being possibly different from one's own and as continuing over time. However, these feelings are perceived as simple undifferentiated states, not mixed ones. For example, one can be happy or sad, but not both. At this stage, the child can take the perspective of another but this is a one-way or unilateral perspective-taking, in that only one person's point of view can be considered at one time. Hence, with respect to conflict, the child perceives it to be caused by one person and felt by the other. Thus, to resolve conflict, one must stop or negate the offending action, protect the victim, restore the other's comfort, and relieve the distress in some way. These youngsters undertook a roster of actions to this end: D. planned to "throw a glass of cold water on my Dad's head to cool him off"; M. planned to invite Daddy over to Mommy's house, and she would make them both a cup of tea and then they would be happy again.) The child cannot

Table 6.3   Preschooler's Behavior and Attitude Toward Both Parents

Type of Behavior and Attitude	Number and Percentage of Children in Each Category		
	(2–3 yrs) n = 23	(4–5 yrs) n = 25	Total N = 48
Alignment	2 (09%)	6 (24%)	8 (17%)
Loyalty conflict	0	1 (04%)	1 (02%)
Shifting allegiances	3 (13%)	11 (44%)	14 (29%)
Temporary reactions	13 (57%)	8 (32%)	21 (44%)
No preferences	7 (30%)	8 (32%)	15 (31%)

simultaneously consider how the perceived "offending party" feels about the situation. Nor is there any concern for whether or not the attempts at reparation are sincere. It is sufficient that the efforts are made.

From the age of four to six years, for the first time, the children become more aware of the content of the parents' dispute, the cognitive puzzle of parents' conflicting claims. (T. reported, "Dad says Mom should get her head examined. Mom said she did and it's fine. He's the one who needs help.") Differentiation between fact and fantasy is difficult to achieve in the chaos of each parent's conflicting account of reality. (L. worried, "Was Daddy's new woman friend really a witch?") They are also now aware of a parent's continuing angry feelings about concrete issues. ("Mom's mad because dad's not on time. Dad doesn't like the clothes mom puts on me.") However, they are clearly unable to take the perspective of more than one parent at a time. Upon returning home from visits, or when leaving the custodial parent's home, they are often upset and angry about the rights and injustices of one parent. They will accuse the other parent ("Mommy said you didn't pay us any money" or "Daddy said you threw him out of the house"). Accordingly, they demand fairly simplistic restitution on behalf of the offended party. ("Daddy says he's sorry and he wants to come back home.") Hence they are easily co-opted into taking sides with respect to concrete issues. However, they are easily "turned around" by the counterarguments of the other parent, and so the alliances are quite unstable (see Table 6.3). Among some of the older children, the swings in preference are so rapid as to be difficult to distinguish from true ambivalence or loyalty conflict. In general, these children do not have the cognitive capacity simultaneously to hold the conflicting views of their parents or to respond to the contradictory implications inherent in attaching to and loving them both. The incidence of clear loyalty conflict was limited in this preschool sample to one girl. Children of this age are typically very concrete and stimulus-bound in their explanations and seemingly fickle in their allegiances. ("I like Daddy 'cause he brings me ice cream." I don't like my other Mommy 'cause she ties my shoes too tight!")

Children's Coping and Defensive Behavior

Children bring a variety of coping resources to deal with the stressors attendant on the divorce disputes. While there is a great deal of variation in the children's type of coping, certain commonalities are associated with age. They also have different concerns at different ages.

Each child tends to respond in one characteristic style, although over time, and depending on the intensity of the parents' fight, some improve or regress, using more or less adaptive coping patterns.[1]

The Two- to Three-Year Olds

The overwhelming concern of the twenty-three two- to three-year-olds was the issue of separation from one or both parents. In play sessions, they tended to be insecure, distrustful of strangers, and watchful to the point of vigilance. Their play was clearly constricted and continually disrupted by checks on the whereabouts of their parents. There was no indication that children below the age of about forty-two months had any verbal or cognitive awareness of the content of their parent's disputes (what their parents were fighting over). At least they did not make this evident in their words or play.

For the majority, play activity was mainly functional, limited to manipulating objects and seeing how objects work or fit together. Despite their efforts to arrange and rearrange the furniture in the dolls' houses, the end product was often disarray. Some merely watched what others were doing or refused to play at all. (Solemn, serious, and silent, three-year-old A. stood in the center of the room for most of the hour, shook his head, refusing to touch the toys himself, but motioned for the counselor to place the dolls in the house.) Others who were coping better showed elements of family role-play: They arranged the dolls or farm animals to be eating, sleeping, toileting, or watching TV, but it had a static, nondramatic quality. Imaginative or fantasy play beyond this level was largely absent.

Four of these younger children (one boy and three girls) were very distressed and unable to effectively protest. They were described by the counselor as "sad, resigned, forlorn, empty, or vacant waifs with dampened spirits." When their parents remained in the room, they sat passively, and showed little capacity to explore or to focus on the counselor. They had little self-efficacy. They reacted to separation with extreme panic, or inconsolable grief and defeat. When reunited with their parents, they were regressed, dependent, and passive, "like a ragdoll," and their most active stance was to protest weakly by clinging and crying. (S., a joyless two-year-old, clung desperately to her father's knees when he attempted to leave. When G.'s mother left, she cried, clenched her fists, and shook. Three-year-old D.'s reaction to his mother's leaving was to crouch in the corner, in a fetal position, and cry desolately and hopelessly.)

A second group of seven children (five boys and two girls) were more contained or resigned as opposed to despairing under stress of separation from parents or in response to parents' disputes. Four of them presented as slightly constricted and inhibited children (unlike the other three who seemed more protected from the traumas inherent in the situation by the presence of older siblings). They were compliant, shy, and did not venture forth or far from their parents. They needed permission and direction in playing with the toys, from the counselor or other children, but avoided play that reminded them of conflict or combat. (A reticent child, S. avoided any play that involved objects making contact or crashing. He could look at but not play with guns, tanks, or other "aggressive" toys.) In general, all of these children could not report any facts about the divorce or the visitation schedule. Some denied it had occurred or ignored the counselor's attempts to talk about it. Neither was there any indication in their play that they had any understanding of the parents' fights or the divorce arrangements. To what extent this was defensive denial and to what extent it was reflective of the fact they were given confusing, ambivalent messages or no information at all by their parents is not known. The following reaction was common:

☐ Three-year-old Paul stared in silence as the counselor demonstrated how the mother and father dolls lived in separate houses and how the baby doll traveled from one to the other. Ignoring the scene, he proceeded to reunite the family of dolls under one roof.

Among some of the three-year-olds described above, an interesting phenomenon of unintegrated or layered responses was observed. These particular children behaved in an entirely different manner at different times, and their discrepant behavior seemed modeled on the polarized parenting and personality styles of their mother and father. It seemed as though these emotional behavioral states existed separately, side by side, and components of both were not easily available to them under stress. Nor could features of one state be elicited while they were in the other mode. Instead they flipped from one distinct state into the other.

☐ Suzy was cool, contained, mature, and very sober, much like her emotionally inhibited, rational father, as she busily organized the play house and carefully washed and ordered the dishes. At other times, like her mother who was flamboyant and hysterical, she was highly emotional, babyish, and regressed, taking on the role of the crying baby who needed nursing.

☐ Arthur was highly active and overexcited, especially in response to his jovial, outgoing father. At other times, he was extremely passive, withdrawn, "staring off into space," reflective of his mother's angry sullenness and depression.

☐ Rita hummed softly as she banged away with hammer and nails at a "construction" she was making in imitation of her carpenter father, an overcontrolled, obsessive man. Half an hour earlier she had been in a despairing state, curled up fetuslike in the corner, refusing to be comforted. Her despair was occasioned by being separated from her emotionally distraught mother.

To varying extents, the remainder of the two- to three-year-olds (ten girls, two boys) more actively, strongly, and directly protested separation from parents: They demanded attention or were bossy, oppositional, or had temper tantrums. In addition to difficult behavior, they began to complain verbally and resist. A small number of children used their elementary language skills to help master the separation experience or attempt to control it. For example, some two-year-olds found relief and comfort in their ability to conjure up the absent parent when they repeated "Mommy work" or "Daddy home." (Poignantly, thirty-month-old L. told her mother, "Daddy in Daddy's house, Mommy in Mommy's house. Too bad!") Some sought to control their world by demanding "Stop!" "Go!" and "No!" Some asked about the whereabouts of the absent parent or angrily insisted, "I want Mommy! I want Mommy!" or they attempted to use the power of words to stop the parental fight and restore harmony. ("Don't shout!" "Mommy kiss Daddy!") This use of words was not limited to those who had more advanced language development. Rather, to the extent parents were responsive to the child's needs, these more active, symbolic coping responses seemed to be reinforced, whereas when parents responded noncontingently or angrily, a sense of defeatism was evident, and the child regressed and did not speak.

Undoubtedly, the saddest observations were the misinterpretations the parents made of these little children's efforts to understand, master, or gain some control over the situation. (When two-year-old N. questioned her mother, "Mama hate Papa?" in order to clarify the situation, her mother stormed that the father was indoctrinating the child. When two-year-old G., who had just helped her father vacuum, was returned home, she asked her mother "Mama vacuum?" Her mother perceived her as saying "Mama, fuck you!" and became furious with the father for "bad-mouthing" her.) Most frequently, the parents misunderstood the intent of the child's actions. Many children, feeling overwhelmed and helpless, became bossy and demanding or held on to some symbolic transitional object that helped them control their world or maintain a connection with the absent parent. (Two-year-old K. clutched a cookie that her father had given her when he left. Her mother snatched it from her, claiming that the father was feeding her junk food because he knew how much it angered her. He was also making her "look bad" when she forbade the child to eat it.)

Several of the three-year-old girls who had been given clear, consistent accounts of the separation and visitation schedule used their verbal skills extensively to clarify and master their anxieties. Indeed, clinicians commented how some of them clung to and repeated the facts of the situation or the schedule over and over as if to hold onto some stable reality. Several others who had been subject to chaotic care were also trying to make cognitive sense of the situation but were extremely confused and had no coherent verbal understanding.

The Four- to Five-Year-Olds

The central concerns of the twenty-five four- to five-year-olds were clearly different from those of their younger counterparts. Although they continued to show fears of separation from and loss of one or both parents, they were also increasingly troubled by other matters. First, most had become aware of the content of their parents' disputes, the cognitive puzzle of parents' conflicting claims. They wondered what was true and what was not; what fact and what fantasy (Did Daddy throw Mommy out of the house, or did another man steal Mommy from Daddy?). Second, they often became urgently concerned about the emotional and physical well-being of a parent (Would Mommy be sad and cry if she was on her own? or "Daddy wants to come back home because he has noplace to live and he said he is sorry"). Third, these fears about the well-being of a parent were often fused with acute fears about their own physical safety and vulnerability to abandonment, especially where they had witnessed violence between the adults or experienced being left. ("Mom wants Dad to move away. She doesn't like him. He has to live in an apartment far, far away. She's hurting him. She gets all riled up, mad, and angry. She looks like she's going to kill herself. I'm thinking I have to stop her. She can't stop herself!")

Fourth, since they were obviously the centerpiece of the parents fight, and given their own egocentricism, a sense of responsibility for the events was evident. (R. said, "They fight about me. I just make them fight!"; P. said, "Dad said not to call Tim [stepfather] Dad. . . . Tim gets mad if I don't. I didn't mean to call him Dad. That started the whole thing!"; G. said, "Mom came to school to pick me up. I didn't know what was happening. Mom told me to hurry up. I talked too much. Then Dad came and said I had to go with him. They got in a fight. I talked too much.") These feelings of enormous power, even omnipotence, however, were paradoxically juxtaposed with a sense of their smallness, helplessness, and overwhelming inadequacy in the face of the intractable fight. ("I told Mom Dad was sad. She didn't answer me. She got mad and yelled at Dad." Later this child told her counselor, "It's hard to fight with giants all the time.") We speculate that the oft-observed compliance and passivity found in these children is related to their fears of their own omnipotence (to hurt or harm) and, in turn, their fear of retaliation.

☐ A. boasted that he would shoot anyone who got in his way. However, when his farm animals were being overrun by another child's advancing army, A. took a little rubber owl and attacked the enemy tanks, graphically portraying his helplessness and the paucity of his resources (a little bird) in dealing with the overwhelming conflicts (armored tanks). This also demonstrated his difficulty in making a counteraggressive move.

Finally, given their parent's continual denigration of their ex-mate, some of these children were clearly concerned with the problem of with whom to identify. (Four-year-old A.'s dream captured the predicament: He was in the center of a battlefield, "But the good people wore bad masks and the bad people wore good masks. I wasn't sure which to follow.") They were either confused, felt shame, or denigrated themselves if they felt they had introjected (become like) the "bad" parent. In these children, clear indices of incipient self-esteem problems emerged. (One four-year-old boy wrote a book about his life. In the "Story of Mike" he reported "I make my Mom sad and mad because I act like Dad who is a frog." Later, he acted out being a frog and leaped into the garbage pail.) The confusion about both parents in some cases was extreme, and the child was preoccupied with issues of identification.

☐ Alice, a very verbal five-year-old. discussed the problem. With respect to her father she said, "Mom doesn't want me to see Dad because he's mean. Dad is mean and he does nice things too. He takes us out, but he runs his errands. Sometimes he grabs my hand too tight. Sometimes you have to rush." With respect to her mother she said, "My little sister throws a fit. Mom smacks her hard. You have to grow up to do that stuff. It gets me mad to see someone smacking." Later, Alice explains remorsefully, "It's not good to hit my sister, but sometimes when you get mad, what are you supposed to do? You just get mad and spank!

The four- to five-year-olds varied widely in the extent to which they were actively trying to make sense of, work through, and master the conflicts surrounding their parents' divorce, the degree to which they were avoiding or defending against their feelings, and the degree to which they found ways of surviving despite the conflict.

The first coping style and the least adaptive reaction to the parents' conflict was observed in three boys and intermittently in two boys and one girl. In response to verbal reference to parents' disputes, or in response to interpersonal conflicts among their peers, these children became highly anxious or panicked and manifested behavior that was chaotic, autistic, or bizarre. Their behavior was diffusely disturbed and disorganized. They had difficulty making eye contact, sitting still, and holding a conversation in a normal voice without grimacing and posturing. They seemed at the mercy of their swirling feelings. Primitive and violent material spilled out with little organization. Aggressive and nihilistic themes or sexual ideation were coupled with infantile regression (for example, baby talk) and inappropriate affect.

☐ Bruce, five years, ran chaotically around the playroom. "I'm a policeman. I'm going to shoot your eyes and brains out. I'm going to shoot myself. Bang! Bang!" He gave himself a trophy for shooting his hand. He grabbed the snacks and ran around again, shooting and disrupting the other children's play.

☐ Fred, five years, arrived with a pout that changed dramatically to a false smile and back again. As he drew a picture of his visit with his father, he verbalized, "I hope I get runned over because I want to be dead. No one can help because I is dead. It fun!" He laughed.

At times they clearly tried to muster primitive defenses like denial. In response to the counselor's questions, they denied both facts and feelings. For example, they denied parents were divorced, denied any parental disputes, denied visits had or had not taken place, and denied they felt upset. They tried to distract or avoid by babytalk or nonsense syllables. (J. answered with "Ditty-dooty" and other childish babbling to every question and flapped his arms in a peculiar, ticlike mannerism. N. screamed "Stop! Stop!" and rolled over in a bizarre manner, interrupting the game, when his peers began to role-play a conflict between parent puppets.) When calmer, these children might try to develop a play theme, but they frequently disrupted it when it became emotionally charged or reminiscent of conflict—that is, they were prone to lose contact with reality in their play and hence frightened themselves.

- ☐ Neil built a fortress for a house. People and dogs were hidden inside. Blocks of wood buttressed the walls and police and Indians with rifles protected the occupants against monsters raging on the outside. He became frantic at the idea of any occupant leaving the house or anyone else entering the building. Increasingly assaulted by his own fears, he abandoned his play and was scarcely coherent for the remainder of the session.

- ☐ Dennis noted that his father had a rifle and only one bullet. He only needed one bullet because he had such good aim. He developed a story about a male cat hunting and hurting a female cat. As he became aware of the conflict (and the parallel situation in his own family), he became overwhelmed with anxiety and characteristically ran around the room for his own protection.

In sum, these children seem to be at an impasse in that they are clearly disorganized by the divorce situation and the disputes between their parents, have virtually no elements of cognitive understanding to organize their experience or bind their anxiety, and are unable to engage in sustained talk or fantasy play in order to express or work through their conflicts.

A second, larger group of children had a characteristic style of avoiding or blocking out the parental conflict and relating to parents in a manner that was either very appealing or very helpful. This modus operandi, or coping strategy, of supporting their parents seemed to ensure they would be taken care of or at least not put in danger of being rejected or abandoned. In general, they avoided or refused to talk about the parental conflict. However, at times they reported very abbreviated versions of the facts of the disputes, though they denied having many feelings associated with the fights. They tended to seal themselves off from their feelings and avoided asking questions or knowing much about what was happening. Hence, they had difficulty accessing their own feelings, particularly their anger and their dependent wishes.

☐ Five-year-old Randy told his counselor that his parents were not fighting and that it was not difficult for him having his parents live separately. When specifically asked, however, he did recall a fight in which his mother called his father a "Hungarian asshole," at which time his father smashed a piece of his mother's artwork. Randy matter-of-factly reported, "A policeman came and took Dad to jail for a little while. He got out. We didn't get to see him that week. The next week, we went out for dinner. Yes, we had a good time." He denied that he felt upset or scared. However, his mother reported that he had been "doubled up with stomach cramps."

Interestingly, there were broadly two different styles of adapting themselves or molding to parents that were mostly associated with children's gender.

Four boys and one girl tended to be cute, charming, bright but nonverbal and somewhat immature. They acted like silly clowns, which amused or distracted their parents, or they excited and entertained them by flirting with danger, infantile swaggering, and seductive provocations.

☐ Sam continually placed himself in potentially dangerous situations. He teetered on the edge of the block bin, balanced himself on top of a rolling truck, stood on a chair and peered out the seventh-story window, and in the waiting room, ran into an open elevator and merrily screamed as the door began to close. His usually depressed and hysterical mother rolled her eyes and laughed.

☐ Fred related in a coy, tantalizing, and provocative manner, running up to his mother, trying to French-kiss her, clowning, and gesturing for effect.

These children tended to be quite engaging but highly reactive to their surroundings. Having trouble modulating their affect, they became "wound up" or overexcited when others in the group became boisterous and quieted when the group calmed. They responded well to structure when it was imposed. Having little capacity to organize and control themselves, they seemed overreactive and dependent on the outside and tended to structure their behavior in response to others' needs and dictates. (Five-year-old J.'s drawings were either imitative of others or hastily drawn, messy productions, with rough shapes. sketchy lines, or globs of paint.) In the play sessions, they were restless, teasing, easily distracted, and unable to engage in sustained play. They seemed to have a superficial sense of relating to others and showed little true engagement and little autonomy and self-direction.

Six girls and three boys, on the other hand, were characterized by being excessively "good," compliant, oversocialized children who sought to placate any expressions of anger and submit to the wishes of others, especially their parents. They tried to please, to be sweet and helpful. They seemed fearful of being any trouble and worried about rejection. At the least this group was marked by a passive stance, at most by a great deal of role reversal with their parents and a pseudo-mature stance of taking care of others.

□ Shy, endearing Pauline was typical. She engaged in little spontaneous conversation and denied what was happening in her family. Her parents were not arguing. She saw her father regularly. She rarely protested and retreated from confrontations. She was extremely patient as she waited two hours in the waiting room for her parents to finish their interviews. In her manner and play, she was invested in keeping everything nice. She drew sweet little hearts and flowers and was overconcerned with looking good and dressing prettily. Her mother reported she was very comforting and supportive of her at home although, at times, she would become whiney and dependent. Her counselor noted that "she slinks into the family system like a cute little extension of either parent."

Their play was fairly stereotyped—taking care of, cleaning, dressing, and feeding dolls and doing chores for the therapist. At times of greater stress, they could not play at all. (Whenever C. witnessed her disturbed father terrorize her mother, she was passive and very lethargic in her play session. She sat and just sifted sand through her fingers.) Under pressure, the veneer of sociability sometimes shattered, and the child's unmet dependency needs and anger were no longer contained.

□ Four-year-old Ellie, previously a very solicitous helper in the group sessions (opening doors, turning off lights, and putting away toys), broke down when her parents resumed their dispute. She regressed precipitously and dramatically into a tough, angry, demanding, and persistent two-year-old who grabbed what she wanted, when she wanted it, with almost no respect for others. She hoarded toys, gobbled her snacks, and treated her counselor as though she were a feeding machine.

In general, however, they were described as somewhat anxious, withdrawn, constricted, and lacking in any direct expression of anger. Themes of mild depression were suggested by such descriptors as "sweet, sad demeanor, serious, subdued, and expressionless."

☐ Beth was a beautiful, gentle, silent Eurasian child who drew copious pictures of flowers and rainbows that she presented to her parents after the sessions. She answered in a barely audible voice, "I forget," in response to any question about her parents' fights. Her mother reported she became extremely passive, limp, and curled up and went to sleep during or after the violent verbal and physical struggles between her parents, which occurred regularly at transition from one home to the other. This massive blocking out of all conflict also occurred in response to altercations among her peers, wherein she became extremely lethargic and passive, unable to defend herself. When alone with each parent and teachers, she was an excessively good, compliant child, meticulously conforming to their expectations.

The third group of children (four girls and three boys) to varying degrees were struggling to make sense of the situation and actively trying to master their conflicts and cope with their parents rather than adapting themselves to the conflict and the family situation. Unable to use their parents' differing versions of reality to gain some coherence, they were forced to make sense of the situation on their own. They were quite verbal about the facts of the dispute and the divorce arrangements, but their accounts were immensely confusing. Many of the central concerns (separation anxiety, worry about the well-being of self and parent, confusion about the parents' counterclaims, sense of helplessness, responsibility and agency, and questions of whom to believe and emulate and whom to denigrate) were inextricably interwoven. Sometimes with a distinctly nightmarish quality, or like an existential drama consisting of seemingly unconnected vivid images and scenes, their verbal accounts reflected both the dramatic conflicts they had witnessed and their fears, fantasies, and magical thinking. These children's play themes were much more coherent and meaningful than the loose associations and stream of verbal consciousness that composed their verbal attempts to explain their problems.

☐ While unable to clearly talk about her parent's dispute, instead presenting a garbled mix of overheard remarks and fears, Cindy developed a story that was a very symbolic rendition of the family's dynamics and inability to settle their conflicts. "This is a story of a witch and a giant who fight and fight and fight. Sometimes they grow tired and sit down to rest in the shade of two trees. Then they get up and begin to fight again." When the counselor asked the outcome of the story, Cindy answered, "Well, they rested and then they fought again."

Their fears and conflicts, more clearly expressed symbolically through fantasy, were often obsessively repeated until they found some way of mastering it. Their projective and dramatic play, which was on occasion truncated or disrupted when they became too anxious, more accurately reflected their perception of their family dynamics. Through play, and often without the verbal interpretation of the counselor, they sought and found ways of resolving dilemmas. In sum, these children were trying to obtain a coherent account of their situation and, to varying extents, were able to talk or use play constructively to repair, control, and order their world. Though these children presented as more painfully confused and anxious than the second group, they were also more differentiated in their emotions, and were obtaining more distance or separation of self from the enmeshed conflictual parental relationships.

☐ Wendy, aged four years, was a slight, pretty, dark-featured Latin child. In response to the counselor's questions about the divorce, she began a long, elaborate and somewhat confused account which included the following excerpts:

"My Daddy ripped my Mommy's wedding pictures. I went into my Mommy's room and started to cry. I was scared he would hurt her." She paused and interjected, "He's changing. He was once a bad guy and now he's changing to be a good guy," but then proceeded, "The pictures got outside on the street. He ripped them and he was still fighting. He was holding my Mommy tight. She called the police. They put him in jail and I was crying because Bob had a picture of him. I wanted to rip the picture of Bob!" (Here the child is referring to a mug shot of the father that the mother's boyfriend had obtained from the police.) The child continued to talk about her father: "Then he got another car. He went away with a green and black car and he came back with a white car. I remember driving in the blue car." The counselor asked when she saw her dad for visits. Wendy answered, "Daddy picks me up Sunday and Wednesday when we have time enough to buy my clothes. My Mommy doesn't come. I don't know why. He picks me up at 10:30 and brings me back at 5 and 8. My Daddy asks me if I could stay there longer and I say, 'Okay, I'll ask my Mom.' I ask her and she says nothing."

"My Mommy has a boyfriend. He is Bob. Pete (an Uncle) told me not to listen to Bob because I don't like him to get a picture of my Daddy (the mug shot). My Mommy doesn't want me to listen to Bob either." (Her mother is upset that she is disrespectful to Bob). In response to the counselor's question she adds, "Bob just visits. He doesn't live at my Mommy's house. My Grandma is going to paint Bob's walls." (She was referring to Bob's mother, no relative of hers).

Wendy then volunteered "I was crying about the cat. He got into the dryer and he got dead and now he's in heaven. God's taking good care of him. He got into the dryer and my Mom's shoes were in the dryer and he got blood on his mouth. We got another cat. His name is Mifi. Humphrey [a third cat] went away. They took him away. My Mommy told me not to look out the bathroom window 'cause they were taking him away. Mifi was mad at Humphrey and Humphrey had fleas." With barely a pause, Wendy continues: "My Auntie Judith is asking me to put my face under water. She promised me a sucker if I put my face under the water, but the store was closed. Yes, she was teaching me how to swim. She made me stand up to see how tall I was."

During Wendy's play session, she placed the mother and baby dolls in the bathtub and had them watching TV together. She used all the furniture (kitchen cabinets, tables, beds, and chairs) to barricade the bathtub, and protect the two dolls. Next she decided it was time for bed. After checking the TV was turned off, she placed both mother and baby in bed and covered them with blankets, commenting, "I sleep with my Mommy in her bed for two days and now I sleep in my own bed every night." (She was actually too afraid to sleep alone at night, and insisted on sharing her mother's bed). Then she pulled blankets over the dolls' heads and placed fences around them and on top of them for protection. Finally, she again used all the household furniture to barricade the scene. A little later she took a large dinosaur and had it creep under the blankets and eat the baby. She smiled. Then she grabbed the man doll and had the dinosaur bite off his head. She smiled again, saying "It's not scary, it's funny." Throughout the session, the child repeated variations of the same play sequence.

From the time Wendy was born until she was about eighteen months, she had been present on numerous occasions when her emotionally unstable father, either drunk or drugged, physically abused her mother. Since that time the father had undergone rehabilitation, and consequently there were only sporadic incidences of physical violence, the most recent triggered by his discovery of the mother's boyfriend. Given this history, there are, of course, a number of levels of interpretation of this child's behavior. For the purposes of identifying her concerns and her style of coping with the parental dispute, we note that Wendy accurately reports the violent incident and expresses worry about her mother's safety, but she is also cognizant that her father is much improved. She is attached to both. She is struggling cognitively to understand the visitation play (for example, her father's comings and goings in different cars), who belongs to whom in terms of family relationship, whom to respect, and whom to dismiss. She is placed in the center of their dispute but feels helpless when she voices her father's requests for increased time and is ignored by her mother. The trauma of the violence between her parents is fused with the trauma of having one of her cats die in the clothes drier and her other cat taken away, which are fused in turn with the loss and shaming of her father who is arrested by the police. The present and past are joined. All of these fears inhibit her autonomy and mastery (like sleeping on her own and learning to swim). These fused fears of destruction, death, and abandonment are more simply expressed in her play, in which she tries to protect the mother and baby doll with fences and barricades from monsters who will devour them. Her attempts at mastery are clearly evident in the repetitive play in which she laughingly has the dinosaur gobble up the dolls, dismissing her frightening feeling that neither the mother nor father (the man doll) can protect her.

Vicious Cycles in Parent-Child Interactions

Some of the most pernicious interactional dymanics involve the manner in which preschool children, in particular, accommodate themselves to their parents and to the conflict in ways that appeared adaptive but place at risk their capacity to develop a solid, consistent sense of themselves. In general, these parents are so preoccupied (with the dispute or their own unmet needs) that they find it difficult to remain connected with their children. They deprive their children of empathic understanding and are not able effectively to mirror and affirm the children's individual concerns: their fears, accomplishments, and needs. While parents give the impression of being very close and bonded with their children, their perceived attachment is often a pseudo-mutual one because they project much of their own experience onto the child and behave as though that were true. Hence, they are unable to respond to the child's changing needs or fully participate with pleasure in the child's individual growth and development. The appearance of closeness to the child obscures the children's essential loneliness, deprivation and sense of not having their own selves acknowledged and nurtured. Although hungry and angry, the children cannot express their needs directly because they fear rejection and retaliation or simply are not heard. In order to have their needs met to any extent, the child has to reflect what each parent needs and wants. Consequently, they become vigilant and highly attuned to each parent, and mould themselves to preserve these ties.

At the same time, the intense disputes typically result in polarization of parenting styles. In opposition to and reaction against one another, parents perceive and treat their child very differently. For example, correcting for one parent's overstrictness, the other parent becomes overly permissive; reacting against one parent's overinvolving the child socially, the other keeps the child from his peers; objecting to one kind of value orientation, the other parent emphasizes another; believing that one parent infantalizes the child, the other demands too much maturity. This split parenting exacerbates the child's difficulty in individuation. What makes for a solid sense of self is undoubtedly continuity and consistency of the environment in relation to oneself. However, these children of entrenched disputes try to fit in with their parents' progressively polarized expectations. The result is a progressively narrowing spotlight in which to express themselves, leading to identity confusion. What is more, the children internalize characteristics of their parents and the evaluation and affect that is associated with these traits. If the mother demeans the father as a man, her son's own identification of himself as a male is demeaned. These complex, split identifications, the idealizations and devaluations of parts of self, contribute to the identity diffusion.

Once this interactional process is underway, the parent and child construct together a unique environment that reflects only parts of the child that are functional or fit with each parent's expectations. The child becomes constricted to certain defined roles or styles of behaving and seldom makes demands, so that the parent's perceptions are never challenged. We speculate that if the children made greater demands, highlighting their own needs, perhaps the parents would act otherwise, and the vicious cycle would be interrupted. Indeed, those children who protest vigorously, and even evidence behavioral problems to which the parents are forced to attend, may be less at risk.

CHAPTER 7

The Dilemma of the School-Age Child

I feel like a candle burned at both ends. It's a weird feeling because I don't know which way to drop

—Peter, nine years old

As children grow older, their understanding of the parental disputes, as well as their age-specific distress and symptomatic behavior in response to witnessing parental fights and to making transitions between one parent's home and the other, change. They develop different patterns of coping and defensive response to disputing parents, and they typically become more involved, even enmeshed, in the parental conflicts and play a significant role in the drama, thereby creating a family impasse.

Children's Involvement in Parental Disputes

The forty-four elementary school-age children in our research sample witnessed more than half the verbally and physically abusive incidents yet less than half the verbal reasoning between their parents. Girls and boys were equally likely to be exposed to the conflict. Very few parents (5 percent) protected their children consistently from their arguments or from the depression and rage that often followed the dispute. Few attempted to explain their disagreements in a non-blaming way. The several children who were not informed of the issues but witnessed the parent's distress seemed the most anxious, perhaps because their fantasies of what was happening were worse than the reality.

Like their younger preschool counterparts, these children were by-standers who witnessed the arguing, insults, threats, and pushing and shoving or overheard angry telephone exchanges. The parents were absorbed in the quarrel at the time it was happening. In the fear and challenge of an angry confrontation, each parent was perceptually and emotionally focused on the opponent and seemed unaware that the child needed protection. Three children were in their mothers' cars when the raging women rammed the ex-spouses' cars. In one instance, the child was injured. A stepfather threw a chaise longue from the second story, striking and shattering the windshield of the father's car, in which the daughter was sitting. The children were also used as passive weapons in the dispute (for example, visits could be threatened or actually restricted if child support was not paid or if the ex-spouse did not conform to certain requests. In two cases the child was the object of a physical tug of war; in five cases the children were kidnapped and secreted from the other parent. Another three children were repeatedly not returned after agreed-upon visits).

However, the older the children, the less likely they were to be only passive bystanders, objects, or trophies in the parental war. Throughout these years (ages six to twelve), the parents, perceiving them to be more mature, drew them into the dispute, burdened their children with requests for support, comfort, and reassurance of their own troubled emotions. ("She's old enough to know the facts!" one angry mother said, and proceeded to tell her ten-year-old about the father's "betrayal of them all"). Children were used as communications channels between parents who refused to talk directly to each other. They carried messages back and forth about arrangements for the visits and holidays; they made requests for extra money, and acted as debt collectors for overdue child support. Like the proverbial Greek messengers, the children were blamed and punished if the message was not to the receiver's liking. Very frequently they were caught in the middle and became the target of the angry exchange.

☐ Six-year-old Mariane was handed the phone by one parent to make requests of the other parent to change visiting times. Each parent, then, seeing the ex-spouse in her, ventilated their anger on her. On Sunday evenings, her father told her, "Check with your Mom to see if you can stay till Monday." Her mother either angrily refused or on Monday blamed the child for being tardy: "You promised to be home on time!"

Finally, some of the older children were used to collect evidence, to spy, to communicate threats and insults. They were encouraged to harass the other parent and were party to long verbal harangues and complaints about the other parent. Some of these children needed very little encouragement to take on this more active role in the dispute: they were willing cocombatants.

Children's Reactions to Witnessing Parental Hostility

All of the younger and two-thirds of the older school-age children were reported to be acutely distressed by witnessing the parental fights and very frightened if physical violence was involved. The younger group (six to eight years) showed a predominantly submissive distress response (79 percent). They became "highly anxious, stared helplessly, or froze." Others cried; one boy hyperventilated. Some had immediate physical symptoms (stomachaches, headaches, asthma and fever). The child's distressed behavior often intensified the fight. (For example, J., seven years old, said, "They fight about me being upset." When asked why he was upset, J. answered "I cry 'cause they fight".) Submissive distress decreased markedly with age, as only 32 percent of the older group (nine to twelve years) showed this response. (See Table 7.1.)

The younger children were more likely to try to control the fight (74 percent) compared to the older ones (56 percent) by distracting (E. put his fist through a window), by telling them to stop (B. tried desperately to drag his drunken father away from beating his mother), or by preventing them from meeting each other (six-year-old K. packed her own bags and waited on the curb for her father). Parents of school-age children compared to the parents of preschoolers no longer were shocked, surprised, or thought it "cute" when their offspring tried to intervene and prevent them fighting. Usually the child became quickly embroiled and was asked to take sides. (Said seven-

Table 7.1   School-Age Child's Observable Response to Witnessing Parental Disputes*

Type of Response	Number and Percentage of Children in Each Category of Response		
	(6–8 yrs) n = 19	(9–12 yrs) n = 25	Total N = 44
Submissive distress	15 (79%)	8 (32%)	23 (52%)
Aggressive distress	4 (21%)	7 (28%)	11 (25%)
Avoidance	12 (63%)	15 (60%)	27 (61%)
Attempts to control	14 (74%)	14 (56%)	28 (64%)
Takes position/co-opted	4 (21%)	11 (46%)	15 (34%)
Excitement/pleasure	1 (05%)	0 (00%)	1 (02%)

*Data are taken from a checklist of twenty-four child reactions to witnessing/hearing parental fights, reported by both parents to the counselor.

year-old S., "It's like sinking in the quicksand." And indeed many of the older children were finally co-opted and took a strong position in the fight (44 percent of the older ones compared to 21 percent of younger ones). Some even took up issues of their own, which helped refuel the dispute (eleven-year-old L. began a stringent diet, about which her parents began to fight).

Other responses did not seem to be age-specific. Almost two-thirds of all the school-age children at times avoided the dispute. They blocked their eyes and ears, retreated to their bedroom, ignored their parents, or knew when not to be around. These were judged to be the most adaptive responses of the healthier children. One-fourth of all children showed aggressive distress responses (angry, willful behavior or hitting).

Reactions to Transitions between Parents

In accord with California state laws, like their preschool counterparts, these children as a group had been given frequent and continuing access to both parents by the court. (Compare Furstenberg et al., 1983). Although sole mother custody predominated (three-fifths), one-fifth of fathers had sole physical custody, and one-fifth of these children were in the joint physical custody of their parents. Except for about three children, who had clear permission to be with and enjoy the time with the other parent, all of these children were often symptomatic at the time of the transitions between parents (see Table 7.2). Since the children were spending on the average twenty-seven hours per week with the other parent, and were making on the average two transitions each week (range, from 1 to 10), this means they were very frequently stressed. When the parents were actively fighting or very tense with each other, the children were much worse. The younger children calmed relatively quickly when the parents settled their differences and behaved in a respectful or more friendly manner. For the older children, the legacy of the tension sometimes remained for months. They were often apprehensive, vigilant, and chronically stressed at the transitions. This was especially so when the disputes had been going on for years, or where there had been a particularly traumatic incident of violence in the past.

The mildest reaction, seen in almost all the children, was a quietening and withdrawal at the time of the transition. This was possibly adaptive, to the extent that the child seemed emotionally to center in on him- or herself and prepare psychologically for leaving one parent and seeing the other. However, in other children this withdrawal was much deeper. The parents reported the child was "spaced out," "un-

Table 7.2   School-Age Child's Reactions to Transitions
Between Parents*

| Type of Reaction | Number and Percentage of Children in Each Category of Reaction | | |
	(6–8 yrs) n = 19	(9–12 yrs) n = 25	Total N = 44
Quiet/withdrawn	15 (79%)	16 (64%)	31 (70%)
Tension/apprehension	16 (84%)	15 (60%)	31 (70%)
Resistance	12 (63%)	14 (56%)	26 (59%)
Somatic symptoms	8 (42%)	11 (44%)	19 (43%)
Regressions	8 (42%)	3 (12%)	11 (25%)
Aggressive/difficult	10 (53%)	9 (36%)	19 (43%)
Happy/positive	8 (42%)	13 (52%)	21 (48%)

*Data are taken from a checklist of twenty-one child reactions to transitions between parents for visitation or time sharing of the child in shared custody, reported by both parents to the counselor.

responsive," "blocked out to the world," "zombielike." (For example, C. impassively head-rocked all the way in the car as she crossed the no-man's land between the two opposing families. It took her at least a day to be more emotionally responsive to her father.)

Other, more distressed reactions were high anxiety, apprehension, tension, and restlessness (84 percent younger, 60 percent older). The younger children also showed more regressive and aggressive behaviors (whining, clinging, contrary behavior, eating and sleeping disturbances) than the older. Parents reported children would return "sullen, uppity, condescending, and carrying tales," which could and often did provoke more bad feeling between the parents. There was high resistance to going on and returning from visits for almost three-fifths of the children. For the early latency group it was manifested by clinging and verbal protests; in some of the late latency group it showed up in extreme physical resistance. The children would hide, run away, lock themselves in the bathroom, or simply refuse to budge. Parents frequently complained that the children took hours and sometimes days to settle after the visits.

More than two-fifths of all the children demonstrated some kind of somatic symptom or exacerbation of a physical illness at the time of the transition. Parents complained that their children came home ill and that it was the other parent's neglectful caretaking that was responsible. We initially suspected the parents' reports were indications of their resistance to sharing the child. But after carefully examining the accounts of frequent colds, high fever, allergy reactions, diarrhea, headaches, stomachaches, vomiting, asthma, and eczema, it was concluded that the reports were likely to be genuine and seemed striking evidence of the degree of stress these children were experiencing.

☐ When Pat returned from visiting her father every other weekend, she was not only highly anxious and withdrawn but would complain of colds and flu. Her mother noted she was extremely lethargic and slept excessively. Her allergy attacks kept her home from school for a couple of days. When the custody fight was active in court, she was confined to her bedroom for several weeks.

☐ Before leaving to see his mother, Fred was quiet and withdrawn and would eat little or nothing. Father reported he would return from visits "white and putrid, often running a high fever. He also threw up and missed school a couple of days." This boy had been subject to two custody investigations after three years of postdivorce disputing.

Parents used the children's symptomatic behavior as the starting point for a renewed dispute. They seldom identified their children's disturbance as reactive to the parental conflict and the problem of moving between two warring homes. Rather, they blamed the other parent for not taking adequate care of the child or used it as evidence that the visits were bad for the child and should be abandoned or shortened.

As with the preschoolers, despite all the symptomatology around the transitions, most school-age children, especially the younger ones, wanted to go on the visits and seemed to enjoy the frequent access to both parents. (The exception was certain older children who had made a strong alliance with one parent against the other. They were highly resistant and staunchly negative to the visits.) After the initial resistance to leaving, parents usually reported they had very pleasant and happy times together, though the children were often distressed at the idea of returning home. By and large, the youngsters wanted set, regular visits. In fact they usually opted for the status quo, whatever that was, and seemed to have a pervasive pessimism that any changes were likely to make the situation worse. They seemed upset by the confusion of a chaotic schedule. The most frantically distressed, lost, and confused children we saw were those to whom access was never made clear, those in situations in which plans kept changing, and those who were snatched back and forth as each parent acted unilaterally with respect to the child. To the children, flexibility meant more parental fighting or being kept from seeing a beloved parent for longer than they liked. They were often concerned about justifying that time spent with parents was fair or equal and felt more comfortable when everyone was following clearly defined rules.

Attitudes and Behavior of the Children Toward Their Disputing Parents

We found very clear age-specific responses in these children to their two angry and competitive parents, partly linked to the child's cognitive understanding of the conflict (Selman, 1980). In general, the younger children (six to eight years) were likely to have less clear preferences, shifting allegiances and loyalty conflicts; the older children (nine to twelve years) were more likely to be in alignments. Moreover, these alignments were likely to be strident and unshakable (see Table 7.3).

The younger school-age children, already cognizant of the details of the parental dispute (visits, money, and so on), could in addition keep an image of the other parent's feelings, beliefs, and attitudes when on visits. They tried to make sense of the dispute and determine who was right and who was wrong. The conflicting stories from each parent were obviously confusing and involved some in an endless search for who was lying and who was telling the truth. Their quest invited

Table 7.3   School-Age Child's Behavior and Attitude Toward Both Parents*

Type of Behavior and Attitude	Number and Percentage of Children in Each Category		
	(6–8 yrs) n = 19	(9–12 yrs) n = 25	Total N = 44
Strong alliance	0 (00%)	7 (28%)	7 (16%)
Alignment	7 (37%)	12 (48%)	19 (43%)
Loyalty conflict	8 (42%)	5 (20%)	13 (30%)
Shifting allegiances	5 (26%)	4 (16%)	9 (20%)
No preference	7 (37%)	7 (28%)	14 (32%)
Rejection of both	0 (00%)	2 (08%)	2 (04%)

*Data are obtained from counselor's ratings. Note that 50 percent of the children showed two categories of response over time.

more pressure from parents who wished to set the record straight ("What do you mean your mother said I gave her no money, let me tell you . . ."). They often incurred the wrath of a parent when they dared defend the other, and there were real life consequences to expressing preferences. ("You want to live with your father? Then go, and don't bother coming back!")

In response, some actively tried to please both sides by carrying stories about the mother to the father and vice versa, greatly exaggerating or completely fabricating the negatives in each home. The outcome of this was usually to consolidate or escalate the bitterness and distrust between the parents. These same children often blamed the stepparent for the problems, thereby provoking arguments in the new family unit, and seemed both fearful and pleased with the family uproar that resulted. Others, punished or threatened with rejection for taking the side of the other parent, became emotionally and behaviorally constricted.

In general, then, six- to eight-year-olds tended to avoid or withdraw from situations involving both their disputing parents, formed unstable coalitions with each parent and projected negatives towards a stepparent, sometimes without dissonance and sometimes with a lot of confusion. These rapid shifts in allegiance to one and then the other parent during the early school years seem to indicate the child's developing ability to reflect on the pattern of relationships in the divorced family as a whole, while their confusion and instability suggest that only partial or unilateral perspectives were being processed at a time.

The middle elementary school years (ages seven to ten) were marked by the child's developing capacity for self-reflexive thinking in social relationships. Not only could he or she take the perspective of the observer of oneself, but the child realized that others could perceive their view. There was an infinite regression of possibilities: "I know that she knows that I know." The relationships that were now possible were reciprocal in that both self and others' perspective could be simultaneously considered. The child could also now acknowledge mixed feelings and degrees of feeling and make distinctions between intentional and nonintentional actions of self and others. ("Dad says he didn't mean it, but he could have helped it if he really wanted"). Hence, with respect to the parental conflict, the child could, for the first time, simultaneously experience the juxtaposition of different interests and abiding conflictual feelings, and sought a solution that would meet the needs of both parents. Moreover, the actions of each parent needed to be genuine or sincere toward the other to be acceptable. ("He says he's sorry, but I don't think he really means it.")

The children capable of this level of understanding are, more than any other group, anxious, torn, saddened and constricted by parental disputes. They feel tremendously uncomfortable, caught in the middle of a dangerously complicated situation and helpless. For the first time the child seems to conceptualize the whole system of emotional relations in the family, and becomes most vulnerable to the unresolved conflict. Consequently, loyalty conflicts are prevalent. These children clearly want a relationship with both parents but seem deeply worried about the consequences. For example, sometimes they would capitulate to the wishes of a mother who did not wish them to visit the father, but did so with much guilt and worry about hurting the father or being rejected themselves. Others would go but not be able to enjoy themselves on the visits, they worried about the other parent and would call home to check their well-being.

In general, these children made several different attempts to cope with the loyalty conflicts, none of which provided any real or lasting solution to their dilemma. Most tried to remain equidistant from both parents, struggling to retain loyalty with both without losing either. They were obsessed with being very fair to both sides, evened out stories as if to keep a balance sheet, and were more likely to favor a split-time joint custody agreement. Others tried to withdraw and keep their feelings and preferences hidden. They seemed on guard, watchful, and extremely careful about what they said lest it be used in some way against the other parent or themselves in retaliation. They hated to be asked where they wanted to live: They either did not know or did not want to tell. Hence, emotionally they appeared constricted, anxious, and somewhat depressed. Others tried to keep their two worlds separate—the mother's from the father's. For example, they could not talk freely, or they could not talk at all, to the parent on the telephone when with the other. They became highly distressed and "frozen" by accidentally meeting the other parent on the street during nonvisiting time. They benefited from neutral drop-off and pickup places so that the warring parents would not have to meet, and they would not have to respond to their two parents at the same time. Only those few children who had been given repeated permission to be with the other parent could express pleasure and talk freely about what happened on visits with the other parent. At this stage, children seemed painfully aware that there were no simple solutions to the fights.

However, pure loyalty conflicts were not sustained for very long.

Instead, from the middle to late elementary school years (ages nine to twelve), alignments typically began to form as the child made a choice for one parent and, with varying degrees of intensity, began to exclude and reject the other. Among one-third of the six- to eight-year-olds and one-half of the nine- to twelve-year-olds, alignments were of moderate intensity and were often secret or private preferences. They involved a definite verbal preference for and behavioral siding with one parent, together with a wish not to hurt the feelings or raise the ire of the other parent. The alignment was accompanied by affective dislike towards, withdrawal from, and resistance to spending time with the other parent. However, residues of ambivalence and loyalty conflict were evident. For example, they did not want to tell the parent directly that they did not want to live with him or her. They softened their preference by saying they wanted to live in the preferred parent's neighborhood, or they asked the counselor to tell the parent. Interestingly, legal custody disputes were often precipitated when a child began to make such an alignment, because the rejected parent, sensing the child's withdrawal, sought to prevent the impending loss by appealing to the court. However, among more than one-fourth of the older children, the alliances were overtly hostile and unshakeable stances in which the child stridently rejected and refused to see or visit one parent. Once formed, these alliances were extremely resistant to change and often continued through the early adolescent years.

In sum, whereas the younger elementary school child attempted to remain equidistant to each disputing parent, suffering considerable loyalty conflict, the older child found it harder to maintain a neutral or even position. The alliances typically seen at this age result from a convergence of developmental facts: the child's capacity to conceptualize the whole system of emotional relations in the family, his or her tendency toward uncompromising moral views of the situation, and pressure from family members to take a more active role in the parental fight. All of these coincide to make it more imperative that the only tenable resolution of the untenable loyalty conflicts for the child is a firm coalition with one parent against the other. Once this occurs, the child has resolved the systemic tension and not surprisingly shows little or no anxiety.

Children's Coping and Defensive Behavior

Apart from these general trends, there was a great deal of variation in these children's responses. A proportion of children remained in shifting allegiances; many did not develop loyalty conflicts; others became involved in intense "unholy" alliances. What accounts for these differences? The clinical profiles of these children's coping and defensive responses provide a more detailed, complex, and informative view. From a content analysis of the clinical profiles, a spectrum of four coping and defensive responses to the parental conflict were distinguished, each less adaptive than the previous. Each child tended to respond in predominantly one way, although among the younger school-age children there was more likely to be a mix of responses, and it was more difficult to determine which children were coping better. Among the older children, clearer patterns emerged, with some taking quite adaptive routes while others became more enmeshed and emotionally vulnerable. Under the stress of the parental fight, some regressed and used less adaptive means. With treatment, they used more functional patterns. The four principal types of response are termed maneuvering, equilibrating, merging, and diffusing.

Maneuvering

About one-fifth of the children (five boys, four girls) were actively struggling to maneuver in the unpredictable and potentially dangerous confines of the parental dispute. These children talked more openly to the counselor about their parents' conflicts, were rather direct and forthright about their predicament and seemed to want to stake out their own territory. (One six-year-old wondered "Who owns me?" a twelve-year-old wanted to take part in the decision making.) At these times, they did not become overwhelmed but appeared to maintain distance by preserving their own view of the situation and managed their feelings while actively manipulating the situation to meet their own needs.

☐ Benjamin, aged ten, was angry at his father for restricting his access to his mother and also aware of his mother's lack of genuine interest in him. He devised all kinds of strategies for inciting her suit for joint custody and spent hours scheming with his younger brother to effect a custody change. He would secretly telephone his mother to report incidents in which his father had been unfair in order to mobilize her into action. He arranged to meet his mother without the father knowing. At the same time, he was both worried about and fearful of his surly, depressed father and took responsibility for managing his emotional state. "I know how to get him out of his sad moods," he said. "I just do something wrong, and then he gets mad and yells. Then he's not sad anymore." He realized that his father could become violent after drinking, so he and his younger brother studied street maps and planned an escape route in the event they needed to flee to their mother. When his mother procrastinated, he turned to reading newspaper advertisements to help her find suitable housing.

They seemed aware of the possibility of being rejected by both sides, or lost in the fight, and took conscious if not always well-advised action to protect themselves. They refused to participate in any alignment, or made strategic alignments with the more powerful parent or with the parent who provided a window of escape.

□ Michael, nine, was well aware of his mother's intensely vindictive behavior toward his father and his father's passivity and
ineptness in dealing with her. He had seen his mother slash his
father's tires and smash his windshield. He was quite adept at
avoiding his mother's anger by focusing her on his athletic pur-
suits about which she was very proud. Behaviorally, he complied with his mother, following her directives to visit or not
visit and affirmed, with no elaboration or trace of rancor, her
views of the father. When with his father, he was warm and
open but simply refused to discuss his mother. He told the
counselor: "She would kill me if she saw me wave to my father
when I pass him on the street! . . . I don't say anything. . . . It's
best this way."

Some tried to please by reporting what either parent wanted to hear. This carrying of tales and stories (lies, fantasies, half-truths) often excited the concern of the parent. Some of this had a sneaky, manipulative quality. During the early school years, children are not very clever at diplomacy or taking political advantage, and thus they often found themselves in a great deal of trouble for lying or being sneaky. This manipulative stance was also in part an outlet or subli-mated expression of their aggression.

□ George, seven, maintained his link with his father by reporting
mistreatment and neglect by his mother. When she learned of
his stories, she was extremely irate, punished him for telling
lies and condemned him, "You're taking after your father!" The
boy then defensively forgot what happened on weekend visits
with his father. His mother then began listening to his phone
calls with his father to try to find out what the father and son
were "up to."

The older children became more astute in this more active and adaptive stance. These particular youngsters developed a more cynical, jaundiced if not realistic view of the situation. Some spoke about their parents' emotional problems and the endless disputing with a startling clarity, emotional insight, and wisdom beyond their years. They watched a lot, and waited, biding their time as if to make their escape.

☐ Benjamin, who was described above as inciting a custody dispute to escape from his father who had a drinking problem, told his counselor, "I've watched some programs on TV about drinking and alcohol. It makes you weak. I am stronger than my dad, not physically but in understanding. I know what is right and I am determined and that determination is stronger than my dad's."

☐ Emanuel, nine, accurately sensing both his parents' disturbance, shook his head and acknowledged, "I don't talk with either of them." He was concerned about getting his mother upset because "she's crazy enough to do something . . . like kick me out!" He was not sure of his dad either, "He does weird stuff and talks peculiarly. . . . What's more, Mom doesn't want me to [visit him]." He took care of his younger brother because "that keeps Mom quiet" and avoided parents' attempts to entrap him in their dispute. In sum, he was straightforward, feeling he had to deal with his "crazy parents," and was not going to do anything to upset the balance.

It seemed as though we were witnessing the birth of tricksters, reminiscent of those cultural folk heroes from myths who survive by dint of their astute social awareness, imagination, foresight, distance from, and manipulation of the system. Our clinical judgment was that at higher levels of moral development (evidenced by principled moral reasoning and empathic concern for their parents), these children looked like clever mediators or diplomats. At lower levels of moral development, we feared the early onset of antisocial tendencies in that some children aimed to get what they wanted without consideration or respect for others. The most active tricksters were boys. One nine-year-old girl developed a clownlike identity, acting silly, and irresponsible in an engaging manner, making light of not only the conflict but everything else. We suspected the training arena for the trickster identity was the long, elaborate, and unusual play rituals in which these children typically engaged. This play involved complicated plots in which the hero had to maneuver in a dangerous, unpredictable world of bad guys, traitors, and monsters and did so by sheer wit, agility, and deviousness. (Guerrilla warfare was the favorite play activity that obsessed Benjamin for three years before he finally ran away from his possessive, dominating father, who refused to allow him to see enough of his mother.) In this way, fantasy was used to practice and achieve mastery.

Equilibrating

Another one-fifth of the children (six boys, four girls) were more passive in their adaptation to the parental dispute. Rather than trying to master the situation, they attempted to master the feelings engendered. They tried to cope with and survive the parental dispute by keeping everything in equilibrium, internally and externally. They often presented as fairly remarkable children in that they appeared composed, organized, and competent. With their parents, they tried very carefully to be fair and equidistant. They searched for rules and safe places. However they could not assert themselves very well and tried to isolate and avoid their feelings. Their careful vigilance constrained and hid chronic anxiety and tension. They also seemed more vulnerable to psychosomatic illness, (among this group was the child with diabetes, another two with asthma, and one with eczema). Their eagerness to stay on good terms with both parents in this anxious and compliant stance belied their underlying guilt about their situation. In fact, they seemed to be fending off not only anxiety, but depression. These were the children who suffered the most obvious loyalty conflicts. The younger ones especially were acutely worried about and felt responsible for both parents.

☐ Lisa, was an even-tempered seven-year-old who struggled to manage the feelings evoked by her parents weekly fights. While not overtly or acutely anxious, she experienced frequent flare-ups of her eczema. She was very loving to each parent, would comply with whatever her parents wanted, and attempted to keep in touch by phone with each during their absence. She felt anxious if unable to reach her parents by phone and alternatively felt guilty if one parent called when she was not in. She did not know whom to love. "If I love Mom, Dad will feel sad. If I love Dad, Mom will feel sad." In each counseling session, she gave weekly reports of her parents' arguments, after which she painstakingly drew pictures. She seemed to gain some relief in these meticulous drawings of children and adults engaged in activities similar to the ones in which she found herself with her parents. These pictures helped bind her anxiety and distance herself from the parental fights. For several weeks, Lisa drew pictures of people at a park saying "Hi, glad to see you!" At this time, in striking contrast, her parents were meeting at a park and ignoring one another in icy silence. Torn by loyalty conflicts, she one day drew a rainbow, placing clouds at either end. In one cloud, she put part of her name, *LI*, and in the other *SA*, graphically portraying how split she felt.

The older children also worried but tended to avoid and withdraw from the fight and remain somewhat separate from their parents, or they held secret alignments. It was gratifying to find that though it was difficult for them to express their feelings and fears in counseling, with encouragement they could identify their wants. They had wisely chosen not to make them known.

☐ Claire, a sad appealing, bright ten-year-old, was handling the parental dispute by minimizing her own needs and anger and by withdrawing. Her mother was a very depressed, angry woman who frequently erupted into rages and tried to involve Claire in her bitterness towards her ex-husband. Her father, while very affectionate, was passive and unwilling to rescue his daughter. He guiltily acknowledged leaving Claire to care for her mother in his place. Though burdened by her mother's depression, fearful of and angry in response to her tirades, and feeling deprived by both parents' unavailability, Claire valiantly tried to keep her distance. She admitted her feelings to the counselor but made few demands on either parent and avoided discussing her wish to be with her father. "There is nothing I can do, so I don't want to talk about it. I don't think about the divorce, or the fighting. I just want to figure out how to be with both of them and just go on. My brother argues and makes things worse."

Merging

More than two-fifths of the children (eight boys, eleven girls) were of greater concern because they tended to merge with their angry parents and seemed more enmeshed in the parental disputes. They learned to please by becoming nonpersons, by making no demands. These children usually presented as good, conforming, and patient. They were seldom identified as having any problems or causing any trouble. Their hallmark was their constriction of affect. Some lacked spontaneity, seemed vacant, joyless, and withdrawn to the point of looking mildly but chronically depressed. They were not only unexpressive of their feelings, they appeared walled off from access to their emotional life. During early latency, these children were like chameleons. They merged with whomever they were with, splitting their lives in two and blocking out the nonpresent parent's world. They expressed few feelings, wants, and desires separate from those of their immediate parent. These children were in shifting allegiances.

☐ Despite the fact that she was injured when her mother side-swiped her father's car, and aside from the fact that she was continuously placed in the center of the parental conflict (asked to exchange messages and questioned as to whether she wanted to visit her father), Mary told her counselor all was well, her parents did not argue, visits went easily and her mom let her see her dad. She expressed few feelings, no pain, anger, or fears about these events. She presented as a shy, retiring, slightly overweight six-year-old who was not in acute anxiety or disstress. Rather, she appeared to be closing off, drifting away into sadness and retreating. Her mother was concerned because she was "blanking out and staring into space," her teacher reported that she "goes into a daze" after visits (and the inevitable parental fights). Her drawings were stylized, her play lacked creativity. She was a passive, lonely child who tried to please both parents. At times she would sit and wait for hours for her parents without expressing annoyance. When cued, she would voice her mother's complaints about father's girlfriends and his lack of attention toward her. When with her father, she fit in with his busy social and work agenda, without protesting his lack of consideration for her.

Many of the older children in this category were prone to making alliances, and taking on the identity of a raging, paranoid, or sullen depressed parent. They parroted the complaints of the aggrieved parent and repeated stories about the despicable behavior of the other "word for word." Some of these stories sounded like family legends of events that had occurred many years previously. Once the strong alliance was formed, these children looked more cohesive, more organized, and intact. They could express feelings, including anger. Many were free of anxiety and cognitively clear as if the alliance had solved a difficult dilemma. However, the need to defend the alliance belied its fragility. A great deal of distortion was often necessary to maintain their solid inflexible stance. They refused to check out the reality of their position and refused visits, phone calls, and letters from the other parent. It seemed as if they had made a split between the good and the bad, projecting each part onto a different parent and taking refuge in the "good one."

☐ Eleven-year-old Christine had been the center of her parents' fight for years before the divorce, expressing her mother's anger at her father and receiving the brunt of her father's hostility toward her mother. She presented in counseling as fully aligned with her mother and as wanting nothing to do with her father. She refused to speak with him on the phone and would leave the house when he arrived to pick up her brother. "I don't want any kind of relationship with him. He was mean to each one of us. We know what he's like. He'll never change." She often used the same language and described the same incidents as her mother: "When I was a baby in a high chair, he hit me for spilling my milk!" and "[He is] hideous vermin." In contrast, her description of her mother was glowing. Her mother was described as "wonderful, full of fun, a good friend, and a good protector. Last week, when my dad came in and said to my brother, 'Wouldn't you like Christine to come with us on the visit?' I wondered how I could say no to my brother. Then my mom came in and told him, 'If she says no, she means no!'" Christine continued to emphasize how great it was to have her father out of the house. "All is calm since he left. There is no pain and no fear. When he was there, I didn't want to do anything. I was scared. I had an uneasy feeling around him."

Christine tried to portray herself as well-adjusted and doing well in school and with peers. "My friends are just pouring in!" In fact, her grades had dropped and she was fairly isolated. In the group sessions, she was very competitive, unable to lose any games, and very self-critical. She continually berated herself for doing "dumb things." She denied feelings other than those that fit with the rosy picture she wished to portray. She became puzzled when her counselor commented that she looked upset and angry after losing a game. "I'm fine, I'm not feeling that way! I feel free to say whatever is on my mind!" In sum, her stance was unshakable. She was happy with herself and her family. "I don't think about the divorce any more because I am happy with the way things are. I hate my father . . . the way he was. I'm glad he's out of the house. That's that! I know you said last week he probably did these things to me because he was angry at my mom. I disagree. I think it was hatred for me, pure and simple." Her defensive, black-and-white view of her parents was working for her. It bound her anxiety and set a clear path of action: Reject her father and side with her mother.

Mergers who did not make strong alliances by the time they were nine to twelve years old appeared clearly the more disturbed. They were observed to be "extremely constricted, immobilized, in a fog and numbed". During an intense dispute, this fog became more pervasive and affected their school achievement and social relations. They showed a marked lack of autonomy and couldn't make decisions, not only about their parents but about many things. At other times the fog seemed to recede and be localized around their parents and issues of the dispute. These children also seemed somewhat depressed and reported many somatic symptoms.

☐ For most of Jeff's eleven years, he felt torn by his parent's contradictory imperatives. "My mom wants me to brush my teeth once a day; my dad says three times; My dad wants me to see him in the middle of the week, my mom thinks it disrupts my homework". Ever since his father's request for joint custody three weeks ago, Jeff reported he'd been "sick with a weird flu. I could barely move, my body ached, and I had to stay in bed and I slept about thirty hours." Jeff never voluntarily visited his father and when with him was guarded, tense, and distant. On the other hand, with a very blank, expressionless face, he talked about wanting to spend time with him. Then he said he felt more comfortable with his mother "because we think the same."

☐ Sweet, gentle, nine-year-old Alan spoke with a soft voice and slight stutter. He sat passively in his chair and his face was immobile. Though responding warmly and compliantly to the counselor, he had remarkable difficulty remembering events around his parents' disputes. When threatened, he merged with whoever he was with. When with his father, he took on all his characteristics, values and views of the situation. At these times, he became very frightened that his mother would kidnap him, a fear directly taken from his father's paranoid preoccupations. On the other hand, when with his mother, he became enmeshed with her and would take on her views. When not aligned with either, he became extremely confused, anxious, and self-destructive. He ran away from home and wandered dangerous streets of the city for several days and nights in a daze.

Diffusing

Less than one-fifth of the children (five boys, one girl) appeared clearly the most disturbed in that they responded to the disputing parents with marked behavioral and affective diffusion. They did not have workable defenses and became overwhelmed. They manifested unintegrated, chaotic attitudes and bizarre behaviors, (some had sadomasochistic tendencies, suicidal ideas, violent outbursts, and infantile regressions). These children seemed highly reactive to the parental conflicts. (For example, E. escaped into a psychotic fantasy when his mother snatched him the second time. A. became completely uncontrollable and wild, shooting himself and the therapist in the head with a toy gun when his parents renewed their fight.) Even the preadolescents continued to manifest shifting allegiances and only very rudimentary loyalty conflicts. It was as though they had not developed a cohesive-enough self to sustain a consistent or allied relationship with either parent. (L., eleven, was furiously angry at and rejecting of her mother and seductive toward and protective of her father. Nevertheless she would curl up in her mother's lap and act like a baby in the session.)

□ Tom was an angry, out-of-control eleven-year-old who responded to his parents' fights (or to discussions thereof) with aggressive outbursts, psychotic talk, and bizarre fantasies. In his initial session, he noted that when his parents fought, he ran to his hiding place in the doghouse with his dog (his closest friend). He fantasied that during one fight "I kicked the whole door down. They came running. I punched a window with my hand. It was bleeding. It didn't hurt. . . . When they are in a fight, I feel like karate-chopping, *bong, ching!*" When discussing what he wanted to do, he thought "I could live in a different town and my friend Pete could drive me to each of their houses. But Pete is a reckless driver. Once he jumped over a lake and a crocodile." At another time, Tom resolved his loyalty bind with the fantasy of "living with Buck Rogers in a mansion in the sky." In the group sessions, Tom regressed to even more primitive modes of operating. He was wild and disruptive: he provoked, hit the other children and knocked down their constructions. His imagery was filled with violence and gore: he built a fort and spattered it with red paint to indicate blood, he talked about eyeballs popping out and karate-chopping his beloved dog. At other times, alone with the counselor, he was sweet and dependent.

The clinical histories of these children suggest some etiological factors in their differential responses. Some of these children seemed physically and mentally inherently more equipped than others to deal with stress. The children who adapted more successfully were on the whole intelligent, attractive, and more skilled socially and in sporting activities, and they achieved well in school. Their self-confidence and more cohesive and independent view of themselves seemed partly to derive from successful achievements and relationships in other areas of their lives. The children who were doing poorly had a history of problems: disturbed peer relations, speech and learning disabilities, were overweight, and so on. They were perhaps more dependent upon the support of their parents and hence were particularly vulnerable to the cumulative stress of the divorce, parental dispute, and parental psychopathology.

Another concomitant feature of these patterns reflects the longevity of collapse in the family structure. Among the better-functioning children (the maneuverers and equilibrators), we noted that the parental alliance (defined as the parents' support of and respect for each other in their executive roles within the family), had only more recently broken down. Prior to the divorce or the immediate dispute, these parents not only had supported each other as parents, but also usually maintained appropriate boundaries between themselves and their children (that is, they were not prone to role reversal). In the mergers' families, the parental alliance had been in disarray for many years or had never really existed in the first place. Instead, one parent tended to form a coalition with the child against the other. Ongoing parent-child role reversal was more likely in these cases. Within the fourth group, the family boundaries were always very diffused. The parental alliance was splintered by long-term marital conflict. A great deal of confusion between the parent-child roles were observed with children often assuming a parental, spousal or sibling role with the adults.[1]

To this point, we have only considered characteristics within the child and the family structure that contribute to the loyalty conflicts and the alignments. Patterns within the ongoing interaction between the parent and child explain a great deal as to whether or not loyalty conflicts are experienced, alignments made, and with whom. Foremost, it was clear that children experienced fewer loyalty conflicts and were not in strong alignments when their parents were not pulling for allegiance and support, and when they were given some permission to love them both. In fact, some of the better functioning parents were able to join together in support of each other, and refuse to allow an alignment to form!

The older children tended to make alignments out of a number of responses to the parent: to protect the parent who was decompensating, depressed, panicked or very needy; to avoid the wrath or rejection of a powerful, dominant parent (often the custodial parent upon whom they depended); and to hold onto the parent they were most afraid of losing (a half-involved father or a self-absorbed mother). However, contrary to some popular myths, we did not find that children often aligned with the more disturbed parent, or for wholly altruistic reasons. In all cases we found that children chose a parent who provided something important to them in the way of empathy. They reported that these parents usually listened to them more, were less critical, made them feel more comfortable, and understood their age-specific concerns. Some of these parents were, unfortunately, also more seductive and capricious in what they provided.

Children were equally likely to exclude the same-sex as the opposite-sex parent. Some concerned and potentially loving as well as emotionally disturbed parents were excluded. Many parents quickly escalated the intensity of the alliance by acting in angry retaliation in response to the hurt of the child's rejection. Other parents who continued to push for visits with a reluctant child in a relentness manner, also polarized the alignment. We have concluded that parents in post-divorce custody disputes have a narrow margin of error with respect to their older school-aged children. They feel that they are on trial, waiting to be judged, and that they need to court their children's favor. Some feel this is undignified for a parent and instead try to assert their authority, which is not acknowledged, and conclude by fighting with their children. Hence, rejected parents contribute by pushing the child further into an alliance.

Finally, we consider the impact of siblings. Half of our schoolage sample were only children, and they seemed particularly vulnerable by being the single focus of the fight. Where there were siblings, it was clear that one child (usually the oldest) was more burdened by the dispute, leaving the other(s) relatively free. Furthermore, as older children withdrew or were released from that position, the burden was often assumed by a younger sibling.

Emotional and Behavioral Disturbance: Prognosis and Outcome

Regardless of great cultural variations, differences in parental pathology, or the intensity of dispute, the children as a group showed two marked commonalities when they were observed during the time of the custody and visitation disputes. First, they were notably lacking in overt agression and conduct disorders. Second, they paradoxically displayed beliefs that they were very important and powerful while at the same time evidenced feelings of vulnerability, helplessness and fear.

Despite all the aggressive behavior they had witnessed between their parents, they were not emulating it (only four children were described as having conduct disorders). In fact, those who had witnessed physical violence were particularly inhibited. In general, the boys presented in individual and group sessions in a very sweet manner, although highly controlled, repressed anger and depression emerged in their fantasy and play. (R., a sweet, sad six-year-old, lined up all the soldiers and very precisely pierced each with a tiny spear. W., eight, disturbed by other children punching the punching bag and refusing to punch it himself, told a story about seeing a baby's head rolling in his front yard. E., nine, drew pictures of gory battles in which everyone perished.) The girls as a group were likewise good, sweet, docile, well-behaved, and eager to please in the sessions. The younger ones spent an inordinate amount of time in the playroom preparing meals, cleaning up, and helping the therapist. Except for an occasional mean, or sneaky act, these girls were particularly submissive and nonassertive. The older ones were dutiful but rather constrained and dull conversationalists. Certainly some of these responses in the girls are the result of taking on female sex roles in this society; however, their compliance was often greater than one commonly sees in other girls their age.

Along with the suppression of aggression and overt anger and the excessive compliance and eagerness to please, these children held exaggerated conceptions of their central importance and high value.[2] The children clearly understood that they were the centerpiece of the parental dispute. Although many denied feeling responsible for causing the parents' divorce, they definitely believed that if were not for them, their parents would not continue to fight. "I wish I was dead, and then they wouldn't have to fight any more" was voiced by several children. Except for a few younger ones, they did not harbor reconciliation fantasies. They realistically acknowledged that their parents could not live together. However, they did long for them to stop fighting and hoped that they might become friends. They felt they had the power to make their parents happy, sad, or angry and this was indeed not surprising because many were burdened by requests for support and emotional nurturance from their needy parents. In response, they postured or defended with more or less grandiose fantasies about their capabilities. On the other hand, they felt helpless, vulnerable, and afraid because they did not have the resources or knowledge to calm the storm and ensure their parents' happiness or well-being. ("It's like when you have to do a math problem and the teacher hasn't given you that lesson yet," nine-year-old M. explained.) Moreover, they feared being precipitously abandoned if they expressed aggression, emotions, and preferences that were unacceptable to their mother or father. They also worried about hurting a fragile parent by imposing too many demands. Hence, they remained in anxious attachment to one or both of their parents.

The longer-term outcomes are of perhaps greater concern. Two to three years later, the children as a group were two to four times more likely to be clinically disturbed in emotions and behavior compared to a normal (nonclinical) population (that is, an estimated one- to two-fifths had scores above the ninetieth percentile according to the Achenbach Behavior Checklist). Furthermore, when the legal disputes were largely ended and the active conflict (verbal and physical agression) between parents was greatly diminished or had ceased, the Achenbach test scores showed that the children were manifesting emotional and behavioral disturbances more predicted by the extent of conflict and aggression they had witnessed between their parents two to three years earlier. This implies that parental disputes have a delayed or latent effect. Although the children were inhibited and constricted during the litigation and mediation, they were more likely to manifest depression, withdrawal, uncommunicativeness, aggression, and conduct disorders at a later time. Perhaps with the diminution of the fights, they felt safer to express feelings.

In general, children of ongoing post-divorce disputes do not benefit from joint custody or frequent access to both parents. At the followup, two to three years later, we found that those children (particularly girls) who shared more days each month with both parents were significantly more depressed, withdrawn, and uncommunicative; had more somatic complaints; and tended to be more aggressive. In addition, the boys' social competence (involvement with friends and outside activities) was more likely to be disrupted by more frequent movement between parents' homes. Part of the reason for the children's increased distress could be attributed to the fact that their parents were more conflictual with one another consequent upon the more frequent access. Consequently, the children (especially the older ones and the boys), were more caught and used in the disputes. Sadly, although fathers, in particular, were more involved and less likely to abandon their children when they had joint custody or frequent visitation, the value of this involvement did not offset the negative effects of the parental distrust and acrimony. (See Johnston,

Gonzalez & Campbell, 1987, and Johnston, Kline, Tschann, & Campbell 1988 for full reports on these empirical findings.)

In sum, latency children in high-conflict postseparation and divorce families are seldom protected from parental acrimony. To a varying extent, they are passively used as weapons or are active agents in the disputes. These children, especially the younger ones, become highly distressed and symptomatic in response to witnessing the parental conflict and in making transitions between parents. A vicious cycle emerges in which the child's distress and symptomatic behavior fuels the parental fight over the custody and access arrangements. From early to late latency, clear developmental trends are observed. Children become less overtly anxious and distressed with age, but at the same time are more likely to be co-opted into the parental dispute and to form alignments and alliances with one parent. This radically changes the structure of the family relations by excluding the other parent entirely or relegating that parent to a relatively powerless position. Both parents contribute to the alignments and alliances formed, and the child's capacity for secure, intimate, yet autonomous relations with one or both parents becomes severely compromised.

CHAPTER 8

Brief Interventions with Children

Our direct work with children is brief, comprising on the average four to six play interviews, and is distinguishable from other therapuetic interventions in that it is focused specifically on helping the child cope with the parental divorce and disputes. Following these brief, intensive weekly sessions, we remain available to children over a longer period to help them with any new crisis or change, at their own or their parents' request. While this brief intervention is probably sufficient for some children, we fear it has barely begun to address the children's problems in those cases where families are severely disorganized by long-term conflict, where a parent is blatantly psychologically disturbed, and where the child is already significantly symptomatic. (For these reasons, those children who need more extensive, ongoing therapy are referred elsewhere. We encourage parents to make such arrangements a part of their mediated agreement at the conclusion of the family intervention.)[1]

Such a rapid entry and exit from the child's life necessitates a working alliance with the child that avoids nurturing dependency or any extensive transference relationship. We try to prevent children developing unrealistic fantasies that we will reconcile their parents or rescue and protect them from the parental disputes by being realistic circumscribed about our goals and cautious about predicting outcomes. At the same time, the therapist needs to be a warm, empathic, and a concerned advocate for the child's needs, sensitive and respectful to the child's problems, and openly sympathetic about how the parental fights are scary, confusing, unfair, maddening, and painful. Additionally, she tries to be a model of objectivity, reasonableness and resourcefulness in coping with the child's dilemmas. Most importantly, the therapist must also maintain the role of a central stable family consultant, one who is able to relate to each family member and show it is possible to have a positive or equidistant relationship with both parents, despite their differences with one another. If the child's therapist cannot maintain each of these roles, he or she should seriously consider withdrawing from the case, because there is a danger that he or she will become enmeshed in the family dynamics and the child's difficulties will be ultimately exacerbated rather than eased.

During the initial assessment session, with children who have language skills (three years and older), we use a play-interview format. In simple words and often with the aid of a family of dolls and two dolls' houses, the children are told that we are "talking doctors" who see children whose mommies and daddies are divorcing (living in different houses) and who are having problems cooperating. In fact, many of the mothers and fathers we see are arguing and fighting. This is a special place where children can perhaps talk about what is happening in their families. We will try to help them and their parents. The children are then promised confidentiality. We assure them that we will not discuss with their parents anything they tell us unless they give us permission or specifically ask us to give their parents a special message. We then ask them about their parents' divorce: Do they know what divorce means? Do their parents live apart? With whom do they (the children) live? When do they see their mom or dad? We are forthright about the parents' fighting, trying to be an objective other who can look clearly at the situation: are their parents able to talk with one another, do their parents argue and fight, and if so what about? This discussion is gently introduced during the first session as they are invited to explore and play with the toys or other children.

Although in our introduction we are rather direct in structuring the purpose of our meeting with the child, we try to be sensitive to the child's burdensome fears, feelings of responsibility, and guilt. For these reasons, the children are never asked their preferences with respect to their parents, and we try not to put them into a position where they feel they must make such choices. Instead, projective play materials are used to suggest their attachment to and comfort with each parent and other important people in their lives. Nonetheless, the direct interviewing is aimed, at the outset, toward making salient the divorce disputes so that we can more directly assess the children's coping and defensive stance. Furthermore, we seek to make some clinical judgments as to what are the children's central concerns, and whether these are part of or separate from the parental disputes. In this way, we try to respect the children's agendas and not be blinded by our own purposes.

Several projective tasks are employed during initial assessment.

The children are encouraged to tell stories in response to projective pictures that typically evoke themes of parental conflict, divorce and troubled parent-child relationships. They are also invited to complete sentences in a story about a child whose parents are divorcing and having disagreements. Finally, each parent and child are seen in a structured observation session in which they are asked to "draw a picture of your family together." Each of these tests are modifications of the Divorce Specific Assessments devised by Huntington (1985). A rapid clinical assessment of the child's developmental level and ego organization is made which will suggest what he can tolerate in the way of direct talk and play about the family situation. We believe that it is important to respect the child's defenses (often manifested in avoidance and denial) by timing the interventions and intervening in ways that are not overwhelming. We also consider what parents can tolerate in terms of changes in their child and do not encourage children to take a stance that might result in their being punished, rejected, or otherwise placed in an untenable situation. For example, although we might sympathize that it is hurtful to hear their father talk disparingly about their mother, we confirm it may not be wise to contradict or criticize their father for doing so.

Following the initial assessment sessions with the child and each parent, an intervention strategy is formulated. In selecting interventions, we are mindful of the constraints of time and the children's and parent's defensive capacities. The overall goal is to help the children obtain psychological distance from the dispute, maintain good relations with each parent, and consequently resume their own growth and development. There are three subgoals: first, to provide the children an age-appropriate explanation of the custody and access arrangements, the status of the divorce and issues of parental conflict; second, to help the children express their own concerns, differentiate among their own troubled feelings, and separate their ideas, feelings and needs from those of their parents; and third, to teach the children coping and survival skills in the event that their parents continue to dispute.

Many children, especially the younger ones, are extremely confused about the facts surrounding the divorce and dispute and have been unable to make sense of what is going on. Some have been given conflicting confusing accounts from each parent; for others the cognitive unclarity is a function of their own avoidance and denial (they do not want to know). Since cognitive mastery sometimes helps emotional mastery and coping, they are helped to understand the facts and distinguish their fears and fantasies. The child's accurate perception of reality is validated. Beginning with direct questions of what they were told about the divorce and issues under dispute, what they saw and overheard, and what they concluded, the therapist tries to promote their intellectual grasp of the problem and then helps de-mystify the situation. This may mean explaining in simple concrete terms where each parent is living and the current visitation and custody schedule. If these are court ordered, we tell the child the judge thinks this is the best temporary plan until the parents can decide together on a better one. If the living arrangements are in flux and there is no clear plan, we try to give a timetable for when one will be formed and how. We explain our role as mediators in helping the parents make the best possible arrangement jointly. To counter the children's often-assumed burden of having to choose between par-ents, we explain that while we want to understand their own ideas and feelings, the decisions are ultimately their parents' responsibility to make, and if parents cannot agree with the help of the mediator, the judge may have to decide.

Other misconceptions the children may have are gently corrected: for example, that it is unfair for one parent to make a unilateral decision to cut off visits to their other parent, or that mother can get a divorce even if father does not want it. In age-appropriate terms, we help the child develop a positive or nonblaming explanation for why the divorce occurred ("Your parents fight over everything and are not happy living with each other anymore"). At the same time, we clarify that they are not to blame for the divorce or the disputes ("It's not your fault that they fight about you"). We try to offer this information in a simple, factual manner, maintaining a neutral or non-judgmen-tal stance to each parent's position. In sum, the goal is to provide children the security of a cognitive map of the divorce and dispute and some simple guidelines of how we proceed to resolve disagree-ments.

A more important objective here is to demonstrate how they are being placed in an intolerable situation and to show them what are appropriate roles for adults and children in families. Where parents make contradictory demands, the therapist can point to the conflicts they create ("If you cut your hair like your father wants, you cannot please your mother, who likes long hair. No matter what you do, you will displease one parent.") When a child feels blamed for the other parent's actions, we may question their assumption of responsibility ("So your mom took you to the doctor when your dad said you were supposed to go to your swimming lesson! What's a kid to do? Kids can't tell mothers what to do!") When a child is made to feel responsi-ble for a parent's well-being, we might gently point out the responsi-bility is not theirs ("When your dad cries, you feel it is your job to make him happy again. Your dad has been sad for a long time and he has to work out his own problems. It's nice of you to be concerned but you're only nine years old! Kids can't fix grown-ups problems!") Or when a parent makes unreasonable demands or has angry infantile outbursts, we may, with sympathy, become offended on their behalf: ("It's not fair to girls for a mommy to scream and cry like that! You thought it was your fault!") Since we do not wish to tarnish the child's good image of the parent, it is often important to emphasize the situational nature of the parent's behavior and provide some hope where appropriate ("Your dad has been working hard and is very tired." "It seems like your mom blows up, but then she calms down. . . . That's probably just her way.").

As we have documented, for many children the legacy of prolonged or intense parental fights is high anxiety, confusion, emotional constriction and difficulty in distinguishing their own ideas, needs, and emotions as separate from those of their angry parents. For this reason, a major goal of intervention is to help the child become aware of, differentiate, and identify the confusing morass of emotions they experience, which includes feelings of fear, anger, sadness, worry, relief, shame, and guilt. There are a number of techniques to help a constricted child express feelings. The therapist can model and label expectable emotional responses when the child talks about distressful events ("That's unfair, outrageous!" "That makes me mad or sad"); by suggesting a number of ways other children have felt in similar situations ("Some kids feel bad/guilty when . . . , others just get mad"); by further questioning ("Were you confused/ happy/ relieved/sad about that?"); or by confronting the child ("You want to change the subject when we talk about things that make you scared"). While identifying feelings often helps children understand themselves and hence forges self-identity, they also can become overwhelmed and frightened by the recognition of, and may need help in containing, intense emotion. This can sometimes be done by structuring their play or changing the topic of conversation. At times we respect their wishes not to talk, to deny feelings, and to close off their inner world. Indeed, these may be the only ways they can assert their separateness, privateness, and some control in the situation. Prescribing "keeping things to yourself" for constricted children may help put their withdrawal under more conscious control and gives them permission to draw and develop personal boundaries. We continually evaluate the wisdom of conscious expression of emotion, and, in fact, have found that indirectly acting out feelings and conflicts in fantasy play is usually far more tolerable for the child.

It is possible to carefully disentangle feelings from those of their

angry, demanding, or needy parents by the counselor evoking repeated distinctions between how the child may feel differently, or the
same, as each parent ("That's what your dad says, how does it look to
you?" Do you think the same as your mom about everything?"). The
unique, individual identity of each child is gently encouraged by
naming and affirming their special and different qualities. For the
preschoolers, this may involve simply making physical distinctions
("You have brown hair, mommy has blond hair, and daddy has black
hair") or identifying their possessions. (One small boy worried
whether his lunch box belonged to his mother or his father. This
began a discussion of what belonged to him, which broadened to
include his feelings.) For older children it includes helping them recognize more enduring personality attributes—of themselves, their
siblings, and parents ("You are quiet and thougtful, your sister is
mischievous, your dad has a quick temper, your mom's feelings get
hurt easily"). In some older children we try to foster their voicing
their individuality, "You are not treating me as me! I don't feel that
way!"

Since many of these children are having difficulty identifying with
a "rejected, demeaned" parent but on the other hand anxiously incorporate or identify with the "righteously angry" parent, special
attention is given to helping them choose among the different qualities of both parents those aspects they admire and respect and want
to emulate. In this way their capacity to unambivalently identify
with aspects of both parents is potentially salvaged from the parental
battle. The counselor-mediator may be one of the few people, if not
the only person, who can maintain a positive relationship with both
parents. He or she can be valuable, then, as a model, showing the
child that it is possible not only not to choose between, but to relate
to, appreciate, and indeed love both parents.

Based on a realistic acknowledgment that many of their parents
will continue to dispute and make emotional demands for their allegiance and support, the goal becomes teaching these children active
coping and adaptive survival skills, skills that do not compromise
their self-integrity, social and moral development, or relationship
with both parents. Foremost, we offer each child explicit permission
to withdraw strategically from the parental conflict, assuring them it
is not their fight, and they are not to blame. While it is important to
affirm their loving empathy and concern for a parent, or their own
outrage at injustice, thus supporting the children's moral development, they are gently reminded that it is not their responsibility to
solve their parent's problems, to maintain the peace, or to be caretaker of their parent's feelings. Their job is to be children and this

means to play, to go to school, to have their own friends, and to take good care of their own business. We strongly empathize with how difficult if is "for a kid to be worried by these things, but that it is not really fair to them" ("Being a six-year-old is a full-time job. You can't do a grown-up's job when you're only six!") Their fantasies of omnipotence may be gently challenged by asking whether their attempts to make their parents stop fighting and get along better make any difference. They generally acknowledge sadly that it does not help. The counselor agrees and notes, in some cases, that neither they, the attorneys, the mediator, the judge, nor all the king's horses and all the king's men can put Humpty Dumpty back together again.

The children are then encouraged to explore specific problem-solving skills that will work: for instance, how to withdraw to one's room, how to keep one's own counsel and remember one's own views, who are safe people in whom to confide, how to avoid lying to protect a parent or oneself, how not to be a messenger or conveyer of parents' angry messages, diplomatic answers to prying questions, and how to negotiate on one's own behalf. A number of these children can be very frightened, even immobilized, by the intensity of a parent's anger and they need ways of coping with these outbursts and maintaining a psychological distance. Seven-year-old Stanley was told to watch the clock and time how long it took his mother to calm after a fight with his father. The following week he reported firmly and clearly "it took just twenty minutes!" Twelve-year-old Frank was told to make notes on his parents' exchanges with one another. He arrived at the next session with a full written report and for the first time could comment with some critical perspective on the "dumb arguments they have!"

As the child begins to feel and act differently, we try to alert parents and help make them more responsive to the nascent changes. In separate or joint interviews, parents are told that in the past their children have kept feelings hidden and now might become more irritable, challenging, and demanding. We suggest it is important for them to see these changes not as manipulations, the voice of the ex-mate, or as silly childish demands; rather, as the children's tests to see if they can be separate persons and if parents can make their needs a priority. For these reasons, parents are encouraged to be more reassuring, tolerant, and gratifying of these needs if possible. Additionally, parents are told how their children feel excessively responsible for their well-being as well as for managing the fight, and they are asked to reassure the children—that, as adults, they can take care of themselves. While some parents are responsive to these insights and pleased by the children's changes, others can become threatened by the child's withdrawal of support and by the child's attachment not only to the other parent but to the therapist. There is a danger the child can be severely punished or at least withdrawn from treatment. For these reasons, with some children, a very minimal intervention, affirming their accurate perception of the difficult situation and reinforcing their adaptive coping, may be all that can be achieved. We had profound concern for a number of these children whose parents could not tolerate the intervention and we were left feeling helpless in reaching and supporting them. Insisting on treatment risks placing some children in further jeopardy, so instead we try to leave open the possibility for intermittent supportive contact.

The majority of these interventions are effected, not through verbal counseling with the child, but indirectly and metaphorically through the play sessions. Many children become highly anxious or defensive if there is direct discussion of their family relationships. A well-furnished playroom is important in both establishing a rapid working alliance with the children and facilitating their engagement in the counseling process. A variety of projective play mediums are made available: dolls' houses, puppets, sand tray and miniature animals, painting and drawing materials, building blocks, and a variety of games. Each may be used in different ways.

Standard equipment in divorce-related work are too dolls' houses with families of dolls, representing appropriate ethnic groups. Household furniture, cars, and trucks are necessary accompaniments. The younger children are drawn to these play materials and spend considerable time trying to organize the furniture and families in the houses, feeding, bathing, toileting, and sleeping the dolls. A symbolic ordering of their world is evident when they can successfully do this. Dolls' houses are most useful in interventions by the counselor to help the child cognitively grasp the reality of the divorce, the facts that parents are living apart and children and possessions go back and forth between the two homes. Doll-house vignettes also help children bring to the surface their fears and aggressive and dependent wishes, affording the opportunity to label problematic areas and simultaneously suggest more effective ways of dealing with their conflicts. For example, children who are otherwise markedly good, compliant, responsible and pseudo mature may resort to sucking the baby's bottle and gobbling the dolls' food, placing baby dolls in dangerous positions on the roof or throwing the mother doll down the stairs. The therapist may comment: "The children are very thirsty and hungry. Let's see how they can ask for more food"; "No one is watching the baby and she is going to fall. Let's find Grandma or the babysitter"; "The boy doll is really mad at the mom today. Let's ask him why he is so mad."

An array of puppets, which include Muppet-like characters, policemen, doctors, nurses, and judges are also useful for the preschoolers. The counselor uses these to help differentiate the concerns and confusing feelings the children may have. One puppet, named Mouse, lives in the counselor's apron pocket and periodically emerges to talk with the children about problems he has for example, separating from his mommy to visit his daddy. Though he typically clings to his security blanket, he bravely talks about mastery of his many fears and demonstrates proudly how he has learned to dial the telephone to talk to his mother. Mouse also talks to the children about his wish to be very good but how he sometimes finds himself being naughty, symbolized by a little devil puppet who pops out from inside him. The children are encouraged to help Mouse figure exactly when the devil comes out (such as when his dad ignores him or when his mommy yells at his dad). Mouse learns more about the little devil, inside himself who becomes less mischievous and angry, and finally the two are integrated, which allows Mouse a greater range of feelings than he has previously shown. Mouse becomes the children's confidante in the group sessions. He offers a standing invitation to share any of their special worries and it is not uncommon for a child to ask to speak to him from time to time. For example, Mouse has been told how visits were frightening for one child whose parent exercised poor judgment by leaving her with strangers and allowing her to watch horror movies. Mouse advised her to tell her mom when she was scared and not wait till she got home to tell her dad. The older children occasionally produce their own puppet plays, vividly portraying scenes of marriage, divorce, and reconciliation. Problem-solving skills are prompted or demonstrated. For example, a tiny puppet may cover his eyes and ears when there is an argument, or may call the neighbor or the police for help if there is physical violence between the puppets. In one remarkable play, the child had the counselor act out the parents' struggle as she refereed the fight. She directed the puppets with considerable insight and managerial skill on how to stop the fight ("Talk nicely! Let that pass! Give her an apple!"). The therapist then sought to clarify the child's wish not to be burdened by her family and her hopes that her parents would take care of themselves and be civil to each other.

Many children, however, find these dolls and puppets too realistic and hence too anxiety-provoking for projective play. Instead we found the sand tray, with its array of small domestic and wild animals, fences, and occasional monsters, was a more useful medium for the expression of the child's fears and fantasies. For many such emotionally inhibited and traumatized children, the tiny miniatures were able to be manipulated and controlled. At the same time, many issues can be vividly portrayed in sandbox scenarios, the children's central fears, sense of boundaries, perception of safe places and safe people, typical defenses and problem-solving endeavors, and their views of the family dynamics. In some cases the sandbox becomes a jungle where wild animals roamed and small lambs and chicks were helplessly at their mercy. More commonly, the sandbox is a battlefield with war toys (armies of miniature soldiers, heavily armed guards, tanks and assorted weaponry) used to play out, over and over again, an unending war in which everyone was annihilated or only the clever trickster survived. In general, we find it counterproductive to interpret directly the symbolic meaning of the children's sandbox play. Instead, remaining within the metaphor of the fantasy, the counselor gently probes to discuss the animals' feelings and fears, helps the child contain overwhelming destructive outbursts among the animals, puts boundaries or fences around the wild, devouring beasts that threaten the more vulnerable animals, and in general explore new ways of mastering the conflicts and dilemmas that are portrayed.

Drawing and painting are selected as preferred activities by a number of children. Sometimes this represents accommodating, safe responses by anxious children, especially girls who painstakingly draw flowers and rainbows as gifts for their parents. For others, it clearly communicates the child's perception of family relationships, as they draw their parents with angry red or sad, subdued faces separated by thick black lines, and helpless children without hands and feet. Several boys expressed abysmal depression, anger, and helplessness or primitive fantasies of bloody, gory battles and dismemberment in their artwork. The therapist sketched cartoons picturing for the younger child the schedule of visits and the activities of each parent and child. For the older child, the network of disputing relations, including extended kin, are diagramed, showing the child at the center, thus graphically portraying their loyalty conflict and vulnerability. More elaborate books are developed by the counselor and child to take home. These contain stories (similar to those proposed by Gardner, 1976) that use metaphor to reflect the family impasse and suggest coping strategies for the child.

When children have difficulty in engaging in fantasy play, they turn to less anxiety-provoking mediums—building forts or safe retreats large enough to contain themselves with blocks and other construction materials, or to play with board games in which the rules are explicitly defined. The therapist may devise other problem-solving board games. In one of ours, the task is to proceed between family homes along paths with the roll of a dice. As they progress, the children acquire coping cards (developed with the counselor) that can be used when they land on "tight spots" (family dilemmas that a child is currently experiencing). It is also important to leave clear an area of the playroom for bouncing balls, target throwing and bag punching for those occasions when children need to release anxiety in a more diffusely active manner.

The following three cases illustrate these interventions. (Although each case involved a family intervention, with parents and children seen separately and conjointly in counseling and mediation sessions, only the direct work with the children will be reported here.)

COLLETTE, FIVE YEARS OLD

Collette was a diminutive, pretty five-year-old girl of mixed Asian and Latin origin. She generally presented as a shy, withdrawn, timid, and traumatized child, afraid of doing something wrong and of being rejected. There was a sad patience to her demeanor as she waited to be noticed, waited for adults to respond to her, and waited for her mother to pick her up after her interview. The child was extremely small and slight for her age and it was reported that she ate very poorly and had not gained weight for more than a year. At school she was somewhat lost in a large class of children, in which she made no demands and was very obedient. However, although she was obviously of above-average intelligence, she was not progressing very well and her teacher recommended that she repeat kindergarten. With peers she tended to manage by being quite passive and following along after the other children. With her mother she was rather dependent, tending at times to be whiney, irritable, and babyish. She was often anxious about her mother's whereabouts but did not cling. She lit up with anxious joy when she saw her father and was extremely solicitous about his welfare.

One month before the beginning of counseling, Collette's young mother left the home precipitously after she finally found the courage to rouse herself out of chronic depression and end her marriage to a violent, jealously controlling, and dependent husband. These young parents had met in high school and pregnancy precipitated their marriage. The father had never worked but depended on his wife to provide for the family financially. The couple continued to live with the maternal grandparents. Collette's retired grandfather had cared for her while her mother worked until he died suddenly when the child was three years old. After that, her father and various other relatives cared for her until she began school. The grandmother worked and was the primary homemaker for the extended family.

Although he had liaisons himself, often disappearing for days at a time with other women, the young man jealously guarded his wife's fidelity. She recounted numerous instances when, after drinking, he bullied and threatened her, destroyed furniture, trashed the home, and followed her when she shopped or went to work. The police were called several times to disarm him and quell his violence. One night she woke in terror to find him sitting on the floor by her bed, holding a gun and talking softly, saying he was sorry for the trouble he had caused, but that she would never have to worry again because she was going to have a long sleep, and that he and Collette would really miss her. She managed to distract him and escape on that occasion. The child had been witness to many of these violent scenes, had often awakened in the night by the sounds of her father's rages, had seen the telephone ripped out and the police arrive to help.

In response to his wife's desertion, this man was distraught and alternated childlike pleas for her to return with bribes of expensive presents, promises that he would change, and ominous threats of murder and suicide if she did not comply with his wishes. His view of her constantly shifted: Sometimes she was his beautiful, good, and wonderful wife-mother; at other times she was the selfish, unfaithful wife who had betrayed him. Serious violence was a frightening possibility given that he carried a gun and was drinking very heavily. At one point, he made inquiries with coworkers about the layout of the department store where his wife worked. It was very much feared that he was plotting a hostage situation.

For a week after the separation, the father kept his child home from school to keep him company, to comfort him. Later he lavished gifts, bribes, and promises of great outings on her but then failed to turn up for the scheduled visits. When the mother would refuse to talk with him, he would tearfully tell the child good-bye, that he would never see her again, but then return the next day to renew his pleadings. If the mother left the child with the grandmother, he took Collette, claiming she had been deserted, but then left her with his own relatives for care. The child was constantly asked to plead the father's case with the mother: "Ask her where do you belong?" "Tell her we love her and want her back!" Collette tried to reconcile her parents. She whispered to her mother not to argue with him, she tried to have her mother kiss her father, and she told them she wanted them to live together in one house. When her father cried and left, she too was inconsolable.

The child's insecurity about her mother had a strong reality basis. Not only was she fearful for her mother's physical safety, but she was afraid of being abandoned by her. When the young wife left the home, Collette had been left with her father as an offering of guilty compensation. It took court intervention to reestablish the mother as primary caretaker. Moreover, this young woman began experimenting with her newfound freedom from the tyrannical marriage. She left the child with relatives more often and began socializing with friends. Occasionally she stayed out all night. Because she was conflicted, both guilty and resentful about her maternal responsibilities, she could not even telephone to say when she would return. In addition, Collette received no explanation for what was happening. Her mother was at a loss to explain the divorce, the father's pleadings, and the fights she and her separated husband were having daily. She felt that in order to protect the child, it was best to deny her own emotional distress and withhold any discussion of her intention to proceed with the divorce.

In the initial assessment session, Collette's demeanor was very quiet and inhibited, and she was anxious but obedient about separating from her mother. Although she clearly reported with whom she was presently living, she did not seem to understand what divorce meant and was confused as to whether her parents were separated. She listened quietly to the counselor's explanation of the facts and then, after much encouragement, shyly approached the toys. Very gradually she began to engage in wordless fantasy play. Ignoring one dolls' house, she set up the other, placing the girl doll in the middle of the living room and the grandparents together on one sofa and the parents together on the other sofa, all surrounding the little girl. Other children and adults were placed in other rooms. The counselor commented that this was, perhaps, how Collette wanted things to be: her mommy, daddy, grandma, and grandpa all together and her safe in the middle. She nodded quickly and brightened. The counselor then talked about the reality of her family situation, that Daddy and Mommy were getting a divorce. Did she remember what that was? Collette looked puzzled and said she could not remember what a divorce was. This was explained again. The counselor continued to talk about her reality, in particular the fact that her grandfather had died and could not be with them any more, and suggested that Collette set up the dolls' house like it really was at home. She quietly identified the dolls as various family members, and took father doll away and placed him in another house where he was subsequently forgotten for the remainder of the session. The grandfather was placed on the roof and she noted that he was now in heaven. The little girl doll was placed with the mother in the house of her uncle, aunt, and cousins. The grandmother was left alone. (This accurately reflected her present living situation.) Collette then that suggested the whole family was going to have a picnic in the park (the sandbox).

For a time she had the girl doll sitting on her mother's lap, surrounded by other relatives. Then she took the grandfather and buried him in the sand. The girl doll and cousins dug in the sand together and discovered the dead grandfather, who woke up. All the family members crowded around to see the resurrection, and with much rejoicing returned to their own homes. At the end of this scene, the counselor talked with Collette about how much she wished this could happen, and then the sad reality that it could not happen. The child soberly agreed and ended the session by building fences around the farm animals in the sandbox.

During the next two sessions the child remained very quiet and constricted in her play. The mother reported in a separate session that the father had on several occasions been very threatening and the police had to be called to remove him from the house. In response, Collette seemed to be quite lethargic and withdrawn. In the session, she only sifted sand through her fingers. Although she seemed pleased about coming and readily, almost obediently began to play, she anxiously enquired when her mother would arrive. When she did play, there was a repetitive theme of little chicks being placed together in various dangerous places. The counselor identified the chicks as being the children and she readily agreed. She then took a policeman on the motor bike and had him circle the group of little chicks. The counselor commented that the policeman seemed to be protecting the children and she agreed. When asked which chick was her, she pointed to the tiniest and meakest, which was lined up behind another larger chick and flanked by a line of others. The counselor noted that the chicks were all alone and asked the whereabouts of their parents. Casting aside the hen and rooster, Collette took two other chicks and placed them on a precarious ledge, suggesting that they were going to fall off. The counselor interpreted this: "These are like your parents and you are very worried about them; and scared something may happen to them." The child nodded in very ready agreement, seeming pleased to be understood. The counselor explained that her Daddy was very sad and mad about the divorce and that the police were helping him control his feelings. The police and her mother were protecting her. The counselor then again inquired gently about the divorce. Collette continued to have difficulty remembering what it meant. She reported that her daddy wanted Mommy to come back to be with him. The counselor asked about her attempts to get her parents back together, to have them kiss and make up. She looked surprised and asked "How do you know about that?" The counselor explained that she saw both her mommy and daddy and they told her these things. The child was then asked if she thought her mother wanted to go back and live with

Daddy and she conceded she did not. This was affirmed and when the reason for the divorce was discussed, Collette remembered that her mother and father had terrible fights. Then she was asked what she wanted, and she clearly answered that she wanted them to be together again. The counselor acknowledged that she wanted this very much and that this made her feel sad. Perhaps she felt mad at her mommy too? Collette denied any angry feelings. The counselor then asked if she thought she could bring her parents together again? She sighed and said she did not think so. Gently, the counselor confirmed that she could not do this but that both her parents loved her and she would continue to live with her mother and visit her father on weekends.

From this time on, Collette no longer denied the reality of the divorce nor took responsibility for trying to reconcile her parents. However, she remained confused about events in her life and anxious about connecting to her mother. Her mother continued to find it difficult to understand, communicate with, and support the child. For this reason the last two sessions were spent with the mother and child together, in order to demonstrate for the mother ways of relating to the child's fears. The strategy was also to give the child an age-appropriate explanation of the current fights between the parents. This was done in a manner not to demean the father but to recognize his problems and limitations, including his anger, impulsiveness, and refusal to accept the finality of the separation. This constituted reality-testing for the child in the presence of the mother. There was an immediate improvement in the child's affective state when this was done. She became more alert, alive, and assertive in the sessions and obviously loved having these discussions with both the counselor and the mother together. The nature of her play immediately shifted. The new theme was to have all the dolls in one house. The mother and father dolls sat together, with the children around them and other relatives nearby. Then a small green devil arrived to terrorize them by banging on the door of the house and screaming to be let in. This was very evidently a symbolic account of the fights that had occurred in the previous weeks when the father had come to the house drunk, banged on the door and roared to be admitted. The counselor interpreted the scene to mother and child saying that Collette wished that the "nice, gentle" daddy could be at home with Mommy but that she became scared when the "angry" daddy banged at the door. Collette was pleased with this commentary. After this, she often introduced the devil figure and had many policemen and soldiers on guard so that the family members were safe. At the conclusion of the intervention, the child no longer fretted about a reunion of her parents and accepted the fact that her parents could not be together without a great deal of dreadful fighting. The mother was able to talk more directly to the child about what was happening and provided her with more security by consistently protecting herself against the father, and staying within the confines of the visitation plan.

Two years later, at the follow-up, Collette continued to be a quiet, gentle child, but happier and more confident. She had greatly benefited from her father relinquishing the fantasy of reconciliation with the mother and his fairly consistent involvement with her as a visiting parent. She had begun to gain weight again, was progressing well at school, and seemed happier and more assertive with her peers. Most importantly, she expressed considerable confidence that her mother, as well as her grandmother, would be there to take care of her.

TERRY, SEVEN YEARS OLD

Terry, an only child, had been the subject of post-divorce disputes over his custody and care for the past three years, this being the duration of his parents' separation from one another. These parents were extremely hostile and depreciating of one another. Their style of fighting involved the father threatening and bullying to get what he considered best for the child and the mother, who refused to be intimidated, blatantly disregarding his wishes. On several occasions this led to violent physical struggles between them, which the child witnessed. Most times they simply blocked and sabotaged each other's activities with the child. When the father signed Terry up for Boy Scouts, the mother withheld his uniform; when the mother allowed the child to ride in her car without seatbelt, the father slashed her tires; when he planned to take Terry for a weekend camping, the mother arranged an outing to the amusement park. The parents were also in continual dispute about the amount of time Terry should spend with each of them. The one issue on which they did agree was that the boy had some anxiety about attending school and problematic relationships with his peers in that he was either a loner or tended to bully other children. He was also both afraid of and negative toward his teacher.

Terry was a sturdy, dark-eyed boy with tense, pressured speech and rigid body movements. During the initial assessment interview he was quite guarded and extremely watchful, to the point of vigilance. He was rather anxious about separating from his father and tended to repeat many of his father's scornful derogatory remarks about the mother. However, he also showed a guilty, ambivalent attachment to her and was obviously concerned about her safety. He found it difficult to talk about the family situation but assented eagerly when invited to play.

Terry carefully sorted all the soldiers, guards, and Indians and set up two sides of a war. For himself he chose all the soldiers with guns firing aggressively, and he gave the counselor the guards who were less well armed. When all the toy soldiers were lined up in perfect symmetry, facing each other, he announced that the war would begin. He insisted that the counselor destroy all of his army, which she did reluctantly. However, when her back was turned, he had hidden all the Indians behind her line of defense. With much gratification he completed the play by having the Indians swoop down and destroy her army, leaving him the victor.

At the following session, Terry immediately selected the fighting soldiers and distributed the guards to the counselor, announcing there would be a major confrontation. He impatiently dispensed with the counselor's suggestion of building a fort, saying they wanted to "fight head on." Again the armies were lined up, perfectly symmetrical. The counselor intervened and asked him why the two armies were fighting. He answered tersely that they both wanted the land. The counselor observed that if they fought they would mostly all end up dead and asked if there was a better way to solve it? Terry sat back a moment and answered dubiously, "They could cut the land in half."

The counselor moved out of the symbolism of the play at this point with an interpretation, "But Terry, you are not a piece of land, you're a person. Your parents can't cut you in half." The boy paused and reflected. The counselor selected a guard from the ranks and talked about how one of these could be a mediator and help the two opposing armies work out an agreement. She interpreted this as being her role with his parents. The war was resumed with a renewed offensive between the two battalions, but this time the boy stopped the destruction with the comment, "This is no good. Everyone's going to get killed. They'll just have to divide the land." He placed a dinosaur as a guard between the two opposing groups of soldiers and built a wall of solid blocks between the two armies. The counselor commented how they were all much safer when they had a wall between them. Terry answered with sudden insight, "This gives me a good idea. We could build a wall between my parents, so they cannot fight. Their anger is like bullets, they shoot their anger. It can kill. They can have a working-out fight but not a fight with angry bullets." Having said this, the child gathered the toy soldiers and put them away.

Although Terry seemed to have achieved some cognitive understanding of his parents' fight and was trying to figure a way out of their dilemma, his insightful comments were, in part, an intelligent response to the counselor's direct interpretations. They were not reflective of his real feelings. On a less conscious level, he was filled with fears about violence and annihilation that he attempted to master with trickery and counterviolence.

For the rest of the hour, he engaged the counselor in play that expressed this theme. He armed himself and the counselor with weapons and set up confrontations with the counselor, who was viewed as dangerous and unpredictable. However, the child invariably devised a master plan that would trick and annihilate the dangerous other. The counselor was alarmed by the intensity of Terry's involvement in this violent fantasy and the sadistic intent of the players. It was obviously difficult for the child to return to reality at the end of the session. He left extremely agitated.

It was evident from these assessment sessions that while Terry had some capacity to utilize the counselor's interventions, he became easily immersed in fantasies of overwhelming aggression, which both excited and frightened him. He viewed the world as an unsafe place in which one has be a trickster or meaner and tougher than everyone else to survive. His sense of fair play had been greatly undermined, if it had ever existed in the first place. The child had begun to identify with the more aggressive aspects of his father and use the deceptive conflict tactics of both parents. During the next four sessions, the counselor elected to intervene using the metaphor of his play because this more adequately addressed his fears and the child continued to be defensive about discussing his family situation directly. Terry's cognitive capacities were engaged in a search for more rational and just ways of resolving conflicts of interest. The strategy was to encourage problem-solving techniques that were nonviolent and based on understanding and empathy with the disputing parties. Consequently, the quality of Terry's play gradually shifted over the brief intervention period.

As in the previous sessions, at first his play consisted solely of armies having direct confrontations with one another, with much violent killing and maiming if the opponent so much as expressed a wish or feeling contrary to his soldiers' preferences. His soldiers were always heavily armed and vigilant least they be tricked and overcome by unknown enemies. The guards were always assigned to the counselor. To begin, the counselor had the guards make overtures of friendship to his armed battalion, expressing loyalty and cooperation. (This was the metaphor for the offer of a therapeutic alliance). Gradually his army began to depend a little on the guards in order to "give his guys a rest." Sometimes they even took time out to have a party, go to the beach and play, or they slept while the counselor's guards stood by to watch out for enemies.

However, for the child, tricksters and enemies always lurked in the background ready to attack, and his soldiers were always prepared to attack and annihilate them first. The counselor set up dialogues between his soldiers and the enemies, suggesting a stay of execution "until we can find out more about their problems." (This represented metaphorically the need for clarification and exploration of the disputed issues.) Consequently, sometimes the enemies were "talked out of their wicked plans." Gradually Terry armed his soldiers with laughing gas, sleeping gas, and blanks rather than bullets. The counselor then helped him institute a policy of capturing the enemy and taking them before a judge and jury, where justice was done. Terry began to develop very positive feelings toward the judge (a grandfather doll), to whom he referred as a "very civilized man." He respected the fact that the judge would always be fair and just. Finally, he began to send his enemies to prison, or to parole them on their promise of good behavior, rather than kill them on the spot. Terry and the counselor talked together about the reasons for the fights and arguments between two opposing groups and brainstormed about different ways of compromising or solving their problems. Toward the end of this period, Terry began using far fewer soldiers and readily assigned armed ones to the counselor and accepted the guards for himself. There was much less angry intensity about his play, and he could be quite diverted by plots that were problematic but nonviolent. (From this it appeared that the child's problem-solving skills had been increased and that he was able to identify with a number of different roles in the dramas, including soldiers, guards, mediators, and the judge).

By this time, the parents had reached a mediated agreement and were no longer in active conflict with each other. They reported that the child was far more relaxed and happy with them both and was getting on better with his peers. To complete the intervention, the parents were included (separately) in the child's final play sessions in order to return to them the responsibility for nurturing the child's social and moral development. First the father and Terry were seen together, and the father was encouraged to play the fantasy games with the purpose of helping the child with his problem-solving skills. This was restitutive for the father, who needed to attend to his own limited supply of problem-solving techniques and provide a better model for the child in terms of relating to others. Finally, in the mother's play session with the child, although she readily developed interesting, constructive solutions to the confrontations he posed in his play, she learned that she needed to listen more empathically to the child's ideas and feelings rather than dismissing him as she often did.

It is not easy to assess the extent to which this brief intervention had an impact on this child. We can, however, report that, except for a brief regression (and brief counseling intervention one year later when Terry became aggressive with his peers), this boy maintained satisfactory progress throughout the two-year follow-up period. The fact that his parents maintained a stable coparenting agreement with a modicum of mutual respect was probably a contributing factor.

WILLIAM, TEN YEARS OLD

William was a tall, thin, pale boy of ten who appeared very constricted and depressed during the initial interview. The projective testing revealed that he was turning angry feelings against himself, expressing wishes of hurting himself, and that he wondered if he was somehow responsible for his parents' divorce. He worried about his mother's cold anger and his father's sadness. Since the parents' separation, he had become more withdrawn and seemed to be losing confidence in his ability to relate to peers. What remained was extreme passivity; he depended excessively on his parents for direction and guidance and found it extremely difficult to make decisions, even small ones, for himself. He daydreamed in school.

Neither parent really understood why the marriage had failed except to note that they had both been unhappy for some time. The separation seemed to have been precipitated by the father's retirement. He was twenty-five years older than his wife. He had been a warm, loving man and a strong protective father figure for his wife two decades previously. She had been very quiet, shy, and dependent. What had originally been a good marriage, mutually gratifying their complementary needs, lost its purpose as the younger woman "grew up," became more independent, assertive, and socially involved. He on the other hand, grew older, retired from work and social activities, and preferred to "putter around the house with various hobbies." He seemed more a grandfather than a husband for his wife.

William's parents were not in overt conflict with each other. They simply could not, or refused to, talk with one another. The father was experiencing a great deal of sadness at the loss of his wife and family. She felt guilty but withdrew and was unable to respond to his needs. Petty arguments between them punctuated long periods of oppressive silence. A simple misunderstanding led to a legal custody dispute. Neither parent could talk to William about the separation other than to give him the barest facts that they were getting a divorce.

William was seen in a small group of boys of approximately the same age for four sessions. The purpose of the intervention was to help him express his confused and angry feelings, give him an explanation for the divorce that would relieve him of feeling responsible, and give him permission to love and identify with both parents.

Children of this age, are more reluctant to engage in fantasy play, especially in the presence of their peers, yet they find talking about themselves awkward and embarrassing. For this reason the group sessions are conducted on two levels simultaneously. On one level, the boys are engaged together in active play, which involved simple card games, artwork, bouncing balls, and target throwing. This serves to diffuse a great deal of anxiety and lowers their defensive resistance. On the second level, they are encouraged to share details about themselves, their school, friends, family, the divorce, parental disputes, and future plans. With the boys' agreement, the purpose is to produce a story about each of their lives, which will be made into a small book for the final session. The counselor undertakes to keep notes for their biographies, retaining as much as possible the children's own way of expressing themselves. The boys illustrate the stories with their own artwork and diagram their family tree. Hence, during their play, the boys are asked to recall their earliest memories, happy times with both parents, changes in their lives, things that made them mad or sad, and problems they had with their parents and peers and how they have solved these.

William was initially very inhibited and unable to take the initiative in play although he was obedient and cooperative. He quickly benefited from being with the other boys, who expressed themselves in more physically active and verbal ways. He was a remarkably agile child and was able to take pride in his physical skills. Throughout the four sessions, he became increasingly more active and assertive. At the same time, he was able to express pleasure, relief, and sadness about the different changes in his family. He was pleased by the book that was produced, which documented his own life in the context of his large extended family.

The final intervention involved the counselor presenting William with a special story about a family of lions in Africa. This story was a symbolic account of the reasons for the divorce, a script that would enable him to identify with aspects of both parents, and resume his own life with peers, more free from worry about his parents. In giving William this story, we were assured by the progress that his parents had made in counseling that it was appropriate and would stand him in good stead.

> Far, far away on the great plains of Central Africa, where the sun burns hot and where the wild animals roam free, there lived a magnificent lion. He was strong and powerful and a capable hunter and a fiercely

independent thinker. He was so strong and so swift that he was really not afraid of anyone or anything.

Though he made some mistakes when he was young, over the years he became very wise and felt so strong and confident in himself that he began to take care of the weaker and smaller animals. He lived alone many years, just keeping watch out for his animal neighbors until he met and fell in love with a beautiful young lioness. She was spirited and loving, but a little afraid and really depended on the great lion for protection. Sometime later, their young son was born—a splendid, tough little fun-loving male cub. The great lion enjoyed caring for and protecting his family. He hunted and brought home good food while the mother lioness nursed her baby cub in the den. These were happy times in this family of lions. When the young cub became older, many times in the early hours of the morning before the sun became too hot, the lion family would go on hunting expeditions together. The father would teach his young son to hunt small prey with skill and patience. The mother lioness, though she was more strict and would stand no non-sense, showed him places to play hide-and-go-seek and took him to swimming holes in which to swim with other young cubs.

As the years passed, the magnificant old lion grew older. Though he was still strong, he was quieter and liked to spend more time lying in the sun. He was gentle and wise. He did not have to fight any more to protect his family and provide for them because he was well respected in his territory.

But the beautiful younger lioness mother was not ready to lie in the sun with her mate. She did not feel timid any more and did not need his protection. She wanted to go on hunting expeditions herself, with some of her many lion friends. The great lion and lioness began to squabble and fight between themselves. Sometimes they wrestled with each other, and the lion cub, who was a young teenager at this stage, was either ignored in the hassle or at times was actually bitten in the fray. It was not a particularly happy situation. Gradually the lioness began to spend most of her time living in another den several miles away. The magnificent old lion, with his flowing golden mane, was quite sad and rather lonely but realized it was best.

Now the young male cub was becoming strong and powerful and more independent himself, but he was not ready for his family to split up like this. He liked the family expeditions they used to have. He felt kind of mad with them both for not trying harder to make it work, and then he was kind of sad and lonely at times. When he was with one parent, he missed the other parent. He felt like growling and biting and snarling, but he knew no one would like him if he did that. So instead he sat very still and tried very, very hard to be good. When he felt sad, he tried not to think about it. He did not practice his fighting and hunting so much because he was scared that his real feelings would come out and that he would become too angry and really hurt someone.

The wise old lion, though he knew how his son was feeling, did not say much. Instead he encouraged his young protégé to wrestle and play with other young male cubs a great deal. The lioness was concerned too. She really wanted her young son to get on with his life and not take too much notice of the fight between the parents.

Gradually the young male cub began to do just that. As he grew older, he spent more and more time with other young male lions. and even romped with young lionesses at times. He grew to become even stronger and a better hunter than his father because he learned not only all of his father's courage and hunting skills but also acquired his mother's energy and love of adventure.

William read the story silently and seriously, then closed it up and took a ball to play. A little later, noting that the other boys were having their stories read aloud, he asked the counselor to read his. As she read, William on his own initiative acted out the roles in mime fashion. He took on the character of the courageous powerful lion who was a magnificant hunter. He giggled in a rather embarrassed manner at the part when the lion met the lioness and had a baby cub. He strongly identified with the little lion cub who was angry at the parent's separation and mimed the scratching and biting with exaggerated fury. Toward the end, he acted extremely proud when the little cub became stronger than the father and more adventurous than the mother. William left this final session particularly buoyant. Parents reported later that he had shared the story with them and was talking much more freely to them both. At the two-year follow-up, this boy had completely recovered his developmental stride, supported by parents who had, in this case, completely resolved their impasse and were successfully undertaking a joint custody agreement.

CHAPTER 9

Impasse-Directed Mediation

The overall goal of our approach to mediation is to help families through the divorce transition to a postdivorce structure that is conducive to their own and their children's changing needs. To this end, we not only help resolve parental disputes over children but enhance parents' capacity to parent and coparent and work directly with children to improve their capacity to cope with their parents' postdivorce conflicts. Hence, the mediation effort is essentially child focused. The completion of a custody-visitation agreement is seen as secondary to, and an outward symbol of, the family's restructuring. The content and format of the agreement nonetheless are important, as they must not only stabilize and anchor the parents' present transactions but also provide guidelines for that coparenting necessary to change family arrangements in the future. The mediation is short-term (approximately ten weeks, with follow-up consultations available), confidential, and separate from legal proceedings.

Compared with most mediation models, this one is different because it combines a therapeutic and counseling effort insofar as we address parents' motivation to fight and counsel them on the needs of their children. While many would not consider this mediation, the short-term nature and goal-directed focus of our counseling toward accomplishing a stable family settlement of the divorce issues, are in fact consistent with the nature and focus of mediation. Given our subpopulation's vulnerability to irrationality and repeated conflict, it is essential to provide counseling services aimed specifically at shifting the factors that converge to create their impasse. We recognize that there is a danger in losing this focus and prolonging or complicating the process by doing long-term therapy with the parties. While the need for premediation education, counseling, and therapy for high-conflict families has been acknowledged by a number of mediators, all have emphasized that it should be done in a separate setting, apart from the actual negotiations. We disagree and see counseling and mediation of a settlement for high-conflict families as two phases of one process. The understanding of the impasse, the parents' personality styles and the children's needs, gained in the counseling phase is invaluable for choosing negotiation strategies and building the actual agreement. Moreover, the process is better coordinated and expedited by having the same counselor-mediator in both phases.

Phases of Mediation

At intake, parents are informed of the goals of the service and its expected duration. A stipulation is signed that communications within the service are confidential and hence unavailable for court proceedings, and a sliding-scale fee is assessed. Each parent and child is then seen separately to obtain an account of the present dispute, a history of the marriage and separation, and a developmental sketch of the child with special attention to the child's response to the divorce and dispute. During these information-gathering sessions, three focused clinical questions guide the inquiry: What is the nature of the impasse? What is the impact of not settling on the child? What resources are available within the family and their social network to help resolve the impasse? The impasse schema ensures a full assessment of the multilevels of the dispute and thereby expands the options and resources available for its resolution. Based on this understanding, a working strategy is formulated for intervening in the family. There are three distinct phases in mediation with high-conflict families, each of which will be described more fully:

1. A prenegotiation counseling phase, in which each parent is prepared to mediate by strategically intervening in the impasse, and in which the child's needs are explored and an understanding developed.

2. A negotiation or conflict-resolution phase, in which specific issues are addressed and a set of agreements with respect to coparenting and child care are negotiated.

3. An implementation phase, in which the counselor-mediator is available to help with interpreting, monitoring and modifying agreements and emergency consultations in the event of new or renewed incidence of conflict.

Prenegotiation Counseling Phase

During this phase, each parent is seen individually, in order to emphasize their need to attain psychological separation. The counselor-mediator readies the parent for negotiations by shifting the parental impasse, increasing the parent's awareness of and concern for the child, confronting the parent with the realities of the situation, and then preparing agendas for the negotiation session.

Impasse-Related Strategies

While we attempt to set forth strategies of intervention in a progression, in actuality, given the systemic nature of the conflict, a number of strategies and techniques are used simultaneously, aimed at different levels of the impasse. In general, the counselor-mediator tries to shift the internal psychological dimensions. However, this is often not possible given the character pathology of our clientele. Hence the counselor-mediator must work around the parent's internal and relational difficulties by family counseling, paradoxical injunctions and other interventions aimed at the interpersonal level. Alternatively, the counselor-mediator can circumvent the enmeshed couple and work primarily with their social network.

By labeling, clarifying, and psychodynamically interpreting the concealed emotional issues and conflicts within the parent or between the parent and ex-spouse, child, or significant other, these underlying dynamics may be surfaced, and addressed, hopefully freeing the individual to respond more rationally. For instance, it is directly useful to show better-functioning parents how they are using the custody dispute to forestall painful feelings of loss, to repair an injured self-esteem, or restore a sense of power, and to help them instead to mourn the loss, reconstitute a better self-image, and regain control over their lives in other more appropriate ways. Helping parents sort out divorce-engendered conflicts from earlier unresolved conflicts allows for more reality-based decisions. Having parents identify how and where they become caught by their ex-spouse or child in a negative cycle of interactions (emphasizing that "it takes two to fight" but only one to "unhook"), gives parents insight and more freedom to act differently. Reviewing the events of a traumatic separation and putting together a more positive, forgiving picture of the marital breakup salvages their self-esteem and mitigates their need to construct a negative view of the separating spouse. Confronting parents with their distortions, reviewing the aspects of the other parent and the marriage for which they most yearn, and helping them find these qualities in themselves or in relationships with others aids those who are clinging to idealized views. Once the nature of the internal and interpersonal conflicts are clarified, some parents can acknowledge, understand, and better tolerate their feelings and become better able to realistically appraise and revise their actions. For some, these methods suffice to shift the dynamics of the impasse and return them to a more rational mode.

As explained in chapters 4 and 5, for other, more emotionally disturbed parents, with longer-term and more pervasive conflicts, insight into feelings leads to major ego regressions and explosions. Some parents are unable to look at their internal life or their contribution to problems without feeling exposed, attacked, blamed, and betrayed. Insight-oriented therapeutic interventions are perceived as confrontations and challenges and are defended against with categorical denial, increased rigidity of position, blatant generalizing ("I know what is best"), or projection of total blame or splitting ("I'm the good one"). A concomitant devaluation of the mediation process, a painful disillusionment with the mediator, a collapse of perspective and the working alliance, and perhaps a flight from mediation may ensue. Alternatively, aggressive and dangerous acting out may result. In fact, with these interventions, the parent becomes more resistant and the dispute more embedded. For this group, alternative strategies for intervening, based on an understanding and sensitivity to their particular psychological vulnerability and disturbance is essential. Overall, the aim of these strategies is to shift not the intrapsychic conflict but the parents' attitudes and behavior. Interventions are designed either to alleviate underlying anxieties or to support, shift, and redirect particular defenses in the service of making a better divorce arrangement for the parents and child.

One strategy is to modify the psychological motivation indirectly. For example, with a deeply humiliated father who seeks to reconstitute self-esteem by proving his ex-mate a "bad parent" in court, the counselor-mediator attempts to restore his narcissistic balance by highlighting his special strengths, reassuring him (appropriately) about his parental role, and redirecting him to new sources of approval. As he is more supported and reassured, his need to "win in court" decreases. Likewise, with a parent who is unable to tolerate loss and who hangs onto the spouse via a custody dispute, the counselor-mediator encourages new relationships (thereby replenishing loss) and supports a sense of competence (thereby decreasing fear of being unable to survive). As underlying fears are reduced, so is the need for the presence of the ex-spouse and consequently, the dispute.

In another strategy the parent's defenses are supported, positively connoted, framed, or redirected in the service of making shifts. Hence, defining an angry, embittered, and resentful parent as "making a noble effort to control her feelings" may sometimes support her capacity to do so. Telling a paranoid and deeply shamed man who is stubbornly refusing to cooperate that he is "a very proud man whose pride sometimes gets in the way" and emphasizing that he "does not want to do anything beneath his dignity," obliges him not to respond vengefully to his ex-wife. Telling an individual that his violence and emotional breakdown are time limited and reactive to a very traumatic separation decreases his defensive need to prove himself by having all his demands met immediately. Showing an extremely self-centered or sociopathic woman what is ultimately in her own best interests may modify her inconsiderate behavior.

A third strategy, again while not changing the underlying psychodynamics, provides a rationale or motivation that enhances disputants' willingness to develop and abide by agreements. Asking whether present problem-solving efforts are producing the desired results underscores the futility of their efforts. Demonstrating to a father that his solution to his wife's limiting his visitation (to grab his child and not communicate with the mother) only increases her anxiety and unwillingness to give more access may alter his behavior. Providing a father who is concerned with his financial and emotional survival a cost-effective analysis of his present pursuit of custody in court compared with other methods of resolving the disagreement dissuades him from his former efforts. Showing a mother how her raiding the family home and taking what is "rightfully hers" only increases her adolescent sons' anger towards her, and their alliance with the father, restrains her actions.

Though these strategies sometimes work, some parents may rigidly resist changing their views and behavior. Unable to shift a parent internally (by working through, around, or with the problem), the counselor-mediator attempts to shift the external world. Here the counselor-mediator circumvents the parents' problems by directly intervening with their former mate, their new spouse, or others. For instance, the counselor-mediator, in a neutral, nonjudgmental manner, may help the ex-mate understand the other's special sensitivities and psychodynamics and teach special ways of communicating that avoid triggering disturbed behavior. The ex-spouses of paranoid and potentially violent persons (often out of fear of their mate's reactions, jealousies, and harassment) hide information, which only perpetuates states of panic and fury in their mate. These ex-spouses are cautioned to give very clear, direct information, to allow the other time to think through plans, set realistic, rational limits, and to avoid any concealment that would suggest conspiracy. The ex-spouses of obsessive-compulsive persons are shown that their changing plans suddenly is very disruptive and can provoke a breakdown into uncontrollably angry reactions. Overall, this strategy helps them develop a critical distance from their situation. In using this intervention, great care needs to be taken not to negatively label the other parent as "emotionally disturbed" and hence reduce all problems to the psychopathology of the other. Rather, emphasis is upon the more reflective parent taking more responsibility (for oneself and one's children) by not provoking the other parent's vulnerabilities.

Finally, in recognizing that others (new partners, grandparents, mental health professionals, and attorneys) can either provoke and escalate parental disputes and hinder or sabotage agreements, or on the other hand, smooth conflict, facilitate negotiations, and stabilize and support an emotionally upset parent, these others need to be strategically involved in the mediation where indicated and become parties to agreements reached (see chapter 2).

Strategies for Increasing Parental Concern for the Child

Interventions with parents are two-pronged. At the same time, the counselor-mediator works with the impasse, he or she increases parents' understanding of their child and helps them extricate the child from their impasse. In general, depending on the parents' response, there is a progression from sensitizing parents to their child's needs, to specific counseling, and to strong advocacy as the mediation progresses.

Initially, the mediator heightens the parents' awareness and sensitivity to the child's experience and needs by asking many questions about their child's reactions to the divorce, the dispute, and the meaning of each parent to the child. As counseling progresses, the counselor-mediator concretely and clearly demonstrates the often hurtful effects of their disputes on the child. This feedback is provided via interpretations of the child's emotions and behavior or, with the child's permission, via the child's artwork. The firsthand knowledge of the child gained from the play sessions allows the counselor-mediator to speak with authenticity with regard to the child's specific needs and often has a strong impact on parents. While care must be taken not to make parents feel too discouraged or guilty, the counselor-mediator highlights the child's perspective, the risks to the child's development, and the pain inflicted on the child by their fights or refusal to settle. A thorough understanding of the impact of disputes on children is therefore essential. In addition, the counselor-mediator provides guidance and education on how to handle the child, how to shield or remove the child from the parental dispute, and how to ease the child's transitions from one parent to the other. Hence, the counselor-mediator points out to polarized parents the actual and potential effects of their inconsistent handling on the child's self-integrity. Showing parents that their actions are potentially destroying their own relationship with the child is also useful.

Despite these efforts to raise and then use their concern for the child as leverage for change, some parents remain unresponsive and a stronger advocacy role is taken. Here the counselor-mediator confronts the parents with specific examples of the child's suffering. In one case, showing parents how their child was preoccupied with disturbing, violent fantasies led to a cessation of their own violent interactions with each other. In two families in which children had been kidnapped and secreted from the other parent, strongly confronting the parents with the legacy of their actions (highly distressed, confused children with psychoticlike symptoms) led eventually to their making entirely new coparenting plans that helped stabilize the children. For other entrenched parents, the counselor-mediator directly advises what children need and can tolerate in the way of custody and access plans, giving a clear rationale why certain options will not work, and asking parents to make sacrifices for their children. Finally, the counselor-mediator refuses to consider any plan that is clearly detrimental to the child.

Clarifying Realities and Preparing the Agenda for Negotiation

For all parents, but especially those firmly entrenched, the final strategy during the counseling phase is to modify their unrealistic expectations and magical wishes by reality clarification and confrontation. Toward this end, the counselor-mediator sharpens the reality of the divorce situation: the facts that the ex-spouse is indeed intent on divorce, the ex-spouse is not going to disappear as hoped, and they cannot make unilateral decisions with respect to the child (they cannot control what happens at the other parent's house). The counselor-mediator clearly orients parents to the reality of who their ex-spouse is: that they could not change him or her during the marriage and they cannot now. Instead, they have to become more astute in dealing with their ex-spouse. The counselor-mediator clearly summarizes or advocates for the child's specific needs. Finally, with care not to give legal advice, the legal realities (laws, policies, and procedures of the court) are clarified: the fact that they do not have inalienable rights and control over their children and that the court may not grant their wishes, despite their convictions. Many parents want guarantees from the court that the spouse will be cooperative, good, and trustworthy. Here the counselor-mediator helps distinguish what are legally enforceable court orders and what are merely illusions of legal authority. Lastly, the mediator encourages parents to check out their unrealistic expectations and fantasies in consultations with attorneys, child protective service workers, or even the court. After clarifying the realities of the situation, which in effect limits options, the counselor-mediator helps them define what they can do for themselves and their children. Under "the shadow of the law" and within the shadow of these realities, an agenda is prepared of what needs to be accomplished during the negotiation of a specific parenting plan.

Negotiation or Conflict-Resolution Phase

Underscoring their need to meet only for the purpose of cooperative parenting, during this phase, the divorcing couple is brought together (usually for the first time) to resolve the specific issues under dispute and to prepare a coparenting agreement. Some regression often occurs at this first joint session, since parents are usually highly anxious and quick to resume the old unproductive patterns that reestablish their impasse. A number of techniques are used to prevent or limit this regression, as well as further prepare some parents for the negotiations.

First, predicting regression can forestall it. Second, the counselor-mediator can intervene directly in the parents' interaction. Often a simple gesture or a shorthand enigmatic statement reminds a parent of earlier discussions about the manner in which they become hooked, thereby averting the restoration of their impasse. (These reminders capitalize on insights gleaned during the prenegotiation phase and underscore the value of having this phase and the negotiation phase in the same service.) Third, positively connoting negative interactions is helpful. (Acknowledging and dignifying their fighting and their marriage can restore a couple's self-esteem and allow them to control their escalating provocations.) Fourth, paradoxical injunctions (such as informing parents of their need to fight and giving them an arena and a specific set of issues to fight about) are often useful. In one case, supporting a father by insisting that he was unable to make a commitment to his ex-wife, who was constantly demanding that he be a "reliable father," paradoxically allowed him to commit himself to an agreement for the first time. Fifth, some couples need to clarify directly with each other the events of the separation or their views of a particular traumatic incident before they can proceed. Having the couple actually apologize to each other usually symbolizes and promotes a breakthrough. Sixth, the use of analogies or stories helps frame, and thereby avoid, a couple's interactional impasse. For example, the counselor-mediator told one couple an Indian folk tale about the unhappy, conflictual marriage between a coyote and a turtle, which typified their problem. She recounted how the elders of the tribe blessed a marriage between two turtles or two coyotes, but frowned upon the marriage of a coyote to a turtle. They were well aware of the frustration experienced by the coyote, who was lively, emotional and playful, in response to the turtle who was cautious and tended to withdraw into its shell. The turtle was over-whelmed by the coyote's need for action and contact. The allegory decreased their defensiveness, heightened their willingness to respect the other's methods, and gave them permission to separate.

The actual negotiation of an agreement is relatively rapid, given the earlier preparations. Generally it proceeds according to the pre-vailing models: Issues are defined, options discussed and evaluated, specific alternatives selected, details clarified, and agreements draft-ed. The mediator chooses from a wide range of well-known conflict-resolution styles and family therapy techniques those that are best suited for the couple and their impasse. For example one-text media-tion (shuttle diplomacy) for highly hostile and enmeshed couples, crisis mediation for those with recent traumatic separations, and a series of trial agreements for those who are afraid of committing themselves have been found useful.

The agreements developed are impasse directed in that they are responsive to the family's vulnerability to conflict. They provide a blueprint for the family's present and future relationships in that they delineate concrete, workable plans and outline procedures for change. Agreements take into account not only the "real" issues (the legal determination of custody, time sharing, and so on), but are strategically framed to incorporate symbolic issues as well (the need-for respect and control, fear of loss, and so on). For a father who needs to be acknowledged, the agreement begins: "We the parents of . . . ." For a mother who needs to feel separate, the agreement begins: "For these parents to develop their separate lives and identities, the following. . . ."

Careful attention is paid not only to the strategic use of language but to the form and content of the agreement. For couples frightened by the finality of the divorce or who fear a loss of power and control by "being pinned down," broad provisional agreements (legally en-forceable) and "gentlemen's agreements" (legally nonenforceable contracts that define how family members will behave toward one another) may need to be the starting point of a resolution. For couples who are far apart, a series of agreements around increasingly prob-lematical issues can move the family by successive approximations toward a final resolution. Here the agreement is open enough so the parents do not feel trapped and powerless, yet narrow enough to begin building trust. In general, the psychological meaning of author-ity and the law to the parties helps determine which aspects of the agreement should be formally stipulated and ordered by the court. Legal protection of the parties is important but not the only consideration. Whereas some are appreciative and respectful toward legal authority and feel safer by having all provisions specified and ordered, others become resentful and impatient with legal restrictions and are provoked to defy them because they exist. Other parties find a court order meaningless and ignore it.

Implementation Phase

The final agreement obtained is taken by parents for review to their respective attorneys, whose responsibility it is to file it with the court where indicated. Following this, the counselor-mediator remains available to the family for emergency consultations and helps with implementing or modifying the arrangements, when necessary. Hence the service remains present, enabling the restraints, controls, insights, and coping skills learned during the brief intervention to continue. While it is important not to encourage overdependency and usurp parents' right to self-determination, in fact the longer-term success of the intervention often hinges on the background presence of a warm, empathic, realistic counselor who has an intimate knowledge of them and their children. Their hostility, mutual blaming, and petty vicious fights are always understood in the context of their sadness, despair, shattered hopes, expectable frustration, and love for their children. Like a valued family physician, the counselor-mediator shares a long history with the family, respects their efforts, and is available for consultation when needed.

CASE ILLUSTRATION NO. 1

Robert, aged six years, had been the subject of episodic custody and visitation disputes since his parents separated three years previously. At the time of the divorce, a court evaluation resulted in custody being awarded to the father, with the mother having visits with her son on alternate weekends, supervised by the maternal aunt. More recently, both parents had remarried and shortly afterward, the mother and stepfather renewed their request for custody, which was contested by the father and stepmother.

During mandatory mediation in the court, both parents and their new spouses were seen conjointly. The mother, a small, slight, dark-haired woman, was very anxious but quite passive in the interview. She depended on her new husband, Mike, to press her claims. He was a large, overweight, red-haired man with a rather officious and contentious manner. They charged that the child was coming to their house for alternate weekend visits with dirty clothes, torn underwear, or skimpy summer clothing on blustery, cold, and overcast days. Moreover, the boy was withdrawn and sullen. He seemed scared to talk to them, and they believed he was being bullied and threatened by his father. For instance, he told them that his father beat him if he did not call his new stepmother "Mom." They had no idea where Robert lived, where he went to school, and what was happening at his father's house but they believed that the child was living "in filth in the slums" and was being "neglected."

The father presented as a warm, emotional, effusive man, supported by an angry, indignant stepmother. They not only denied the accusations, but countered that the mother was likely to be "violent and dangerous." She had a "drug and alcohol problem." She did not know where they lived because they "were scared to death she [would] come and try to kidnap the child." They cited the court investigation completed two years ago as supporting their claims. It found the mother "emotionally unstable" and recommended that the maternal aunt supervise the visits. They reported that there were restraining orders preventing the mother from coming near their home. They complained that the extended family (which included the maternal aunt and cousins) was stirring up trouble by siding with the mother and insulting them when they picked up Robert from visits.

With these accusations and counteraccusations, the argument between the two sets of parents escalated into an angry battle. Hostility and outrage increased as each of the opposing sides became more entrenched in its position. When the mediation session ended, both families were more agitated and incensed than when they arrived. Following the session, there was a barrage of phone calls from the stepfather demanding that the mediator take action to protect the child from "neglect" and them from "slander." At this point they agreed to pursue extended counseling and mediation with our service before proceeding with litigation.

The parents, child, and several key relatives were then seen separately to take a brief history with the purpose of understanding the evolution and layering of the impasse. It emerged that the mother, Elise, was the eldest daughter of a large matriarchal family, dominated by the maternal aunt. This elderly aunt controlled all her adult nieces and nephews by employing them in her large family business and granting and withholding credit as she saw fit. In the large extended family, there were strong demands for loyalty and support of kin. In actuality, Elise was a dependent, guilty woman who had been dominated by this maternal aunt ever since the death of her own controlling mother. She was torn by opposing injunctions: On the one hand she owed allegiance and submission to the maternal aunt (and to her dead mother); on the other hand, as the eldest daughter, she was expected to command the respect of the family. Normally, she was very afraid of confrontations and avoided conflict. However, when she had a few drinks, she became quite aggressive and postured in a rather supercilious and autocratic manner.

Elise had met and married the father, John, shortly after her own mother died. He was a warm, emotional, rather histrionic man, and the marriage was characterized by a great deal of romance and excitement for the first several years for both of them. However, the maternal aunt constantly interfered in their relationship. She offered John a position with the company and financed the young couple's new home. Indebted to her and dependent on her, they found it difficult to escape her many demands on their time. The marriage deteriorated quickly during Elise's pregnancy with Robert. She had to cease working in the first trimester because of a medical condition, and the couple were soon in fairly severe financial difficulties.

After the baby was born, Elise found it difficult to cope. Baby Robert was fussy and would not nurse. She was inundated with advice and criticism from her kin. When her young husband, John, began to assume more of the child's care and household responsibilities, she felt even more inadequate. She was depressed, began to drink more, and smoked marijuanna. The couple entered counseling but only attended a few sessions because the cost was prohibitive and they had no medical insurance. Arguments between them erupted into physical struggles as he tried to stop her drinking. She, on the other hand, became more aggressive when drinking, and smashed glassware and kitchen appliances when she felt he was trying to take over her role in the house. John was very conflicted about the marriage and ambivalent and guilty about leaving. He sought the advice of an attorney who supported his departure from the marriage and helped him plan a strategy for his escape with the child. They were granted an ex parte hearing before the judge, without Elise's knowledge, on the claim that the mother was emotionally unstable and likely to abduct the child if she knew her husband was considering divorce. The father was awarded temporary custody at this hearing. At seven o'clock the next morning, while Elise was served with the petition for divorce together with the order for father custody at the front door, John grabbed the child and escaped out the back door.

Elise was distraught to the point of being out of control. She felt extremely betrayed, abandoned, and threatened violence. The father obtained restraining orders and kept the whereabouts of his new residence unknown to her. A court investigation documented the mother's erratic behavior and concluded that she was emotionally unstable and unfit to care for the child. It was recommended that the father retain custody with alternate weekend visits to the mother being supervised by the maternal aunt. Defeated, Elise retreated at this time and submitted to the domination of her aunt and the authority of the court. In actuality, she stopped drinking, resumed working, and became emotionally more stable. For the following two years, there were few disputes between the parents. The child's visits continued, and the maternal aunt gradually relinquished her overseeing responsibilities without the father's knowledge. Since, there was no communication between the parents, they never met or talked, the father remained uneasy, convinced that the mother was a violent, dangerous woman from whom the child had to be protected.

What triggered a renewal of the dispute was the remarriages of both Elise and John to new partners. John and his new wife established a new home together with the hope and expectation that they could provide a new and better family unit for Robert, in particular one in which the "defective" mother was replaced. They tended to ignore and dismiss the mother and stepfather and assumed proprietory rights to the child, refusing to discuss his school progress, his medical appointments, or even to inform them when and where they were going on vacations with the child.

These proprietory attitudes were intolerable to Elise's new husband. This man was controlling, officious, and easily offended. In fact, he had all the features of a man with a severe narcissistic vulnerability in that he was hypervigilant about the possibility of being insulted and constantly fended off any implied attacks on his self-worth. He was extremely affronted by what had happened to Elise, his wife, with respect to the initial custody decision. He felt personally insulted by the manner in which John had left the marriage. He reviewed the early court reports that found Elise a less than adequate mother and was outraged. In fact he wanted to rewrite history by obtaining a new custody order. He found it preposterous that there were restraining orders on Elise and that she was not allowed to know where her child lived or what school he attended. All of this he felt to be a fundamental and intolerable attack on her worth and, by association, on him. After all, this implied that he had married a woman whom another man found to be damaged and had abandoned. This threatened man began to project the blame and bad outside himself. He became preoccupied to the point of being paranoid about his wife's first husband. As he and Elise discussed this together, he helped her crystallize a negative, polarized view that John must be "strange, bizarre . . . he must live like a pig . . . he and his new wife were neglecting the child."

In the absence of any communication with the other family, the stepfather turned to the child for information. He literally interrogated Robert about details of his life with the father, and eventually the child broke down or was tricked into telling where he went to school and where his sitter lived. Robert was extremely upset and guilty about revealing what he had been explicitly forbidden by his father to reveal. He became sullen and unresponsive to both sets of parents; at other times he told stories that aimed to please and placate each parent about his mistreatment at the other's house. In actuality, this increased their mutual apprehensions. Before and after visits to his mother he would complain about feeling ill with stomachaches.

As the stepfather became more intensely agitated, he elicited the support of Elise's large extended-kin network to his cause. He demanded their allegiance as well as the counselor's absolute loyalty to his expressed mission of rescuing the child from "the slums." In defense, John and the stepmother sought the assistance of friends and an attorney to counter the barrage of accusations. They became increasingly concerned about the wisdom of alternate weekend visitation and sought to have the child's contact with the other family eliminated or at the very least further reduced.

It was clearly evident to the counselor who interviewed both of the opposing families that the accusations about abuse, neglect, violence, drinking, and drug-taking were greatly exaggerated or virtually unfounded. Elise had been far more stable since her remarriage. The home she and her husband owned was tastefully furnished and carefully maintained. They obviously loved Robert in their own way. They provided him with expensive clothes and toys and took him on many Disneyland-like outings. They did feel hurt by his lack of responsiveness, withdrawal, and failure to declare his allegiance to them. John, on the other hand, had established a small apartment in a working-class suburb. He and his wife devalued material possessions and dressed the child in simple, secondhand playclothes. They, too, obviously loved the child and indeed showed more capacity to empathize with the child's feelings.

Basically, these were two families that triggered in each other severe interactional pathologies that destabilized the situation and placed the child at grave risk. In sum, all three levels of impasse in dynamic equilibrium are illustrated in this case. First, at the intrapsychic level, there was a hostile dependent woman (the child's mother) who was dominated by her family and her husband and who became assertive only with the help of alcohol or drugs, at which time she became overly aggressive. She had remarried a man who had extremely threatened self-worth and constantly needed to prove that he (and his wife) deserved respect and esteem. On the other side, there was an emotional man (the child's father) who overreacted to threats and challenges. Second, at the interactional level, the traumatic separation experienced by this couple (especially the mother) resulted in the formation of extremely negative views with subsequent fear, avoidance of each other, and periodic fights. Given the lengthy time since the parental separation and the defensive needs of the parties to construe the other as negative, it was apparent that these polarized images were fixed and not easily amenable to change. Finally, at the external level, as the conflict escalated, the mother's extended kin (with whom she had permeable boundaries) became overly involved and helped consolidate and maintain the dispute.

Having formulated the nature of the impasse, the questions became: Where are the leverage points for intervention? Who should be included in the mediation? What techniques should be used? First, it was apparent that conjoint sessions with both families present were destructive. The stepfather, in particular, experienced the defensive countering of accusations as very threatening. He reacted by projecting more of the blame and manufacturing more demands. As a result the impasse was becoming more firmly embedded. The strategy was to have separate sessions with the two warring families in order to apply selective counseling techniques with the different parties.

With the father and stepmother, this counseling was more straightforward. Both were psychologically better equipped and had the capacity to accept some clarification of their contribution to the disputes. The counselor showed them how John's emotional overreactions were threatening and challenging to both Elise and her new husband. She was being made to feel inadequate again and needed to assert herself in the only way possible for her, which was to become slightly intoxicated and use very nasty language. Similarly, their refusal to share any information with the stepfather was very demeaning to him. He became more suspicious and placed more and more pressure on the child to find out what was going on. In sum, the other family's very obnoxious behavior was reinterpreted as being directly in response to how belittled, inadequate, and unnecessary they were made to feel. John and his new wife were then educated on how their child was feeling caught in the middle of a dangerous situation, disloyal to both parents. Robert needed permission to be with his mother and to love her. Despite Elise's shortcomings when he was a very young child, he had remained very attached to her and had grieved when she suddenly disappeared at the time of the separation. He now felt insecure and conflicted about her but also longed for her. They could not replace his mother, no matter how damaged they thought she was! The counselor shared with John and his new wife the great efforts Elise and her new husband had made toward this child during his brief visits (handmade Christmas gifts, special outings, and a special room of his own). They needed to respect these efforts as symbols of love and concern. Next, the changes that the mother had made since the divorce were emphasized: She was much more stable, working regularly, and drinking very little. The father, in particular, was skeptical about the extent of such change. Finally, the counselor stressed that there were no magical solutions and emphasized the realities of the situation. The mother was not presently acting in a manner that would justify the court's reducing visitation. In fact, as the child grew older, access would be increased to include summer vacations and more holidays. The father needed to take responsibility for having married this particular woman and for having given his child this particular mother. He could not simply dismiss her. This was "the cross he had to bear." Since the father was a strongly religious man, this reframing of the problem had considerable impact on him. Henceforth he often talked about accepting the burden of his cross with more grace and stoicism.

These interventions with John and the stepmother were quite fruitful. They were amenable to considering these new insights into the dynamics of the two families. However, when they began to act more reasonably and graciously toward Elise and her new husband, they were met with a barrage of more demands and criticisms that undermined their new willingness to cooperate. In fact, their refusal to play out the stepfather's projective fantasies were very threatening to him, because this indicated that the fault might not be entirely outside himself or his wife. This was intolerable to him, and he warded off this threat by reciting a litany of complaints about John that extended back into the marriage, for example, how the father had always lied, cheated, and stolen valuables that belonged to the mother. He also construed the offers for more flexible visitation with Robert as the father's and stepmother's capitulation and evidence of their admission of guilt and inadequacy. This reinforced his own claims for custody on behalf of his wife.

The counselor was forced to review her strategy. The narcissistic vulnerability of the stepfather, now more apparent, was seen as the central energizing component in the current impasse. Clarification and insight into the dynamics were too threatening and increased his need to project blame. Support of his position was dangerous because it reinforced his conviction that his worldview was completely right. If the counselor did not then take action on his behalf, she was seen as betraying him. It was also important to note that the stepfather's concerns about the child were a bogus issue, in fact a paranoid projection. Attending to these bogus issues was making them more real and increasing his paranoid preoccupation. The counselor made three stategic interventions.

First, the counselor complimented the stepfather on how much he loved and cared for his wife. He loved her so much that he was prepared to take on and fight her battles for her, to right the wrong that had been done her. All of this "horrible business had nothing to do with him," but as a caring person he was trying to fix the matter. The counselor also complimented the stepfather and mother on what they were trying to do materially for the child. The stepfather relaxed somewhat in response to this and decided to allow the mother, henceforth, to take more responsibility. In dealing with the mother directly, a particularly supportive, nonconfrontational relationship was established. Diagnostically, she had the borderline personality's tendency to relate in terms of different states or roles. Sometimes she was the whining, crying child who elicited caretaking, sometimes she was an officious policewoman investigating a misdemeanor, and other times she was the responsible, courteous businesswoman (manager of the maternal aunt's store). It was the latter role that the counselor called forth in the sessions. She asked Elise to consider her ex-husband as a difficult customer with whom she had to do business over the next ten years. Elise responded well to this stance and was far more courteous and less insulting and aggressive in her dealings with John. Second, the counselor reacted honestly and dramatically to the stepfather's angry tirades during the sessions and his paranoid attacks that she was biased on behalf of the other family. During one such interview, the counselor told him she was extremely upset by his bullying manner and was insulted by what he was saying. Noting that she did not have to tolerate this unfair portrayal, she rose to leave the room. The stepfather immediately quieted and resumed the discussion in a more reasonable manner. This intervention involved symbolically holding up a mirror to the stepfather's hostility and showing him how it affected other people. Third, the most important tactic was to stop intervening with this family and allow the whole situation to "cool down." Interviews were spaced over several weeks, with a month off for the holidays. Elise and her husband were encouraged to become socially involved with other people and to do things for themselves. The counselor insisted that nothing more could be achieved with the other family; the situation would not change, and they needed to find how to live with it. The goal was to allow the paranoid preoccupations with the child and the divorce situation to shift to another matter. This is precisely what happened. Several weeks later, the stepfather exploded in a very angry confrontation with his landlord. This quarrel, which resulted in litigation, diverted his attention for some months. During this time, Robert's visits to his mother went smoothly and the child became more relaxed and happier. Finally, using shuttle diplomacy (since the parents could not meet together), the counselor mediated several small modifications to the visitation schedule. This became a carefully worded document that omitted any reference to the mother's inadequacy or emotional instability and framed the child's need for a loving relationship with both parents. During this mediation, the counselor advocated very strongly on the child's behalf, saying that a change in custody or substantially increased visitation was contraindicated because of the extreme distrust, hostility, and lack of communication between the two families.

The above interventions involved eight sessions, spread over four months. Robert was seen separately in individual play sessions with the purpose of teaching him how to cope with the parental conflict. The counselor then remained available by telephone to review and reinforce the insights gained and gradually transfer responsibility for communicating between the two families back to the parents. Elise and John were able to negotiate several minor changes to the visitation schedule on the telephone. One year later they agreed to meet face to face for a mediation session. Both stepparents willingly excluded themselves from the interview. This proved to be a very positive meeting, during which both parents supported each other's involvement with the child. What was most intriguing was the gradual shifts in perception of each other that was affirmed by these positive exchanges. John no longer perceived Elise as violent and dangerous. Elise and the stepfather were more gratified with the respect they were being accorded. At the two-year follow-up, the child continued to have access to both parents, with only sporadic disagreements that were fairly easily negotiated.

CASE ILLUSTRATION NO. 2

Mary and Keith, the parents of three-year-old Eric, had been separated for eighteen months. The mother had been awarded custody, and the father had been given visitation with his son every Saturday from 9:00 A.M. to 5:00 P.M., following a court recommendation. He returned to court to cite the mother for contempt because she frequently withheld the child. He was also demanding alternate weekends with overnight visitation with his son to be effective immediately, "like every other normal father gets!"

Keith was a tall, thin, morose man with dark features and an agitated demeanor. He was terse and impatient in the intake interview and gave a somewhat jumbled, illogical account of the separation and legal dispute. He alternated demands, threats, and foul language with apologies and promises to "go along with anything the counselor decreed." Then he would demand to know by what rights anyone could tell him when he could see his child.

Mary was extremely apprehensive about the father's visits with Eric. She was obsessed with fears that he would not watch the child carefully enough, that the little boy would be hurt or become ill in his care. She reported that she and the father never communicated. Keith would arrive punctually to pick up the child, grab him out of her arms, and would not even allow Eric to say good-bye. When she tried to question him about where he was going or give him instructions about Eric (such as his need for medicine), he invariably swore at her. She admitted she often swore back. On several occasions she had been so provoked by his stream of foul language that she slapped him and he had slapped her back. When this happened Eric would scream, terrified, and cling to whichever parent was holding him. Mary called the police a number of times for protection. She also routinely had her mother or one of her sisters stand by to supervise Eric's transitions between parents. Keith seemed more provoked and even less willing to talk in their presence, although it restrained them from hitting one another. Mary had no idea where the father lived and had no phone number where he could be reached. Eric arrived back from visits tired, dirty, and often ill. She had no idea whether he had napped or what he had eaten. Moreover, Eric was usually uncontrollable when he arrived home, frequently dissolving into temper tantrums, soiling himself, or having nightmares. It took a day or two for him to settle. Mary admitted that she kept the child from visiting the father for almost two months during the winter because Eric had frequent colds and ear infections and she could not be convinced that his father would take adequate care of him.

Mary, who was an attractive young woman, related these concerns in a coherent, rational manner, albeit with a great deal of anxiety. She seemed warm and empathic toward her child and ex-husband. She expressed considerable guilt about leaving the marriage and deserting Keith. She was extremely sad for him because she knew he had been unhappy and conflicted for a long time, and she felt she had compounded his problems. She described how as a child he had been continually criticized, bullied, and demeaned by his stepfather and how he had tried to protect his mother from her abusive husband. As an adult he continued to have very poor self-esteem and was alternately angry, guilty, and depressed. However, she was also very afraid of him because he had been violent during the separation period. She spoke tearfully about how, on their final night together, he had tried to choke her while she held the baby in her arms. Then he smashed every mirror in the house and left. Several hours later he called to apologize. For weeks, he would telephone her twenty and thirty times a day, alternately asking to reconcile and leaving death threats on her answering machine. Most of all, she was afraid that he would kidnap Eric and she would never see the boy again. At this point in the interview, Mary broke down into uncontrollable crying. She explained through her tears that they had lost their first baby, Erin. She had drowned when she was two years old in a neighbor's swimming pool. The baby-sitter had been negligent.

This case incorporates many of the components of a typical impasse. At the intrapsychic level, Keith, the father, had many of the characteristic features of a borderline personality disorder, with obsessive-compulsive traits when he was functioning at his highest level. These character defenses barely covered his anger and shame at himself. He had long-standing problems with very poor self esteem, and difficulty maintaining an integrated view of himself. He continually tried to defend by projection and a bullying, aggressive stance. On the other hand, he was painfully conflicted and ambivalent, often apologizing for his outbursts, making repeated efforts "to do the right thing" by his son and his son's mother. The pathos of his struggles with himself, his depression, and his pain engendered protective and mothering responses in others, especially women.

It was these qualities that drew Mary to him in the first place. She had the capacity to nurture and had fantasies of rescuing this man from himself. She could possibly have continued to nurture and nourish him had she not regressed herself in response to the tragic loss of their first baby. This event was the turning point of the marriage, the precipitant of the separation, and the seed of the current impasse. Mary regressed in response to the loss, becoming more needy, dependent, and insecure herself, but Keith was not capable of meeting her needs. They were both guilty about the baby's death and felt vulnerable and abandoned by each other. Mary clung to the marriage until her second baby arrived and survived his first year. Then she provoked, counterreacted, and pushed Keith out. The humiliation and shame of the rejection was awful for him. His obsessive defenses were completely broken down and he reacted with violence.

The traumatic separation laid the groundwork for the parents' negative reconstruction of each other's identity. For Keith, his negative views of Mary were largely ego-defensive; for Mary, her negative views were based on the very frightening scene when he tried to choke her. Eighteen months later, he had been able to restore most of his obsessive defenses and regain control, but Mary could not believe this. She could not trust him with the child and would find every excuse to forestall the visits. Any slight fever or possible illness in the child activated both parents' concern for his survival. Both would panic and become angry with one another. Actually, Mary could not trust anyone to keep her baby safe, but Keith took this as a personal affront. It renewed his guilt that he was in some way responsible for the death of his first baby or not capable or worthy of caring for a child. He remained deeply humiliated, guilty, and furious. Moreover Mary often made promises to him, which she did not keep, that he could have Eric for holidays. This further threatened his brittle defenses, precipitating anger, verbal threats, and occasional physical abuse. Afraid of losing control, the father tried to keep his distance. Hence he needed to grab Eric and run when they exchanged the child because communication with his wife was too painful.

As the fights escalated, he became more panicked and unstable. The couple became involved in a series of court actions, which drained their meager financial resources. Keith was further shamed by the involvement of counselors because this, too, implied that he was deficient. His doubts about his autonomy were reactivated by contacts with authorities (judge and court evaluator) and he alternately submitted obediently and rebelled. Outside of court, relatives and friends were involved. Both parents gave very biased accounts that would enrage supportive others and engage them in combating with or protecting against the other parent.

Eric was at serious risk because of the ongoing, escalating parental fights. He was often exposed to the parents' uncontrolled anger and verbal and physical aggression. This made it difficult for him to master separating from each parent when he left and returned for visits (a task normally difficult for a three-year-old). Furthermore, the parents could not communicate sufficiently to ensure his safety and provide for continuity in care when he went on visits. (Mary could not even determine whether prescribed medication had been administered.) Finally, neither parent could respond to the child's needs in the aftermath of the dispute. (When Eric cried for his mother, the father could not comfort him, and neither parent could tell him when he would see the other again). Apart from the parental conflict, we also had considerable concern about the father's ongoing emotional instability and, to a lesser extent, the mother's overprotectiveness of the child, a reaction to her earlier loss.

The interventions with this divorcing family had three phases: information gathering and assessment, brief counseling and mediation of a visitation plan, and a rather extensive follow-up during which the trial visitation plan was monitored and the counseling interventions reinforced. During the first phase, the counselor undertook a careful assessment of the father's quality of parenting. Because Keith was so blatantly emotionally agitated and difficult interpersonally, there were some serious questions about his capacity to meet the child's needs. The counselor wondered to what extent she should be encouraging the mother to give him frequent access versus encouraging more protection of the child. What the counselor found was a surprising amount of loving, warmth, and bonding between this father and his son. Keith was very protective of Eric and, in fact, his obsessive routines were an important source of security at this point in the young child's life. He obviously enjoyed going on the visits, even though he was tired when he returned. He was most negatively affected by the parental fights and the disappointment of being prepared for visits which were then canceled by the mother. When Keith was not provoked, stressed, or shamed, his parenting looked more adequate. However, we had considerable doubts as to this father's longer-term capacity to be responsive to his son. As the boy grew older and sought to separate and develop independent views, we predicted that this man would be very threatened and this child would be increasingly exposed to the father's erratic behavior. Believing that there was insufficient evidence at this time to restrict the father's access to the child in court, and wanting to preserve as much as possible of the father-son relationship, we opted to support a regular visitation plan.

The counselor shared this assessment with Mary and then pointed out that there were clear limits to her ex-husband's emotional disturbance. In fact, he had many strengths. She had the power to distress him and unhinge his defenses or she could help build on his resources. It was noted that he could follow rules, and wanted to "do the right thing" by his son. He was well organized, always punctual, and predictable when he was not demeaned or threatened. If Mary could guarantee to carry out her side of an agreement and not withhold the child, he could be most trustworthy. It was pointed out that the violent episodes were his distraught responses to the separation and that now, almost two years later, he was under control again. Step by step, the counselor showed how she could help restore the best of this father's functioning. Since Mary was an intelligent woman, with a capacity for insight and some measure of guilt for hurting Keith and depriving him of their child, she was amenable. She acknowledged that he loved Eric and that the little boy was attached to him.

At the same time, the counselor focused on this mother's inordinate and excessive fears for the child's physical safety, interpreting it as an overreaction in response to her first baby's death. She fairly readily conceded that this was so and worked out guidelines with her pediatrician as to when the child's minor illnesses would warrant him being kept from visits with his father. To reinforce this intervention, the counselor talked in more detail about the longer-term emotional sequelae of over-protectiveness.

Keith could not tolerate any form of clarification or interpretation of psychological dynamics, especially his own contribution to the dispute. He projected the blame entirely onto Mary, saying that she was a "selfish, spiteful, and crazy woman." At the same time, he was most anxious to obtain reassurance about himself. The counselor acknowledged that he was a protective, loving father and that Eric was attached to him and felt safe with him, as long as he and Mary were not fighting. In particular, the counselor emphasized that Mary's distrust of his caring for the child was not personal; she trusted no one since the tragedy of their first baby's drowning. (In fact, the counselor added, she would not trust the Archangel Gabriel with the child!) Finally, the counselor insisted that the parental fighting was dangerous to Eric. Keith's grabbing and running with the child and refusing to communicate with the mother was making him very anxious. It was also difficult for three-year-old Eric not to say good-bye, not to take his security blanket with him, and to witness the anger and abuse between the parents. This moderate amount of confrontation of the father's contribution to the problem was almost more than he could tolerate. Several times he became very angry at the perceived judgment and abruptly terminated the session. Because this intervention was gentle enough and interspersed with realistic acknowledgements of his strengths, he invariably phoned back later and asked to proceed. However, he was very impatient, repeatedly demanding to "cut out all of this shit! When am I going to have my son for overnights? If this is not going to happen, I am going back to court!"

During three joint mediation sessions, Keith and Mary were able to put together a visitation plan that involved the child having a steadily increasing amount of contact with the father over the forthcoming year, at which time alternate weekend visitation with an overnight would be achieved. Safeguards were built into the agreement, specifically requiring a reassessment of the plan if the child became symptomatic. The language of the agreement was carefully worded to protect the father's extremely vulnerable self-esteem. During this mediation phase, Mary, her sisters, and the maternal grandmother were seen together in order to answer the many questions they had about the advisability of the father having any access to Eric. In this way, the loving support of Mary's family was used to bolster and reinforce the contract that was being entered into.

For the next eighteen months, this agreement was kept except for several brief problems. Eric was initially very clingy, regressed, and demanding after overnight visits. It was suggested that Mary did not prepare him sufficiently for this. She was encouraged to play visiting games with him with his toy animals and to read him bedtime stories about children leaving and returning to their mommies. During the winter months, Eric had frequent colds, and again Mary tried to keep him home from visits. A brief telephone call reminded her how important it was to be consistent with the father and that she needed her pediatrician's sanctions to cancel visitation. For the rest of this period, the parents usually conversed briefly but amicably. In fact, they began to make a practice of having breakfast together at a local restaurant on the day of the child's transfer.

At the two-year follow-up, we found the visitation plan worked reasonably well until Mary became involved in an intimate relationship with another man. When they decided to live together, she was faced with the quandary of how to explain this to Keith so that he would not feel he was being replaced as a father. She tried to tell him gently during a telephone conversation. He listened silently and hung up the phone in the midst of her explanation. On the following weekends he did not appear for the visits and refused to answer any letters or phone calls from either Mary or his son.

Eric was extremely confused and suffered a severe grief reaction when his father failed to visit. He asked again and again where his daddy was, waited patiently for hours at the window, and cried when it was obvious he was not coming. His self-esteem was clearly affected: he was overheard explaining to his grandmother that "I'm an ass because my father doesn't visit me." Eric became obsessed with the fantasy that his father had died, asked many questions about death, and had nightmares about dying himself. He also developed severe separation anxieties from his mother. He was generally so anxious and difficult to manage that we advised treatment by a child therapist. The father was also contacted and he resumed contact but visited at irregular and infrequent times. The child's therapist and mother helped the child cope with this situation.

In sum, the impasse that resulted in the dispute over the child was largely resolved because of the shifts that Mary was able to make. She gained insight into her own contributions to the impasse and to a large extent overcame her own anxieties and fears about the child's visits to the father. She tried very hard to preserve the best of the child's relationship with the father and handled this vulnerable man in a very gentle manner, attempting not to provoke his emotional disturbance. In doing so, she inadvertently rekindled his fantasies of reconciliation and his great loss and sadness about losing her, his son, and perhaps also his deceased daughter. His fantasies were abruptly confronted when she revealed she had a new intimate relationship. Keith could not tolerate the situation and withdrew completely from her and his child. What is left of the impasse lies within the intrapsychic pathology of this man's borderline character structure. He found it intolerable to become too close to the mother and the child because it made him too sad and too angry. He probably also feared his enormously angry impulses toward them, sensing he might do something to harm them if provoked. Having only intermittent contact with his family protects both himself and them.

This case illustrates the unhappy dilemma faced by many of these children and the limits of any short-term intervention. There is a choice of two evils. If Eric continued to have frequent contact with his father, the long-term consequences would no doubt have been mixed. There was already evidence that as he grew older, the father was telling him negative stories about his mother and her family and depending on him to relieve his depression and support his distorted views of others. On the other hand, when the father failed to visit, Eric felt abandoned, rejected, and unworthy. He experienced severe separation anxieties and fears of death and dying. Until we know more about long-term outcomes, counselors and mediators are left with imprecise criteria for helping parents and the court choose between two unhappy alternatives and piecing together family arrangements that are least detrimental to the child.

CHAPTER 10

Multifamily Mediation

The rapid growth of mediation services in both the public and private sectors has led to a proliferation of approaches to the mediation process. To date, however, all these dispute-resolution models are for individual families or divorcing parents in conjoint sessions. While groups have been used for some time to educate and provide therapeutic support for divorcing parents and their children, and more recently groups have been used to prepare parents for mediation the group method has not been designed specifically for dispute resolution, in which the negotiation of divorce agreements is conducted. However, the group format promises to be not only cost- and manpower efficient, but is in itself a potentially powerful mechanism for change.

We found it optimal to treat five divorcing and disputing families at one time, using the group method. While the parents meet in adult groups for a total of seven sessions with two counselors, children meet with their peers in play groups for a total of four sessions with their own therapist. In recognition of the influence grandparents, other kin, and new spouses have on divorce disputes and their resolution, significant others are invited to join the groups where it is strategically appropriate. Two counselor-mediators lead each parent group. Having two leaders means authority can be diffused, biases counteracted, resource possibilities increased. In fact, group leaders do not always present a united front but maintain separate identities and at times disagree (and find agreement) with each other. In this way they serve as models for conflict resolution. Having an interdisciplinary team of clinical psychologist, sociologist, mediator, and attorney is particularly useful.

Prenegotiation Counseling Phase

During the prenegotiation counseling phase, divorcing spouses meet in separate but concurrently running groups for the first four of the seven sessions. These subgroups are carefully composed of mixed-sex and custody arrangements to ensure a balance of perspectives among the members. The explicit purpose is to prepare each parent for the mediation of a coparenting agreement. To this end, the group leaders undertake direct, focused interventions with each parent for a brief period of the group's time. The other group members function as a participating audience who support, reflect, confront, provide ideas and problem-solving options, and act as models for new ways of relating. The commonality of experiences, problems, and ages of children encourages parents to borrow from and share with one another. A strong spirit of camaraderie usually develops among the parents as they actively engage with each other's problems. In fact, we have come to view these groups as a "transitional family," which supports and anchors the parent during the crisis of the divorce and the stress of the custody dispute. The leaders have a clear agenda for each group session.

First Session

The aims of the first session are to raise parents' awareness of their children's needs and reactions to the dispute and to orient them to the task of protecting their children from the parental discord and to the importance of developing sound child-care plans.

One of the group leaders begins by introducing the group members to one another with the observation that they are all present because they have children about the same age about whom they care deeply, and that they are all having difficulty developing the best arrangements for their children following divorce. In this respect the parental role is elicited from the outset. In a short monologue (ten to fifteen minutes), the leaders describe the age-specific consequences of divorce and disputes for children, thereby informing parents at the outset about the ramifications of their conflicts for their children. This lecture material, specifically designed for the group membership, is made more salient by including symptoms that their particular children are showing. Parents are then asked what they have noticed or are worried about in their children, and what problems they have to solve with regard to their children.

Beginning with structured material and requesting concrete observations of their children raises parents' consciousness and encourages them to attend more carefully to their children. The initial impulse for many parents is to attack or blame their ex-spouse. Asking parents to describe the experiences of their children redefines this purpose and direction. In this way, their parenting role rather than their spousal role is made salient. Those who cannot describe their children in other than global generalities are given a homework assignment of making more structured observations or asked to bring reports from teachers, relatives, and baby-sitters. The structured lecture material and tasks additionally help contain anxiety and forge contact between the group members. Asking parents what they have to solve increases their task orientation and sharpens their sense of responsibility to find solutions.

With this introduction, a special atmosphere is created. Group norms, ideals, and rules are being established. Within the direct lecture materials and within our responses to parents' observations about their children, we positively reinforce certain child-centered values: children's need for both parents, for stability, continuity, a coherent life-style, and parental cooperation and responsibility. These values can then become available as ideals toward which parents reorient their thinking, potentially stabilizing their erratic behavior and giving them direction. Later these group-established values and norms are used as principles in mediated agreements.

Most importantly, we have found that groups naturally provide limits and controls that constrain potential violence and acting-out. While members strongly empathise with each other's fierce anger, frustration, and violent fantasies, we find that they do not support or fan that anger. Rather, they seek to soothe the angry outbursts and direct the irate parent to more viable solutions. One father, for example, had a gun and revealed that if provoked again by the mother's lover, he intended to use it. The other group members, with great concern and support for the father, discussed the effects of his potential action on his son and on his relationship with his son. They gently argued and coerced until he placed the gun with a trusted friend, out of his own reach. When another man rose in fury, unsure whether to strike his mate or to flee the room, two other men quietly laid their hands on his shoulders in sympathy as well as constraint. In the same way, group members pass tissues to, and sometimes hold, a weeping parent, strongly identifying with and vicariously experiencing the other's grief. In many respects each other's sadness, anger, or outrageous behavior is a mirror in which they view reflections of themselves. Hence the ego capacity to observe and more critically evaluate self is developed.

We found that the more psychologically minded members educated other parents or became role models when they put aside painful experiences to resolve child-related problems. This promotes a helpful normative climate in the group and often proves useful to the models as well as to the witnesses. They find themselves compelled to behave in accord with their public testimony. However, the use of members as models involves dangers. While for some, playing a role or grafting on group ideals is curative, giving them direction, for others there is no integration of the group values. In fact, some parents avoid confrontation with their own problems by hiding behind the role of "good parent." Their well-motivated, cooperative, and knowledgeable exterior obfuscates their own difficulties, which they deny and avoid. The leaders as well as the parent remain blind to the role-player's disturbance. Therefore, in developing group values and princiqles, it is important to avoid making one couple or individual group member the model, and instead create a group ideal by selectively affirming characteristics from each group member. In this way the ideal is independent of individuals and emerges from the group rather than being preached, or just imitated. This additionally fosters the group's cohesiveness and each parent's pride.

A second danger lies in the leaders or dominant group members reinforcing their own sociocultural values or ideas about childrearing. The primary safeguard here is to be aware and respectful of family values from different ethnic and cultural backgrounds. To this end we have the group members talk about their own culture's uniqueness, and its particular strengths in terms of child-rearing and family practices.

Second Session

The aim of the second session is to increase parents' awareness of their impasse or need not to settle the divorce dispute. A fifteen-minute lecture describes typical intrapsychic, interactional, or external dimensions of parental conflicts. In this material, the confluence of parental motivations and interactions that lead to disputes, including those represented among the particular families present, is described. The parents are then helped to identify their own impasses and where they become caught in conflicts, and how they can resolve the negative cycle of interactions with their ex-spouse or extended social and family network.

Whenever possible, we seek common themes and similarities in the impasses of the group members, and we work with group members in pairs. Coupling group members around a theme decreases humiliation and increases communication between them.

One common intrapsychic theme that locks disputes revolves around parents' difficulties in separating. In one group three women, each in her own way, failed to accept the fact that their marriages were over, and this interfered with their capacity to protect or plan for their children. One mother, fearful of being on her own, would flee and then return to her marriage, leaving her child feeling confused and worried about abandonment; a second was unable to tolerate the rejection involved in her husband's request for a separation and in retaliation would reject the father by withholding visits; a third, guilty about hurting her ex-husband by leaving, would submit to his unreasonable demands, leaving her child unprotected. In this group we explored how some parents remained in marriages that were unfulfilling because they feared being on their own, were unable to face the narcissistic hurt inherent in divorce, or could not tolerate the guilt of wanting to leave and thereby hurt another. In addition to clarifying their dynamics, we supported the first mother's capacity to be independent, the second's self-esteem, and the third's right to leave her troubled marriage—critical interventions for each.

Another common secenario is at the interactional level. Two parents in one group, during very traumatic separations, had acted in a disturbed and dangerous manner, engendering in their ex-spouses a wish to exclude them from their children's lives forever. In a frank though nonblaming way, the "disturbed" parents were told that events had happened, during very hard times, which broke down trust. Now they needed to rebuild trust, not by demanding their rights all at once, but by showing their former spouses piece by piece that, in fact, they were now different. In turn, while agreeing with the aggrieved ex-mate that the "disturbed" parents needed to prove themselves trustworthy and that the children had to be protected, they had to distinguish where adequate protection for the children ended and revenge for all previous abuse began. Moreover, because of the separation, it was difficult for the aggrieved spouse to know whether problems had been ameliorated. We encouraged them to observe their children carefully to see how they were responding to renewed contact with the other parent.

On the external or social level, some impasses involve extended family systems. In one group, parents had children under two years of age, and almost all were living with grandparents who, rather than providing support, were fueling the discord by demanding the parent take escalatory actions. With these parents, we clarified the dynamics of their situation (their need to cling to their family to replace the lost spouse, their blind identification with their own parents' position and values, or their ambivalent submission to their family's demands as the price for returning home) and then supported their capabilities, independence, and need to assume their own parental authority. Encouraging one parent to take an assertive role with her kin benefited others in the same situation. Group members also provided one another with factual information on survival (for example, how to locate housing, work, child care, and so on).

One hazard involves the therapist or group labeling or agreeing with one parent that the ex-spouse is disturbed and reducing the impasse to the "psychopathology of the other parent," thus failing to have both parents take responsibility. Parents are helped to recognize and accept the need to cope with the reality of each other's strengths as well as limitations, noting that the other parent (even if he or she is "disturbed") is not going to disappear but must be dealt with. Additionally, we highlight the conditional or situational nature of the other's "pathology," first by showing how the "disturbed" parents' problems are triggered and sustained by the present parents' actions, and second by developing various group principles that underscore the interactive nature of disputes. Disputes are viewed as two-way streets, "while it takes two to fight, it often requires only one to unlock a dispute," and "even if a parent is not part of the problem, he or she needs to be part of the solution." These principles foster parents' recognition of their responsibility and power, a first step toward change.

A second, related danger arises if group members blindly support each other's views. In forming the groups, mixing the custodial status and sexes of parents provides a variety of feelings and attitudes, which helps prevent a "group paranoia" from developing. Joking that all problems are in the other subgroup (where their ex-spouses are meeting) highlights and often dissipates the group's projection of blame. As part of group members' mutual support, they can come to view the group leader as biased or siding with their ex-spouse. Here the group experience provides its own safeguard. A member's claim, for example, that the leader favors mothers is challenged and corrected when the leader supports a father's importance in another case.

A third danger involves the group inappropriately challenging (or failing to support) a fragile or disturbed member. Formulating a good clinical assessment of each member during the intake sessions, together with an understanding of the limits of each parent's tolerance, constitutes a necessary step toward protecting the group's most vulnerable participants. Indeed, some parents could not tolerate clarification or insight into their own contribution to the impasse, and needed more supportive, empathic acknowledgment of their positive efforts. In addition, brief individual sessions are made available to assist these parents during particularly stressful times.

Third Session

Developing and integrating the themes of the previous two sessions, during the third session we aim to increase parents' understanding of the impact of the parental dispute on the child and to
help parents extricate the child from the parental conflict. Interventions with parents are two-pronged. On the one hand, we try to shift
the internal and interactional dynamics underlying the parental impasse so as to resolve or circumvent the parental dispute. On the
other hand, we clarify the ways the children are experiencing the
dispute, along with their needs and developmental risks, in the hope
of using the parents' concern for their child and their concern for
their relationship with their child as leverage for change.

☐   The resolution of Mrs. W.'s anger toward her husband over the
separation was to refuse to communicate with him and to mini-
mize his contact with their six-year-old son. Feeling insulted
and mistreated by her husband's "desertion," she felt her needs
now had to come first. Her son, a pale, inhibited child, was very
attached to his father and feared losing him. In response to his
mother's angry actions, the child was turning to his father and
becoming progressively more distant from his mother.

In the mother's group, we acknowledged her terribly distressful separation but then confronted her with our concern
that not only were her anger and depression in danger of becoming chronic but she was in danger of losing what she was
trying to protect: her child and her relationship with her child.
We noted that she seemed to want the boy to witness how victimized she felt and to show how terribly she had been treated
by his father, perhaps thereby having the boy ally with her in
her anger at his father. Her strategy, however, was backfiring.
The message the boy was receiving was that his mother was
helpless, unavailable, unloving. Each time her son approached
her, she was angrily depressed, which he experienced as rejection. She needed to improve her relationship with her child, not
fight with her ex-husband.

With the father, in his corresponding group, we clarified how
his indecisiveness over the separation and continual unclarity
about his plans threw the mother into a state of turmoil. He
needed to understand that his frequent presence precipitated
the mother's depression and anger. He often lingered during
exchanges to comfort the boy and calm the mother. This, in
effect, provoked the mother's rage and hence the boy's need for

comfort. We advised the father to teach his son how to cope with the mother's upset, to reassure his child that his mother would be better once he left, and to leave quickly after visits.

As illustrated in the above cases, an array of interventions is used within the group. Feedback regarding the children's specific needs is both verbal (interpretations of the children's behavior) and graphic. Children's artwork as well as photographs of the children playing in their groups are given to parents to discuss. Group members are asked for their own observations of each child's pictures and productions and to evaluate each other's ideas. Provision of this concrete data on the reality of the child has proved especially effective in countering parents' tendencies to deny the seriousness of their children's reactions. Mr. W., for example, was given a photograph of his son, whose fragility was clearly evident in the boy's apprehensive, sad smile and in the fort the child again and again tried to build but never managed to make solid. The child's sadness and insecurity, so graphically portrayed in the picture, were directly connected to the parental impasse.

Similar parent-child dynamics are often identified during this session. In one group, three parents were experiencing (and precipitating) the withdrawal of their preadolescent children into an alliance with the other parent. Each parent, in response to the pain of the child's rejection, was contributing to the development of the unwanted alliance by angry, demanding, retaliatory attacks on the child. In the group, we discussed the understandable nature of their hurt, the consequences of their assaultive behaviors on their child, and alternative ways of coping with the situation (for example, the need to withdraw while maintaining a more nurturing and less demanding stance vis-à-vis their child). Group members became involved in sharing better strategies for coping.

Commonalities in the children's symptomatic responses and coping styles emerge. In one group, for example, all the little boys presented with very sweet exteriors, which masked the intense anger and frustration revealed in their fantasy play. In another group, the little girls presented with hypergirlish behaviors, entertaining and caring for their parents (and therapists), paying the price in their own constriction, lack of autonomy, and individuation. Linking a child's problems to those of others expedited parents' acceptance of their own children's difficulties.

Alternatively, important differences among children are seen in bold relief in groups, laying the groundwork for parents to seek individual solutions and plans. For example, it was clear that Mr. M.

could not have a joint custody situation like Mr. B. because the M.'s could not work cooperatively as the B.'s could, and the B.'s child's coping was not that of the M.'s. Frequently, this offsets parental demands for their rights, "because that's what's given in court now." The group setting helps parents realize that they are different, their children are different, and therefore their plans need to differ.

Technically, one of the difficult tasks of this session is how to provide feedback without making parents feel too discouraged, guilty, or angry. Connecting feedback about the child with possible resolutions to the problem and with positive aspects of the situation often reduces parents' guilt and anger. Thus, for example, in the W. case we reminded the mother of all the good work she had done in the early years with her child and helped her to focus now on improving her relationship with her son, together with considering how this might be accomplished.

A second danger lies in the fact that many children do not look troubled or symptomatic to their parents. While some children were indeed not symptomatic, others were developing symptoms that were not recognized because they were socially adaptive. As discussed in chapters 6 and 7, many of these children are compliant, undemanding, inhibited, and quietly withdrawn. Moreover, parents do not recognize that though their children are not currently symptomatic, they are at risk for problems if the fight continues. Here the group experience is invaluable, as parents can view firsthand how other children are becoming symptomatic under the stress of parental disputes that have continued for longer periods of time. By this time, there is usually a "Greek chorus" of warnings from other group members to support the need for preventive action.

Towards the end of the third session, tensions begin to mount. Parents usually become more emotionally involved in the group process. Group leaders, while maintaining a warm, noncritical friendliness, are becoming more focused and directed—presenting new ways of looking at the dispute and focusing on the fact that the parent may be contributing (if sometimes unwittingly) to the impasse. Gently though firmly, parental externalizations and rationalizations are not accepted; parents are asked to look further. Some internalization and owning of responsibility is required. Parents accept these confrontations because groups are inherently supportive, the support emanating from their peers as well as the leaders. Parents are told this is their impasse. Whether part of the problem or not, for the child's sake, they have to become part of the solution. The time pressure creates an urgency: The joint mediation sessions are forthcoming.

Fourth Session

As parents enter the fourth session, many are near resolution of their impasse or responsive to the needs of their children; others are not. For the former, we label and describe their impasse (to aid them in cognitively putting it aside) or offer clarifying interventions that help crystallize a resolution of their emotional conflicts. For example, for parents who feel they have failed and go to court to succeed, we underscore the failure of their marriage, not themselves, and redirect their search for success toward finding a resolution to the parental conflict. Parents are then asked (despite residual feelings) to move on to consider realistic plans for their children for the upcoming mediation sessions.

For those parents who are still firmly entrenched or who are unable to make the needs of their children central ("I have to think of myself," "If I'm happy, my child will be happy"; "I have given him [spouse] too much, he is not getting one more thing [child] from me"), we have found that the best strategy is to confront them with the reality, the unalterability, of their situations. They may then better assess the relative costs and benefits of future actions.

The aim, therefore, of the fourth session is to help parents reality-test, to confront differences between the realities of their situation and their fantasy constructions, wishes, and convictions. A second aim is to prepare specific agendas for the joint mediation sessions.

Again, we look for common themes among the group members, often focusing on one or more of three areas: the reality of the divorce situation, the reality of the ex-spouse, and the reality of the law and the options in court. Many parents deny the separation or its consequences. Some cling to reconciliation fantasies and forestall planning, while others, who want out of the marriage, expect not to give up anything (for example, time with the child). Some (who do not know what is expected during divorce) feel hurt when the ex-spouse does not behave as he or she did during the marriage. Others hope that with the divorce they will not have to deal with the other ever again. They refuse to coordinate any plans for the child or even to communicate with the spouse, hoping magically that the other will "disappear" or "drop dead." Parents may make unilateral decisions and become incensed when their plans are interfered with by the other parent. Here we facilitate the other group members pointing out that as a parent they have no choice: They have to find some way of relating to and making agreements with the ex-spouse. In fact, they need good-parenting contracts, which specify access and the kind of relationship they are going to have. Rules for how they behave and communicate need to be built into these parenting agreements.

In a neutral, nonjudgmental manner we discuss who the other parent is as a given fact. When an ex-spouse is emotionally disturbed, for example, we help the parent understand some of the dynamics of the other's disturbance and how to deal with that parent to avoid triggering the ex-spouse's special vulnerabilities. For example, Mrs. V., in dealing with her paranoid husband, was cautioned to give him very clear information about her living arrangements with her male friend and her plans for the child's visit. Out of fear, Mrs. V. often hid information and kept secrets from him, which only triggered his suspicions; clear contracts allayed his anxieties. To avoid a total negative reification of the ex-spouse, we then outline those areas in which the troubled mate, though disturbed, could still be an effective parent. When parents complain about the other's irresponsibility, lack of availability, or critical demeaning attitude, they are reminded that these were reasons they left the marriage. They could not transform their spouse then nor can they now. Hence, they have to become more astute in dealing with him or her. Basically, this strategy helps parents develop some critical distance from the ex-spouse and helps them avoid their conditioned responses.

Despite the interventions thus far, a few parents continue to insist on the "neglectful, inadequate caretaking" or the "immoral and pathological influence" of the other parent, with little or no evidence in reality. Hence they seek to curtail the child's access to the other parent or demand very stringent and restrictive conditions on that access. Other parents—for example, young mothers—can harbor unrealistic expectations as to their inalienable rights to their young children, despite prevailing laws that emphasize "frequent and continuing access to both parents." For these parents, the realities of the court situation—the content of the laws, norms, philosophy, and procedures of the court—is important information that helps shape a more realistic framework within which to enter the actual mediation sessions. Here the combined group experience is especially useful in reflecting on possible court responses to their dilemmas, since many parents in the group have been to court repeatedly in the past, at great financial expense and generally at even greater frustration with the outcomes. On the other hand, great care needs to be exercised to avoid giving legal advice and to avoid frightening away parents who need to return to court to protect their children adequately. For this reason, and to avoid the tyranny of biased information, parents are strongly encouraged to verify their beliefs with their attorneys and court workers. Moreover, the parents' right to go to court is underscored, and if mediation efforts break down or are not successful in protecting the child, we in fact recommend a return to court for a legally enforceable order.

After discussing the realities of their situation (that is, the facts that they cannot change the divorce, their ex-spouse, the laws of the land, and so on), which in effect limits options, the group begins to help each of the members define what they can do for themselves and their children. A specific agenda is prepared of what needs to be accomplished within the mediation sessions. Clearly defining areas to be covered and problems to be resolved rather than specific plans to be sought avoids the danger of parents entering mediation with unrealistic expectations as to outcomes or with preformed solutions to which they become intractably wedded. Expressing the belief that there are a number of creative solutions to their dilemmas encourages brainstorming and sets the stage for a mutual exploration of options.

Negotiation or Conflict-Resolution Phase

Following the prenegotiation counseling phase, the two parent groups are combined for three three-hour joint mediation sessions. The children's group ends and the children's counselor joins the enlarged adult group to provide direct information about the children and to help evaluate whether the child-care plans being developed are appropriate for the child. Hence, the joint mediation sessions involve five divorcing couples; several new spouses, grandparents, or significant others; and three counselor-mediators (that is, as many as fifteen to eighteen people might be present at a large conference table).

The aims of the joint mediation sessions are twofold: to provide couples with the experience of cooperatively resolving problems together and to help each couple develop their own specific parenting agreement. There is a great deal of drama and ritual to the joint sessions, reflected in the fact that attendance is high, energy is focused, and parents are dressed for the occasion. There is considerable excitement and curiosity about each of the parents' ex-spouses. Parents enter in procession accompanied by supportive and protective peers with whom they have developed a relationship over the preceding four weeks. This makes facing the ex-spouse easier.

In the context of this formality and ritual, a clear working agenda is set. Parents are told that the aim of the meetings is to develop a coparenting agreement that will improve their present situation, plan for the future, protect their children and foster their capacity to mediate. As in the first parent group session, starting with an agenda and providing a positive task focus contains anxiety, forestalls regression, and gives direction. We then review the content and possible forms agreements can take.

On one end of the spectrum are highly specific, formal written plans that concretely and clearly define: (1) access agreements (weekly, holiday, and vacation schedules); (2) specific procedures for how the couple are to work together and to negotiate future problems; and (3) legally enforceable safeguards aimed at alleviating central concerns. (For example, if Mr. M. does not return Johnny to school on time on Monday, he loses his Sunday overnight visit. If Mrs. G. finds a stable place to live, Tommy will be able to visit overnight, and so on.) On the other end of the spectrum are more general, informal working agreements that describe the principles that guide the couple in making their arrangements and coparenting their children. For some the agreement might entail delaying a final decision, developing instead a temporary plan that could give a mother time to reestablish herself or a couple time to rebuild trust. Whether written or unwritten, formal or informal, a set of "gentlemen's agreements" is also developed—specific agreements that are not enforceable in court but that are essential for building trust and important in shielding the child from conflict. Unique to each family's vulnerability to conflict, these agreements structure parental behaviors during potentially conflictual interactions so as to further their continued working together. Often they define very explicit family rules for behaving and communicating that place a set of restraints on the family (for example, parents will not speak negatively of one another in the presence of the children; parents will terminate their conversation for twenty-four hours after the mother's third request to the father to stop yelling). We convey the expectation that all will mediate some kind of parenting plan. However, even if couples do not formulate an agreement, they are reassured that they will have a clear plan of how to proceed.

In actuality, the joint mediation sessions comprise two stages: an initial transition from intensive counseling into mediation (session 1) and the actual mediation (sessions 2 and 3). The initial transition to negotiation affords group leaders the opportunity, for the first time, to see the couples together. This is especially important when the factual basis of a case keeps shifting (that is, when there are blatant contradictions as to events from each parent). The group setting provides an especially safe forum within which to request clarification of hotly disputed issues because the group norms, members, and leaders limit and restrain acting out. (For example, in one such meeting a father and stepfather were able to clarify a violent incident between them by explaining that each perceived he was being attacked by the other and was really trying to protect himself from the aggressor.) Some regression is seen in this first mediation session, as couples meet together often for the first time in many months. They are highly anxious and resume old, unproductive patterns that threaten to, or succeed in, reestablishing their impasse. Publicly predicting this regression is usually effective in minimizing it. In practice, therefore, the first joint mediation session is devoted to limiting this regression as well as preparing parents jointly for negotiations. We directly intervene in the couple's interaction, frame their impasse (thereby once again extricating it from the business at hand), clarify misunderstandings, air grievances, exchange apologies or forgiveness, and develop agreed-upon rules for how they will communicate during mediation sessions. The supportive and public nature of the group aids this process.

By the second joint session, group leaders move from the role of counselor to that of mediator and clearly inform parents that negotiations are under way. The leaders become more task oriented and operate more on an issue level: What do parents need to resolve? How are they going to go about it? What are their options? The plan is given central focus. At this point, emotional issues are clearly isolated and defined as separate problems to be worked on at another time and place. However, the intimate understanding the group has developed about each other's vulnerabilities during the preceding weeks is invaluable in helping parents determine where emotional and irrational themes are intruding into their decision making. Often a simple gesture or a short statement is sufficient to remind parents of earlier discussions about their impasse.

During the actual negotiations, each family situation is dealt with one at a time. As members have different timetables and readiness to mediate, we begin with families who have some capacity for sharing and who are most able to cooperate and settle. These couples pioneer and anchor the group, serving as models for others. When these couples are conciliatory and cooperative, showing resolution is possible, it has a ripple effect that increases the entire group's motivation to proceed. In fact, when one couple reaches a solution, a realization that there is nothing magical to resolution ensues, and others, given hope, want to know the route.

In practice, couples in groups receive four or five living demonstrations on how and how not to mediate. Couples are thus provided not only with a roadmap of where and where not to go but also with successful mediation strategies, tactics, and solutions. Further, observing others mediate on issues not their own provides couples with the opportunity to develop a more abstract understanding of the mediation process. This understanding guides their future negotiations. As with individual family mediation, a wide range of mediation styles and intervention techniques drawn from conflict-resolution theory and practice are useful in groups (for example, "one-text shuttle diplomacy"; developing agreements from areas of "overlapping self-interest" [Haynes, 1981]; sharpening a conflict and then considering the "best and worst alternatives to a negotiated agreement" [Fisher & Ury, 1981]). Here we focus on those techniques that emerge from the group structure and process.

The group medium affords new options and maneuverability. If a couple becomes highly resistant, stalemates on an issue, or reaches a plateau, attention is directed to another couple with a message to the former to "take a rest, and observe other couples make decisions together." If a parent proposes an outrageous solution, we also move to another couple; the message here is that no one is willing to listen. If a parent becomes overwhelmed emotionally, we suggest a short time out while another couple's parenting plan is being developed. If parents become involved in a tedious and angry debate over trivial issues, we draw their attention to the fact that they have one half hour of the group's time and are entitled to spend it however they wish. In actuality, the audience that witnesses these petty debates usually becomes bored, uncomfortable, and impatient. However, these exchanges reflect in a vivid manner their own futile exchanges, making them more likely to avoid this pitfall.

During the second and third mediation sessions, there is generally a crescendo of activity as five parental agreements are being developed simultaneously. To ensure that each receives proper attention and is individualized to the family's needs, once the general framework for an agreement is reached, the couple is invited to take time between sessions or during the session (in a corner of the room) to complete the details (for example, a specific time-sharing schedule). A most promising technique is that of delegating another group member, frequently the new spouse or grandparent, to act as mediator for the parents in these aside meetings. In this way the responsibility for making and keeping agreements is turned back into the natural extended kin network.

There are four dangers to the mediation sessions. First, some parents make agreements to save face, in submission to group pressure, conformity to group norms, or in obedience to the mediator, only later to refuse to honor the agreements. It is important, therefore, to test parents' compliance early in the mediation by asking them to make small changes. Moreover, discussing the rationale behind proposed agreements brings unspoken reservations to the surface. Second, some parents take time to deal with trivial issues, leaving little time to mediate important ones, while others hold out until the end and then refuse to make an agreement. A clear understanding from the start about what needs to be resolved (and in what order) helps avoid this problem. Third, some couples refuse to cooperate as they remain invested in the fight or resist being helped. The mediator can present the couple with a paradoxical intervention that either acknowledges his or her inability to help or directs the couple to continue the fight. To prove the mediator wrong, the couple often mediates. Alternatively, the mediator can directly confront or have the group confront the couple with their refusal to settle and its implications for themselves and their children. Fourth, sometimes there is emotional pressure within the group to resolve the conflict. (For example, the child's therapist wants to rescue the child, or the group insists on some "obvious solution" rather than allowing parents to create their own solutions.) In this way couples are deprived of the opportunity to work through issues and discover their own paths. The mediators' task, then, is continually to return responsibility to the parents, not only for the agreements they make but also for the consequences of their refusal to settle.

As this suggests, the group model can be potentially coercive and used with tyranny as group leaders or members pressure parents to submit to their interests and values. The primary safeguard here lies in the good clinical training of group leaders, a training which emphasizes understanding, self-awareness and support as major elements in change. Allowing parents time for continued mediation after the termination of group sessions to rework their agreements provides a second safeguard.

Implementation Phase

Following the last group mediation session, a counselor-mediator remains available to individual families if necessary for one or two postgroup interviews to draft or finalize agreements, for more ongoing mediation, to help implement or modify arrangements, and for emergency consultations in case of new or renewed incidence of conflict. We found that approximately one-third of families had some postgroup contact with our service. Although in our research design we did not include a reconvening of the group during the follow-up period, this would be a very appropriate addition to the group model. A number of the parents voluntarily remained in contact with each other; many more enquired about each other with great interest and concern at the formal two year evaluation. An ongoing peer-support group, led by successful "graduates" of the program, would be extremely useful in stabilizing long-term disputing couples and supporting those that are particularly dependent or borderline in their functioning as parents.

CASE ILLUSTRATION

A court mediator referred Jack and Marcia to our services with an editorial note: "This father is one of the most pathologically angry men I have ever seen, and the mother is emotionally unstable. I am concerned about the devastation of their entrenched fight on their five-year-old son, Sam."

This couple had been disputing in court over logistics of visitation for almost two years. With respect to the current dispute, Marcia, the mother, wanted to switch alternate weekends because she had to attend seminars on the weekends she was scheduled to have the boy. Jack, the father, flatly refused, saying he had been "jerked around enough by that bitch!" He said he had repeatedly arrived to pick up Sam for the visits at the agreed-upon time and place only to find that both the boy and his mother were not there. In fact, he had not seen his son for three months, including the Christmas holidays, because she continually "messed up the visits." When the couple did meet, they invariably became involved in mutually demeaning verbal assaults on one another that would often progress to violence. (She would wag her finger and chide him, he would call her names, she would slap his face, and he would punch her.) The police were routinely called to supervise the child's transitions amidst a great deal of drama that excited the interest of the neighborhood.

Upon presentation at our service, this man was imposing. He was a large-framed, burly truck driver with a macho, swaggering gait. Brusque, rude, and evasive in the initial interview, he took a rather cynically amused, condescending attitude toward the woman counselor. When he did deign to speak, he was a man of few words, and those few were mostly threats and foul language. "That slut won't tell me what weekends I can see my son. If she were here, I would punch her in the mouth! It would cost me three hundred dollars to get her face fixed but it would be cheaper than this process. It's a waste of time to come to counseling! I've tried decent ways to get a response from her. I want to take her to court where they'll really stick it to her and throw her in jail. Let her learn that she can't do this to people!" Later he fussed, "The court system doesn't help. It's filled with little people, cogs in wheels. They told me if we don't get a settlement, they would recommend me not seeing my son!"

Marcia, the mother, presented as a colorful and hysterical woman, rather heavily made up, dressed in a flamboyant manner, and adorned with excessive costume jewelry. Emotional lability characterized her functioning. At times she was gay and amusing with self-deprecating asides that bespoke self-esteem problems; at other times she would burst into tears or become very angry and rigid. Most notable were the rather vague, dismissive accounts that she gave as to why Sam, her son, was not seeing his father. She said she had tried to cooperate but there were various mix-ups. Once she had forgotten, another time Sam had a birthday party, another time she or the father had been confused about the time and place of the exchange. Other times, she claimed that the father did not turn up when expected and Sam was left at home for the weekend, quite disappointed.

A brief history from both parents revealed their impasse dynamics. The couple had a brief turbulent marriage of three years in which there were ongoing narcissistic struggles, each refusing to acknowledge the other. The marriage ended precipitously when she discovered her husband's lover. In retaliation, she cleared out his bank account and all the furniture from the home and drove away in his prized truck. It took extensive litigation and court orders to compel her to surrender these possessions and to establish child support payments, which he had refused to make. His final counterrevenge was to distribute her court-ordered financial settlement to her various creditors rather than giving her the lump-sum payment, so that in effect she received no money. Meantime, their five-year-old son became the prized trophy in the battle of wits between them in their ongoing attempt to salvage pride.

With each countermove, Marcia felt more rejected, abandoned, humiliated, and angry. Jack, on the other hand, felt extremely manipulated by her and experienced her moves as assaults on his masculine self image. Threats to terminate his rights as a father were the "last straw," and he became uncontrollably angry toward the court mediator who suggested the possibility. Underneath the anger in both parents, we sensed considerable sadness and guilt as well as shame. This was manifested in their tendency after particularly angry exchanges to wait for each other in the parking lot or telephone to offer small concessions. There was also a sense of a great deal of erotic attraction and excitement generated by the dramatic fights, which helped stave off depression and loss, especially for Marcia.

Both parents denied any impact of their disputes on their child. Jack simply insisted, "He's a normal kid," and did not perceive the boy's high anxiety or discern the boy's attempts to please him by acting tough and brave as dangerous and symptomatic. Nor did the mother connect his hyperactivity, restlessness, and problems in concentrating at school to the parental fights. She was entertained by his impish antics. (This was the child described in chapter 6 who flirted with danger and distracted his mother from her depression, which inevitably followed the parental fights.)

There were a number of interventions made at several levels into this impasse. Here we will present some of the central strategies that were used within the group to effect change. Jack and Marcia were assigned to two different concurrently-running groups for four weeks of pre-negotiation counseling. Our agenda with the father was to have him understand the extent to which he provoked and incited the disputes with Marcia and to show him how the conflict was affecting his child. At the same time, we wanted to support this man's continued relationship with his son. There was a threat that he could walk away from the whole situation and the child would be left solely in the care of this emotional, hysterical mother. On the other hand, we considered that his implicit demands for the boy to be tough and supermasculine were a problem. We wanted to draw out his more nurturing qualities which we sensed existed beneath the aggressive posturing.

Actively engaging Jack in the sessions was an obvious problem. He initially sat back from the group with a condescending little smile or read the evening newspaper, hence distancing himself from the others and dismissing the value of the group's enterprise. We judged it unwise to confront him or tell him straightforwardly about the child's problems and what he should do about them. (He already felt controlled and demeaned, especially by women.) Instead, a strategy was devised in which each of the two leaders took actively opposite viewpoints about his situation and each led the group members in a lively debate. Hence, the father was a passive audience to his own family dilemma. While one counselor insisted that the father provoked the mother (for example, by writing four-letter words on the child-support check), the other countered that the mother was the one who "set him up" (by changing the times and dates of the visits). One group member commented that it was obvious that Marcia was still very much in love with Jack, and fighting was her way of staying in contact. (This man cited his own ex-wife's analysis of the situation, since she attended the other group with Marcia.)

Turning his attention to the effect of the parental fight on the child, the counselors then "wondered" about the meaning of the child's school problems, and why Sam was so restless and hyperactive. Other group members offered suggestions, very aptly linking the child's anxiety and attempts to entertain, distract, and please his parents as responses to the ongoing feud and his mother's depression. Finally, while one counselor voiced the opinion that the father was too tough and demanding and was not affectionate and supportive enough with the little boy, the other counselor strongly disagreed and insisted that the mutual teasing and roughhousing between the boy and his father were "ways in which men express affection toward one another; anyone could see that this father loved his boy, was going through a great deal to see him, and had much to offer!"

This playing out of the family drama and this man's ambivalences inevitably drew Jack into the group process, and he became actively involved despite himself. He sheepishly admitted he did write insulting remarks on the child-support checks; he was flattered that his ex-wife still found him attractive, and he argued that he was affectionate with his son (for example, they made pancakes together and always kissed goodnight even though they both joked "Yuck!" and wiped the kisses right off). He was especially gratified during the third session when he reported yet another incident in which his ex-wife did not have Sam available for the visit, and the other group members became properly incensed on his behalf. In response, this large burly, aggressive man sat back and meekly asked, "What should I do now?" The leaders suggested a clear and specific visitation agreement with safeguards to protect his relationship with his son and helped him draw up an agenda in preparation for the mediation sessions.

Within the corresponding group in which Marcia, the mother, participated, she created quite a stir with her sardonic humor, tears, and peppery outbursts. The other group members responded supportively to her fears to the extent her feelings resonated with their own. When asked about the dispute over the child, Marcia immediately launched into a detailed account of her traumatic marital separation with enormous emotional intensity, as though it had happened yesterday and not three years previously. The leaders commented on this fact and talked about "shattered dreams," this being a shared theme among the impasses of these particular group members. As Marcia wept, another woman teared in recognition of her own sadness and loneliness, and another man (who was still in love with his wife twelve years after the divorce), grandly passed her a large red handkerchief saying, "You haven't gotten to my story yet!" A strong sense of comradrie developed between these particular three group members as they exchanged stories and mourned together their disappointed hopes. Later, the group leaders were able to confront them on their holding onto the past: "Marcia has cried for three years, Maria for five, and Ted for twelve years. How much longer do you want to devote to mourning your lost dreams? What keeps you from turning away from your ex-mates and putting together a new life, dating, and making new friends?" To Marcia, in particular, "You deserve more than this, why do you continually put yourself down or into a situation where men put you down?" At the same time, the group leaders spoke with respect and admiration of her capacity to work and financially support herself as a high school teacher: "You are obviously an intelligent and independent woman."

During the third session, a less productive aspect of this strong alliance between these particular group members became apparent when we, as leaders, began to discuss the children's need for both parents. Since Marcia and Ted were holding on to their children partly as replacements for and as punishments to their lost spouses, they tended to focus group opinion in ways that justified denying visits to the other parent. The strategy with Marcia was to remark that we were very glad her negativity toward the visits was "out on the table." Up until this point, she had denied she had purposefully kept the child from the father and instead insisted on many other sundry reasons for the aborted visits. This led to a frank discussion with her about what were real and what were unrealistic fears of Sam being with his father and her own fears about being alone. Then we discussed likely negative consequences if the boy did not continue to see his father. She conceded he needed to visit and was ready to prepare an agenda of issues to be addressed in the upcoming mediation sessions.

In general, the public nature of the group mediation gratified this couple's exhibitionistic desires and provided a dramatic ritual that celebrated the ending of their marriage. When the two parents' groups were joined to form one large group, Jack and Marcia played a special role that facilitated the mediation sessions. First, their continued attraction for one another as well as their competitiveness with one another was evident from the manner in which both had dressed for the occasion. Second, they immediately engaged in a series of petty verbal brawls that quickly degenerated into mutually degrading insults. Resisting the temptation to confront them on this, the group leaders instead observed to one another that they really never understood how much fun Jack and Marcia got out of fighting; that they must have had a particularly lively, exciting marriage. Marcia stopped, laughed ruefully, and admitted it was so. She remembered that their dinner parties were of great amusement to their friends and that several little neighborhood children used to "play Jack and Marcia fights" in imitation of them. Jack smirked in agreement. Henceforth, the group positively connoted their frequent fighting, usually laughed with them at the next series of barbs, and marveled at the ingenious ways they devised to provoke each other. To the extent that their marital relationship was honored as special, Marcia's self-respect was increased. When she felt less humiliated, she provoked him less, and he felt less manipulated and had less need to demean her. In this way, the vicious cycle was disrupted. Additionally, the other group members were able to gain some critical distance on their own petty disputes as they joked about Jack and Marcia's. At the same time, the counselor-mediators seriously addressed the fact that while their fighting was entertaining, they also tended to "hit below the belt." They said and did things to one another that really hurt and the fight degenerated to mutual humiliation and sometimes to physical fights. Besides, their son didn't always know when they were having fun and when they were serious!

The actual mediation was brief given this preparation but it was strategic. Because we believed that this particular couple could easily disrupt and rescind all previous agreements made, we did not give them this opportunity. Instead the leaders began the negotiations by passing them a written copy of their present agreement and asked them about "the adjustments they needed to make to this plan that would make it more workable". They were able to make mutually acceptable changes relatively easily. Because we remained concerned about Marcia's hysterical tendency to agree to something on one level and undo it on another, unconscious level, we predicted there would be further upsets and built in special safeguards that would, in particular, protect the father's contact with the child (that is, a clause that specified the consequences of either parent failing to comply and provisions for further mediation at our service). Three years later, although the parental relationship continued to be fiery, physical aggression had ceased, verbal insults were rare, and Sam was having fairly regular access to his father.

Outcomes Two to Three Years Later

A brief evaluation of the outcome of our mediation services was made six months following completion of the active intervention at which time the counselors reported on the status of the dispute, whether agreements were maintained and court recidivism. Data was available for all eighty (100 percent) families at this point. A full evaluation was conducted between two and three years later, during which time parents and children were interviewed. Seventy-seven of the eighty families were located during this follow-up, and at least one member from seventy-five of those families agreed to participate fully in the outcome assessment. This constitutes a return rate of 94 percent of the original sample. In total, 85 percent of the mothers, 74 percent of the fathers, and 70 percent of the children were interviewed at the second follow-up.

The relative success of the interventions was assessed first by the number of parents who mediated agreements, the number who maintained or were able to renegotiate these agreements over the follow-up period, and the number who returned to court during the follow-up period. Second, we evaluated the extent to which the coparenting relationship had improved, assessing the relative levels of parental conflict, cooperation, satisfaction with the agreement, and amount of sharing of the children. Third, we tried to assess whether the different interventions affected the children's adjustment at the follow-up, and fourth, we examined the relative cost-effectiveness and efficiency of the interventions. Finally, we critically evaluated the extent to which the impasse had been resolved at the two- to three-year mark.

What was our overall success rate? At the end of the intensive counseling-mediation, 82.5 percent of the families had reached agreement. Two years later, 44 percent had kept the plan developed with the service, 16 percent had renegotiated on their own using the original plan as a basis, and a small group (3 percent) had sought another private mediator. Hence, almost two-thirds were managing on their own. Thirty-six percent had returned to court, half to a court mediator, and half to a judge (after further mandatory mediation failed). Those who returned only to mandatory mediation usually attended only one brief session, often at the suggestion of the counselor who wanted to enhance a parent's reality testing. Thirteen percent of the sample returned only once to court, and 23 percent went two or more times over custody and access matters. We regard this remainder, approximately one-fourth of the sample, as comprising the subgroup our impasse-directed model of mediation was unable to help.

At the two- to three-year mark, in the sample as a whole, there was a marked diminution of expressed hostility and conflict. From the Straus Conflict Tactics Scale, we find that verbal aggression had decreased from an average of once every week at baseline to once a month at the followup. Physical aggression had virtually disappeared, from once a month or more at baseline to less than once a year at followup (see Table A.1). These rates of aggression are now more commensurate to those in a normal divorcing population (compare Gonzales, Krantz, & Johnston, 1984).

Comparing the Individual Family and Group Service Models

During specified periods of the initial intervention, either the individual family mediation service was available or, at other times only the multifamily group service was offered. A total of forty families were assigned to the individual model and forty to groups. There were no significant differences between the families who were as-

Table A.1   Verbal and Physical Aggression Between Parents*
(Mean number of incidences during previous twelve months)

	Baseline (before mediation)		Two-Year Follow-Up	
	Mean	SD	Mean	SD
Verbal reasoning	25.03	22.7	11.42	10.57
Verbal aggression	54.48	45.4	11.93	17.43
Physical aggression	11.31	17.58	.84	2.61

*Data are from the Straus Conflict Tactics Scale (Form N). Both parents' responses are averaged.

signed to the two treatment models in terms of their demographic characteristics (ethnicity, occupation, employment status, and income) and dispute-related data (length of separation, length of parental dispute over child, content of dispute, and conflict tactics). Figure A.1 summarizes the structure of the two models and shows how families move through the services from intake to follow-up.

At the end of the negotiation phase, 80 percent of those divorcing couples in the individual service and 85 percent of those in the group service reached agreements. After six months, 70 percent and 75 percent of the families in the individual and group services respectively had kept agreements or renegotiated the plan by themselves. Two years later, the stability of the agreement and ability to renegotiate outside of the court had changed to 63 percent for the individual and 64 percent for the group model. The number of families who returned to court to either the court mediator or to the judge showed similar trends. Statistical tests revealed no significant differences between the individual and group models in terms of mediated agreements, ability to negotiate on their own, and court recidivism. (See Table A.2.)

In terms of improvements in the coparental relationship (in particular the levels of parental conflict, cooperation, and satisfaction with the agreement), we found that the group model showed better outcomes than the individual model. At the two- to three-year mark, group members compared to parents seen individually were significantly less likely to be verbally aggressive with one another, even after controlling for the initial levels of aggression ($F = 6.2, p < 0.05$). They were also less likely to be in dispute over child support at follow-up ($x^2 = 6.0, p < 0.05$). The fathers, but not the mothers, who had group treatment, were significantly more satisfied with their custody and access arrangements ($t = 2.44, p < 0.05$). Parents experiencing the group treatment were more likely to discuss and share decision making about their children and also to talk together about other unrelated matters ($t = 1.8, p = 0.06$).

Documenting the differential effects of the individual and group treatment intervention for the children was more difficult. The children's adjustment at the two- to three-year mark (as measured by the Achenbach Behavior Problem Checklist and Social Competence Scale) was not significantly better in the group or individual model. However, since children benefited when parents decreased their verbal and physical aggression toward one another, we conclude that the group treatment had a greater indirect positive effect on child outcome. (See Johnston & Campbell, 1987 for further details.)

Figure A.1   Flow Chart and Structure of Two Service Models

Phases	Court Referral	
	Intake	
	Information-Gathering Interviews	
	One or two individual interviews conducted with each parent and each child. Significant others invited to participate in counseling. Standardized measures and questionnaires completed.	
	Individual Family Impasse-Directed Mediation Model	Multifamily (Group) Impasse-Directed Mediation Model
I. Prenegotiation or Counseling Phase (preparation for Negotiation)	Each family member is seen in individual and, when appropriate, conjoint interviews.	Five families of mixed sex and mixed custodial arrangements are seen together. Parents seen separately from exspouse.
	Length of service depends on the family's individual needs.	Four two-hour weekly parents' groups conducted.
		Four two-hour weekly children's groups conducted.
	One counselor-mediator sees the entire family.	Two counselor mediators lead the parent group; one counselor conducts children's group.
II. Negotiation or Conflict Resolution Phase	Conjoint interviews are conducted (if appropriate) with parents to finalize plans and draft access agreements.	Three three-hour joint mediation groups conducted with the two parent groups combined; all three counselors-mediators are present.
	On-Call Consultation	
III. Implementation Phase	A counselor-mediator is available to the family for emergencies and continued mediation.	
	Six-Month and Thirty-Two-Month Follow-Up	

Table A.2   Comparative Outcomes of Individual and Group Services and Overall Outcomes of Impasse-Directed Mediation

Outcomes	At end of mediation		At six months postmediation		At thirty-two months postmediation		Total
	Individual / Group		Individual / Group		Individual / Group		Individual / Group
Completed mediation with service	32/40 (80%)	34/40 (85%)	—	—	—	—	66/80 (82.5%)
Kept or renegotiated agreement	—	—	28/40 (70%)	30/40 (75%)	24/38 (63%)	25/39 (64%)	49/77 (64%)
Managed by themselves	—	—	—	—	10/38 (26%)	13/39 (33%)	23/77 (30%)
Used private third party (service, therapist, mediator)	—	—	—	—	10/38 (26%)	3/39 (21%)	18/77 (23%)
Dropped issues under dispute	—	—	—	—	4/38 (10%)	4/39 (10%)	8/77 (10%)
Returned to court	7	2	3	4	4	8	28/77 (36%)
To mandatory mediation only	1	0	3	3	2	6	15/77 (19%)
For judicial decision	6	2	0	1	2	2	13/77 (17%)

The most important difference in outcome of the group compared to the individual service was in the arena of cost-effectiveness and efficiency. To test the relative cost-effectiveness of the two models, we compared the number of staff hours of direct service to each family and the number of months that each family took to complete the intervention. All face-to-face service hours, including intake, counseling, mediation, and implementation were included in these analyses. Nondirect service hours (for example, staff strategy conferences, telephone consultations with clients, attorneys, and significant others) were not included. The group model required preparatory discussions among team members, especially for those novice to the method. For experienced leaders, approximately one hour of staff conference time per group session is needed. Given that the individual model also required staff-staff consultations as well as far more phone calls, we estimate near equal nondirect service time was required for both models.

On the average, the groups required 17.3 hours ($sd = 4.5$) per family compared to 27.6 hours ($sd = 19.2$) for each family seen individually. This highly significant difference ($t = 3.28$, $p < 0.001$) indicates that in terms of paid staff hours, the groups were more than 40 percent cost-effective than the individual service. As for the duration of treatment, families in groups maintained contact with the service for an average of 6.4 months ($sd = 4.6$) compared to an average of 12.1 months ($sd = 10$) for those families seen individually. The groups hence took about half the time to accomplish the same task, also a highly significant difference ($t = 3.28$, $p < .005$). Part of the reason for this greater efficiency is that the groups seemed to be more intensive and goal directed, the leaders' role more defined, and the parents more task oriented. The individual model was more drawn out, with parents becoming more dependent on the service, requiring more outside phone contact and a longer period of monitoring the implementation of the agreements.

In sum, on all success criteria, the group model proved to be either equal to the individual model (with respect to parents' ability to develop and maintain agreements and stay out of court) or better than the model in which families are seen individually (with respect to the parents' capacity to co-operate and co-parent with diminished aggression). Most significantly, the group model proved to be far less costly, in terms of staff hours required and the time taken to effect change. In addition, as counselors and mediators, we felt that multifamily mediation compared to individual family mediation reduced worker stress and burnout, a particular problem in working with these families.

The Status of the Impasse at Followup

There was wide variation among the families in the qualitative changes in the impasse and the degree of resolution achieved two to three years after the initial mediation.[1] We estimate that a minority (one-fifth of the sample) had completely resolved their impasse, in the sense that there was no longer any active dispute and parents were working cooperatively together, able to flexibly renegotiate changes in the schedule and respond to their children's changing developmental needs. Generally, at least one of these parents had gained some understanding of the dynamics of their dispute and were able to act so as to free themselves, the other parent, and child from the impasse. Some understood their own contribution to the impasse. For example, they saw their previous attempts to protect their child were inappropriate or realized, "I didn't need the court to confirm I was a father." One mother who had desperately clung to her ex-husband two years earlier realized after he left the state that she could live alone. She then negotiated visits more rationally. Some parents had undergone a religious conversion, taking on a new philosophy or standard with which to evaluate their actions: "I had to give up my anger and let go." These changes set off a positive chain reaction in the ex-spouse. Others better understood their ex-spouse: "I thought he was violent, now I realize he's a mouse trying to be a lion," and this woman was now more supportive of her ex-mate.

Sometimes both parents had resolved their interactional impasse, for example given up the idealized or devalued view of the other, and had formed an effective working partnership on behalf of the child. These parents knew what calmed and what incited the other parent and consciously decided not to provoke. In part, they already knew all too well the dangers of not working together. In part, positive experiences with one another were motivating, and they became invested in keeping a good relationship going. They not only valued the co-parental alliance, but they valued and respected each other more. These positive attitudes helped heal the narcissistic injury, self-esteem was elevated by the other's acknowledgement. Beneficial, rather than vicious, cycles of interaction were created and layers of the impasse unraveled.

These were not problem-free partnerships. In fact, these parents soberly and realistically acknowledged each other's vulnerabilities and problems, but despite these and the frustrations they engendered, they had found a way of working mutually. In fact, this level of resolution was not only characteristic of those who were psychologically more intact. Some parents with long-standing and serious psychological difficulties were able to be extremely cooperative with and supportive of one another. In these particular cases, we found success was partly due to the continued availability of a skilled therapist who functioned as a mediator and executive coordinator of the family during times of stress and crisis. Here the therapist absorbed parental angers, balanced their competing needs, and provided them with an auxiliary ego or new guidelines for behavior. Most importanily, they provided a feedback mechanism between the parents' separate worlds, allowing the parents to coordinate decision-making around the children. Effective family or child therapy hence was one of the mechanisms for resolving emerging new conflicts and increasing both the stability and flexibility of co-parental functioning over the longer term.

For a much larger group (approximately two-fifths of the sample), there was marked improvement but the resolution was less than optimal. We could identify many of the elements of the original impasse in the present family dynamics, although the disputes engendered were more covert, milder, or less frequent. Some families were stable but very sensitive to stress and vulnerable to renewed conflict. While their custody and access arrangements worked smoothly and they were not fighting, their bitterness, anger, distrust and disagreements lay dormant and potentially could be reactivated with little provocation. There were a number of factors responsible for the overall reduced conflict and the improvement that we observed.

Several parents explained that their children were now older and could better fend for themselves, hence they felt less compelled to protect their children from their ex-spouse. In fact, as these children grew older (into early adolescence and teens), they did assume more responsibility for arranging visits and making schedule changes, thereby reducing parental contact and potential for dispute. Providing they were allowed to negotiate these changes freely, unfettered by parent's opposing demands, the children seemed to do this reasonably well.

However, for some children, the peace between parents had come at a price. It was worrisome to note that a number of these children had assumed the burden of maintaining the precarious balance of family stability. To varying extents, they had sacrificed their own needs (time with their friends and pursuit of their own interests) in order to accommodate to their parents' wants and schedules. For example, they had accepted split-time joint custody schedules or rigid every-other-weekend visits or even refused to visit a parent in order to please and placate. They went back and forth without protest (or protection) between their parents' two separate worlds and could not easily make requests that would allow them to change the visits in order to attend special events with their peers. Some remained as the primary companion, confidante or surrogate spouse to a dependent parent. Some continued to act like chameleons, passively merging with whichever parent they were with, remaining constricted, subdued and unaware of their own feelings and ideas. Some became very proficient at actively orchestrating the various demands of their competing parents and appeasing both, but seemed sadly burdened by these responsibilities. (Wallerstein, 1985a, 1985b, has made similar observations). Hence our predictions about the accommodating stances of many of these children described in chapters 6 and 7, together with the constriction and diffusion of their sense of themselves, were to varying degrees borne out. The longer-term effects of the sacrifices these children were making warrants serious investigation.

More commonly, the decreased intensity of the dispute was achieved by parents avoiding each other assiduously. They never met or talked with one another, did not interfere in each other's lives, and pursued their own style of parenting. Rather than joint decision making around the needs of the child, each followed a policy of noninterference with the other. This "parallel parenting" worked partly because they had a very structured time-sharing agreement and partly because, as noted above, the children did not protest or make other demands. These parents accepted the inevitability and routine of the children's visiting arrangement, while voicing to the counselor when asked that they objected to many aspects of the situation. However, they felt it was futile trying to change the situation ("She'll never change! It's not worth it!"), because they did not want to fight anymore or because they were invested in a new relationship elsewhere. The fact that their children lived in two separate worlds did not seem problematic providing that those two worlds never crossed and the children were not caught in contradictory expectations. However, in these cases, visiting schedules were often extremely rigid and unresponsive to the child's changing needs. Where a fixed visiting schedule was not in place, the child often found it difficult to summon up the courage to initiate contact with the other side. Hence visiting became less frequent or gradually ceased entirely over time.

Several parents, all but one of whom were fathers, withdrew their demands to see the child. They withdrew in frustration with their ex-spouse, because they were driven away by the parent-child alliance, or because they felt depreciated and angry at a court order. Nineteen children were not visited by one parent at follow-up. In those cases where the children were very young (under two) and had never become bonded to this absent parent, they did not seem upset. In fact, they seemed to benefit from the absence of conflict, especially if the remaining parent was emotionally more stable and had remarried successfully. However, the larger group of children, who had been attached to the abandoning parent, showed many distress symptoms. They were depressed, grieved the loss, and exhibited poor self-esteem, feeling unworthy and rejected. They also felt guilty that they were somehow responsible for driving the parent away. They worried that they had not fought hard enough or taken a strong enough stand to show they cared, hence felt they had disappointed the parent and caused him or her to leave.

The remainder, almost two-fifths of the families, showed no obvious improvement. In fact, 15 percent of the total sample had actually deteriorated over the follow-up period. The impasse had not shifted, and they either continued in chronic conflict or had cycles of cooperative and conflictual exchanges. Among the few couples who deteriorated, there was severe conflict: new or renewed accusations of abuse, neglect or sexual molestation, repeated litigation, involving the extensive participation of mental health professionals, attorneys, police, and court personnel. The impasse had spread to involve ever-widening circles of others. Some families expanded their disputing network over three court systems and two states. In general, these families who showed no improvement were disrupted also by more stressful life events (unemployment, illness) and loss of important sources of support (the family home, breakup of new relationships). Psychologically, many of these parents became more depressed, embittered and entrenched, unable to go on and find a new life for themselves. These families remained disorganized: decisions were made by default, and often impulsively and unilaterally. It was no surprise that their children were the most symptomatic and often seriously disturbed. This, in turn, intensified the stress and parents' mutual blaming, becoming another active component of the impasse.

Overall, these evaluations of outcome are both gratifying and sobering. On the one hand, approximately two-thirds of these families have achieved some degree of resolution of the impasse and have maintained coparenting agreements or can renegotiate further problems on their own. There was also a dramatic reduction in levels of overt conflict (verbal and physical aggression) between the parents. Hence, to this extent, the hazards to children's development were reduced by preventing the parental fight from becoming chronic. This "success rate" is gratifying given the relative brevity of the intervention and the disputatious nature of the sample. Recall that this subpopulation of divorcing families, from the outset, was selected because they had not been able to complete their child custody agreements despite the efforts of their attorneys and court mediators. In fact, at intake they had met many of the criteria used to predict poor prognosis in mediation: they had been enmeshed, litigious, had high levels of anger and violence and were ambivalent about their separation. They were also assessed as having moderately severe pathology, personality disorders and/or stress reactions and to varying extents had problems in separating their needs from their children's. On the other hand, the outcomes are sobering. From the qualitative evaluations, we conclude that when divorce disputes are settled, the structure of post-divorce family relationships stabilize into many different forms, some of which had worrisome implications for children. Whether stable or no longer in overt conflict, the disturbed functioning of a number of these families threatens their children's longer-term psychological and social development. Hence, counselors and mediators need to examine the kinds of family structures that emerge during the resolution of the divorce impasse and ensure that the family's restructuring is appropriate for the children.

This book has addressed the plight of an increasingly large population of families for whom divorce is not a relief from an unhappy marriage because it does not signal the end of parental disputes. Instead it may signal the beginning of chronic struggles over the children between distressed parents, or disturbed patterns of parent-child relationships where the children bear the long-term burden of preventing their parents from destroying themselves and each other. The outlook for these children is ominous, even grim, with disturbing implications for the next generation unless we can find better ways of helping them.

Notes

Chapter 2

1. This divorcing population is very unlike that in Wallerstein and Kelly's (1980) study, in which only 10 percent of the families had extended family networks geographically available during the marriage.

2. The roles taken by new partners and extended kin in the custody and access dispute were qualitatively described by the counselors and rated on a five-point scale. All the rates reported were obtained from the consensus judgments of two clinicians.

3. In our group, some 12 percent of ex-husbands and 10 percent of ex-wives had kin who fell into this category.

4. Less than 20 percent of ex-wives, and about 10 percent of ex-husbands, were so affected.

5. This kind of extended family structure may involve either a strongly matriarchal or patriarchal culture which unbalances the nuclear family, making divorce more likely.

6. Our focus has been on the conditions under which disputes spread and become more intense. Conversely, it is important to note the conditions under which conflict is dampened. Aside from situations in which kin and others temper parents' anger, some parents did not press for custody because their new partners did not actively want the child. Given their own considerable guilt and ambivalence about the divorce, parents were more likely to receive only ambivalence or weak support from others. When the kin networks of both parents were intertwined by marriage and friendships in a close community, the polarization and splitting of the networks were less likely to occur. Finally, when there were multiple cross-alignments of support given by kin to ex-spouses (for example, the mother was supported by the maternal grandmother and paternal aunt, and the father was supported by the maternal grandfather and paternal uncle), the elements of support seemed to cancel each other out.

Chapter 3

1. The basic theory about this sociopsychological process is developed by Berger (1988) and Johnston (1988).

Chapter 4

1. Interrater reliability for the broad distinction between presence and absence of indicators of personality disorder ranged from .88 to .96.

Chapter 5

1. Wallerstein (1985b) has referred to this phenomena as the syndrome of the overburdened child.

Chapter 6

1. Common concerns and different styles of coping with those concerns for each group were identified by consensus among three clinicians. Interrater reliability between two clinicians who independently evaluated the extent of each child's coping was .89 (Spearman's *rho*).

Chapter 7

1. Minuchin (1974) has discussed in detail the implications of these structural disturbances for intact families; Isaacs, Montalvo, and Abelsohn (1986) have detailed their implications for divorcing families.
2. These clinical observations were supported by their excessively high test scores (mean = 85th percentile) on the Piers-Harris measure of self-esteem (Piers, 1984).

Chapter 8

1. Half the children in our study were seen individually; half were seen in small groups with their peers.

Appendix

1. These evaluations were made by consensus among the three counselors who interviewed the families at the two- to three-year follow-up.

Selected Bibliography and References

Achenbach, T. M., and C. Edelbrock. (1983). *Manual for the child behavior checklist and revised child behavior profile*. Burlington, VT.:, Queen City Printers.

Ahrons, C. R. (1981). The continuing coparental relationship between divorced spouses. *American Journal of Orthospychiatry* 51: 415–27.

American Psychiatric Association (1980). *Diagnostic and statistical manual of mental disorders*, third edition (DSM-III). Washington, D.C.: American Psychiatric Association.

Berger, J., S. Rosenholtz, and M. Zelditch, Jr. (1980). Status-organizing processes. *Annual Review of Sociology* 6: 479–508.

Berger, J. (1988), A theory of normative control processes. In *Studies in expectation-states theory*, ed. M. Webster and M. Foschi. Stanford, Calif.: Stanford University Press.

Berger, P., and H. Kellner (1970). Marriage and the construction of reality. In *Recent sociology* 2, ed. H. P. Pretzel, 50–73. New York: Macmillan Co.

Bienenfeld, F. (1983). Child custody mediation. Science & Behavior Books.

Bohannon, P. 1970. Divorce and after. Garden City, N.Y.: Doubleday.

Booney, L. A. (1985). Child custody mediation groups: A model for supplementing case-by-case strategies. *Conciliation Courts Review* 23:47–54.

Brown, D. G. (1982). Divorce and family mediation: History, review, future consideration. *Conciliation Courts Review* 20:1–44.

Cauble, A. E., N. Thoennes, J. Pearson, & R. Appleford (1985). A case study: Custody resolution counseling in Hennepin County, Minnesota. *Conciliation Courts Review* 23:27–36.

Cooglar, O. (1978). *Structured mediation in divorce settlements: A handbook for marital mediators*. Lexington, MA.: D. C. Heath.

Cooley, C. H. (1964). *Human nature and the social order*. New York: Schocken Books.

Fisher, R., & W. Ury (1981). *Getting to yes*. Boston: Houghton-Mifflin.

Folberg, J., & A. Taylor (1984). *Mediation: A comprehensive guide to resolving conflicts without litigation.* San Francisco: Jossey-Bass.

Furstenberg, F. F. Jr., J. L. Peterson, C. W. Nord, & N. Zill (1983). The life course of children of divorce: Marital disruption and parental contact. *American Sociological Review* 48:656–668.

Gamson, W. (1969). A theory of coalition formation. *American Sociological Review* 26:373–382.

Gardner, R. A. (1976). *Psychotherapy with children of divorce.* New York: Jason Aronson.

Gold, L. (1984). Interdisciplinary team mediation. In *Procedures for guiding the divorce mediation process,* ed. J. A. Lemmon, *Mediation Quarterly* 6: 27–46. San Francisco: Jossey-Bass.

Goldstein, J., A. Freud, & A. J. Solnit (1979). *Beyond the best interests of the child.* New York: Free Press.

Gonzalez, R., S. E. Krantz, & J. R. Johnston (1984). Predictors of post-divorce conflict. Paper presented at the Western Psychological Association Meetings, San Francisco, April.

Hansen, C. M. (1983). The effects of interparental conflict on the adjustment of the preschool child in divorce Ph. D. diss., University of Colorado, Boulder.

Haynes, M. M. (1981). *Divorce mediation: A practical guide for therapists and counselors.* New York: Springer Publishing Co.

Heider, F. (1958). The psychology of interpersonal relations New York: John Wiley.

Hetherington, E. M., M. Cox, & R. Cox, (1982). Effects of divorce on parents and children. In *Nontraditional families,* ed. M. E. Lamb, 233–288. London: Lawrence Erlbaum.

Hodges, W. F. (1986). *Interventions for children of divorce: Custody, access and psychotherapy.* New York: Wiley-Interscience.

Huntington, D. S. (1985). Theory and method: The use of psychological tests in research on divorce. *Journal of the American Academy of Child Psychiatry* 24:583–589.

Isaacs, M. B., B. Montalvo, & D. Abelsohn (1986). *The difficult divorce.* New York: Basic Books.

Johnston, J. R. (1985). Personality attributes and the structure of interpersonal relations, In *Status, rewards and influence,* eds. J. Berger & M. Zelditch, Jr. 317–349. San Francisco: Jossey-Bass.

Johnston, J. R., L. E. G. Campbell, & M. C. Tall (1985). Impasses to the resolution of custody and visitation disputes. *American Journal of Orthopsychiatry* 55:112–119.

Johnston, J. R., & L. E. G. Campbell (1987). Instability in the networks of divorced and disputing families. In *Advnaces in group processes: Theory and research,* vol. 4 ed. E. J. Lawler & B. Markovsky, 243–269. New York: JAI Press.

Johnston, J. R., R. Gonzalez, & L. E. G. Campbell (1987). Ongoing post-divorce conflict and child disturbance. *Journal of Abnormal Child Psychology*, 15:493–509.

Johnston, J. R. (1988). The structure of ex-spousal relations: The integration and application of a set of expectation-state theories. In *Studies in expectation-states theory*, ed. M. Webster & M. Foschi Stanford University Press.

Johnston, J. R., M. Kline, Tschann, & L. E. G. Campbell (1988). Ongoing post-divorce conflict in families contesting custody: Does joint custody and frequent access help? Papers presented to the 65th Annual Meeting of the American Orthopsychiatric Association, San Francisco, March 30th, 1988.

Jones, E. E., and K. E. Davis (1965). From acts to dispositions: The attribution process in person perception. In ed. L. Berkowitz, *Advances in Experimental Social Psychology*, vol. 2., New York: Academic Press.

Kalter, N., J. Peckar, & M. Lesowitz (1984). School-based developmental facilitation groups for children of divorce: A preventive intervention. *American Journal of Orthopsychiatry* 54:613–623.

Kalter, N. (1987). Long-term effects of divorce on children: A developmental vulnerability model. *American Journal of Orthopsychiatry* 57:587–600.

Kaslow, F. (1979–81). Stages of divorce: A psychological perspective. *Villanova Law Review* 25:718–751.

Kelley, H. H. (1973, February). The processes of causal attribution. *American Psychologist*, 107–128.

Kelley, J. B. (1983). Mediation and psychotherapy: Distinguishing the differences. *Mediation Quarterly* 1:33–44.

Kernberg, O. (1967). Borderline personality organization. *Journal of American Psychoanalytic Association* 15:641–687.

Kessler, S. (1975). *The American way of divorce: Prescriptions for change.* Chicago: Nelson-Hall.

Koch, M. P., & C. R. Lowery (1984). Evaluation of mediation as an alternative to divorce litigation. *Professional Psychology: Research and Practice* 15:109–120.

Kohut, H. (1977). *The restoration of self.* New York: International University Press.

Kressel, K. (1985). *The process of divorce: How professionals and couples negotiate settlements.* New York: Basic Books.

Kressel, K., N. Jaffe, B. Tuchman, C. Watson, & M. Deutsch (1980). A typology of divorcing couples: Implications for mediation and the divorce process. *Family Process* 19:101–116.

Lemmon, J. A. (1985). *Family mediation practice.* New York: Free Press.

Little, M., N. Thoennes, J. Pearson, & R. Appleford (1985). A case study: The custody mediation services of the Los Angeles Conciliation Court. *Conciliation Courts Review* 23:1–14.

Lyon, E., N. Thoennes, J. Pearson, & R. Appleford (1985). A case study: The custody mediation services of the Family Division, Connecticut Superior Court. *Conciliation Courts Review* 23:15–26.

Mahler, M. (1971). A study of the separation-individuation process and its possible application to borderline phenomena in the psychoanalytic sitation. *Psychoanalytic Study of the Child* 26:403–424.

Masterson, J. F. (1981). *The narcissistic and borderline disorders*. New York: Brunner/Mazel.

McIsaac, H. (1981). Mandatory conciliation custody/visitation matters: California's bold stroke. *Conciliation Courts Review* 19:73–81.

McIsaac, H. (1983). Court-connected mediation. *Conciliation Courts Review* 21:49–59.

McIsaac, H. (1987). Toward a classification of child custody disputes: An application of family systems theory. *Mediation Quarterly* 14/15:39–50.

Mead, G. H. (1934). *Mind, self and society*. Chicago: University of Chicago Press.

Milne, A. (1978). Custody of children in a divorce process: A family self-determination model. *Conciliation Courts Review* 16:1–16.

Minuchin, S. (1974). *Families in family therapy*. Cambridge: Harvard University Press.

Mnookin, R. H., & L. Kornhauser (1979). Bargaining in the shadow of the law: The case of divorce. *Yale Law Journal* 88:950–997.

Morris, J. D., & M. R. Prescott (1975). Transition groups: An approach to dealing with post partnership anguish. *Family Coordinator* 24: 325–330.

Moore, C. W. (1986). *The mediation process*. San Francisco: Jossey-Bass.

Pearson, J., & N. Thoennes (1980). Mediation project—update. *The Colorado Lawyer Family Law Newsletter*, 712–721.

Pearson, J., & N. Thoennes (1982). Mediation and divorce: The benefits outweigh the costs. *Family Advocate* 4:26–32.

Pearson, J., & N. Thoennes (1984). *Final report of the divorce mediation research project* (90-CW-634), 1–74. Association of Family and Conciliation Courts, Research Institute, Research Unit.

Pedro-Carroll, J. L., & E. L. Cowen (1987). The children of divorce intervention program: Implementation and evaluation of a time-limited group approach. In *Advances in family intervention, assessment and theory*, 4:281–307. New York: JAI Press.

Piers, E. V. (1984). *Piers-Harris children's self-concept scale, revised manual*. Los Angeles: Western Psychological Services.

Rice, J. K., & D. G. Rice (1986). *Living through divorce: A developmental approach to divorce therapy*. New York: Guilford Press.

Ross, L. (1977). The intuitive psychologist and his shortcomings: Distortions in the attribution process. In *Advances in experimental social psychology*, L. Berkowitz ed., 10:173–220. New York: Academic Press.

Saposnek, D. T. (1983). *Mediating child custody disputes: A systematic guide for family therapists, court counselors, attorneys and judges.* San Francisco: Jossey Bass.

Selman, R. L. (1980). *The growth of interpersonal understanding.* New York: Academic Press.

Selvini-Palazzoli, M., L. Boscolo, G. Cecchin, & G. Prata (1978). *Paradox and counterparadox.* New York: Jason Aronson.

Sprenkle, D. H., & C. L. Storm (1983). Divorce therapy outcome research: A substantive and methodological review. *Journal of Marital and Family Therapy* 9:239–258.

Straus, M. A. (1979, February). Measuring intrafamily conflict and violence: The conflict tactics (CT) scales. *Journal of Marriage and the Family*, 75–86.

Waldron, J. A., C. P. Roth, P. H. Farr, E. M. Mann, & J. F. McDermott, Jr. (1984). A therapeutic mediation model for child custody dispute resolution. *Mediation Quarterly* 3:5–20.

Wallerstein, J. S., & J. B. Kelly (1980). *Surviving the breakup: How children and parents cope with divorce.* New York: Basic Books.

Wallerstein, J. S. (1985a). Changes in parent-child relationships during and after divorce. In *Parental influences in health and disease*, ed. E. Anthony & G. Pollock, 317–347. Boston: Little, Brown.

Wallerstein, J. S. (1985b). The overburdened child: Some long-term consequences of divorce. *Social Work* 30:116–123.

Wallerstein, J. S. (1986/87). Psychodynamic perspectives on family mediation. *Mediation Quarterly*, 14/15:7–21.

Weiss, R. (1976). *Marital separation.* New York: Basic Books.

Welch, G. J., & D. Granvold (1977). Seminars for the separated/divorced: an educational approach to postdivorce adjustment. *Journal of Sexual and Marital Therapy* 3:31–39.

Wiseman, R. S. (1975). Crisis theory and the process of divorce. *Social Casework* 56, 205–212.

Index